The Gun Digest

BLACK POWDER LOADING MANUAL

by Sam Fadala

DBI BOOKS, INC., Northfield, Illinois

STAFF

EDITOR
Robert S.L. Anderson
LOAD DATA EDITOR
Edward A. Matunas
ASSISTANT TO THE EDITOR
Lilo Anderson
ASSOCIATE EDITOR
Harold A. Murtz
COVER PHOTOGRAPHY
John Hanusin
PRODUCTION MANAGER
Pamela J. Johnson
PUBLISHER
Sheldon L. Factor

ABOUT THE COVER

Our covers feature something familiar to a lot of shooters—GOEX Black Powder. Still referred to as "GOI" by most shooters (you'll find it that way in this book), GOEX has been marketing their product since 1976. A subsidiary of Pengo Industries, GOEX is in the unique position of being the only black powder manufacturer in the North American continent. Without GOEX, the hobby of black powder shooting might well have been less than what it is today.

DEDICATION

For Professor Charles J. Keim, Alaskan Master Guide, outdoorsman and teacher, who handed me the first muzzleloader I ever touched, and who suggested that I should look into the past for a special understanding of the future. That original plains rifle led me to the great sport of black powder shooting, for which I am grateful.

ACKNOWLEDGEMENTS

Special thanks to three of my black powder friends:
To Admiral RJ Schneider, USN Ret., for unselfish sharing of knowledge and experience.
To Melville "Chuck" French, for his skillful hands which constructed so many useful black powder items for us.
To Val Forgett for his continued faith and encouragement.

Since the author, editor and publisher have no control over the components, assembly of the loads or ammunition, arms it is to be fired in, the degree of knowledge involved or how the resulting loads or ammunition may be used, no responsibility, either implied or expressed, is assumed for the use of any of the loading data in this book.

Arms and Armour Press, London, G.B., executive licensees and distributors in Britain and Europe; Australasia; Nigeria, South Africa and Zimbabwe; India and Pakistan; Singapore, Hong Kong and Japan.

ISBN 0-910676-50-X   Library of Congress Catalog Card #82-072296

CONTENTS

CONTENTS

chapter 1

Black Powder Shooting Success

MUZZLE-LOADING IS right for the times. The sport is deeply rewarding as an *addition* to general shooting. I know of no dedicated shooter whose activity would not be enriched by at least a handshake acquaintance and occasional rendezvous with the muzzleloader. The sport of black powder shooting is both of the past and the present. It is a living history practiced by modern enthusiasts, and I find that when someone says, "I don't like muzzle-loading," chances are he has never tried muzzle-loading—or, he tried it, but enjoyed little success at the game.

A friend of mine forever tells me that black powder shooting is a giant step backwards. His favorite quip is, "Sam, I

Recently, it was determined that most newcomers to black powder shooting intend to do some form of hunting with their new muzzleloader. Hunting with a black powder arm can be very rewarding. Here, the author poses with a 14½-inch antelope buck taken with a custom 54-caliber modified Lancaster rifle built by Dennis Mulford.

gave up muzzleloaders when I was still in knee pants." I feel sorry for the guy. He did not give up black powder shooting. He never even gave it a chance. Now he lives with a misconception about the whole thrilling sport of shooting the old-time guns. He doesn't know what he's missing. It's too bad.

On the other hand, I have met shooters who did give the sport a try and then gave it up. Some of these shooters return to enjoy a lifetime of charcoal burning. Others do not. But why did they divorce themselves from the sport in the first place? The reason is often glaringly evident. They did not have much success at the sport, and the shooter wants success. Furthermore, he is entitled to it. That is what this book is all about, black powder loading and reloading with *success*. The success comes on the heels of tested information, with black powder voodoo and alchemy getting a boot in the behind.

When a shooter separates himself from black powder and tosses the old smokepole into a dusty place of dishonor in the attic, he has usually completed the negative part of a standard evolution that most black powder shooters go through. This evolution goes something like this:

In the beginning, the black powder quitter fully enjoyed the thrills and rewards of the sport. He liked the classic lines of the firearm and its link with the past. The rifle (usually), handgun or shotgun felt good to the touch. There was more romance in the smoke and flame than an old pirate movie. But those early impressions waned and faded when Mr. Shooter found that he could not group his shots or punch a hole through the X-ring, or bring home the bacon with his frontstoker. It was like meeting a beautiful lady who soon revealed herself as shallow, vain, mean and selfish. All the charm went out the window and the initial aura faded into a dull gray lackluster hue of little remaining attraction.

Shooting heavy loads in a Navy Arms New Model Ithaca Hawken flintlock is enjoyable work for the person used to muzzle-loading. Here, the smoke from 110 grains of FFg hangs in the damp morning air. Such maximum loads are entirely safe in *well-constructed* firearms, and do not constitute an overload. Black powder shooting success comes especially when *safety* is stressed above all else.

I would have quit the smokepoles, too, had my freezer never seen the rewards of a black powder harvest, and had the bull's-eye never had a clean round hole chewed out of its middle. I wanted to enjoy the same attributes in my black powder shooting that I had experienced with my modern shooting irons—accuracy with a reasonable ballistic authority. Certainly, the old-time guns would not keep up with the modern ones in these categories, nor did I expect them to. But I demanded fine accuracy at closer ranges and plenty of hunting power at those same reasonable distances. And that's what I got.

But it took some work. It took some testing. The results of that work and testing are the very backbone of this book. Every chapter, every ballistic chart is designed to help the shooter create the best possible load for his own personal black powder firearm. All he needs is a reasonably decent and mechanically safe firearm to start with. No amount of loading care will turn an inherently inaccurate wallhanger into a *safe,* respectable black powder shooter. What we seek is a lasting aesthetic romance with this slow-loading mood-maker. We don't want the romance fading faster than a daisy at the coming of winter because success is unattainable, for who cares about the beautiful lines of an antique-styled classic when the target grouping is more evasive than a swamp hare chased by two beagle pups?

This book is designed to help the reader build his own pet load for his personal firebreather—a safe and accurate load. The tabular data reveals velocities and energies which are also useful to the shooter, for he can apply this information directly both in the hunting field and on the target range. The data helps in sighting a firearm, in letting the shooter know what he's up against in wind drift, and by giving him an idea of energy ratings both at the muzzle and downrange. The shooter is also given an "optimum load" in the commentary. This figure is one of the most important, if not *the* most important in the book, as will be discussed soon.

A while ago, a reader wrote me with a question about his favorite black powder firearm. Accuracy was there with the bottom loads, but with hunting loads, the pattern looked like someone had simply tossed the round balls through the target haphazardly. I asked for a sample of patches collected from that hunting load. The patches looked as if they had been used to clean up acid after a high school chemistry lab experiment. In short, they were eaten up. I advised a buffer between the patch and the powder charge.

Later, the reader told me this: "Dear Sam: Your advice worked out. My rifle shoots better now than it ever has before. Thank you for the advice. The only thing that bothers me about all this testing, though, is that in a way it kind of spoils the fun of black powder shooting. Black powder shooting isn't a science. It is a sport just for fun . . ." The letter made me think for a moment. I knew what the gentleman was getting at. However, I had to respond to the remark about spoiling the fun of black powder shooting with tests, and the answer came in the form of five questions:

1. Is it less fun to have an optimum load that will deliver sufficient ballistics for target work and hunting? Does that spoil the fun of black powder shooting?

2. Is it less fun to cleanly harvest big game in the field with a load that is both powerful and safe, too? Does that spoil the fun of black powder shooting?

3. Is it less fun to *know* your load and to understand its trajectory, ballistic authority and potential? Does that spoil the fun of black powder shooting?

4. Is it less fun to have a group instead of a scattering of holes on the target? Does that spoil the fun of black powder shooting?

5. Is it less fun to know that your load is capable of target accuracy and hunting accuracy? Does that spoil the fun of black powder shooting?

My conclusion was that it is far more fun to understand the black powder load and to build a premium load chain for the personal rifle, gaining the most from its power and accuracy

Novelty shoots are popular at the black powder rendezvous, as well they should be, for it was the original black powder shooters of the land who invented most of the basic novelty shoot ideas. Here, a shooter attempts to split a round ball on the exposed blade of an axe so that the two bullet halves will break the two clay pigeons attached on either side of the blade.

potential. No one is trying to destroy the basic enjoyment derived from the "pureness" of this sport. But I do not think that testing harms this purist approach to black powder shooting. As an example, one newcomer to the sport suggested that he liked everything about the game, except the clean-up, only he placed a couple of strong adjectives in front of the word "clean-up." "I've been using the method described in *The Complete Black Powder Handbook,* and it works. But wouldn't a shortcut be OK?"

I had tested many short-cut methods, and they were all right, but they did not get the bore "squeaky clean." However, I thought, maybe I should try again. I took two rifles, a 36-caliber squirrel rifle and a 50-caliber "Hawken" type rifle and shot and cleaned them for a year's time using an abbreviated clean-up method. I live in a very dry climate, and my findings might not hold up in a humid environment; however, at the end of a year neither firearm showed any signs of rust and both had a clean bill of health following inspection with a bore light.

The test was not scientific, but I had fired two rifles for a year off and on without total clean-up and both survived. I am still strongly in favor of a real hot water rinse clean-up from time to time, but I'll no longer leave my black powder shooting irons home because I'm afraid of the cleaning time afterwards. The shortcut method only took 10 minutes at the most.

With "rubbing alcohol" and Ox-Yoke cleaning patches, the bore was swabbed out. It usually took from one to three saturated patches to remove the bulk of the fouling. Then, with dry patches, the bore was swabbed again several strokes. Using a properly sized Hoppe's bore brush (nylon bristle), the dry bore was worked out a couple times and if a dry patch showed signs of fouling knocked free from the bristles, then I wet the brush with "moose milk"* and stroked the bore a cou-

*"Moose milk" is water soluble machinist's oil and water, 10 percent/90 percent respectively.

ple more times. After some drying patches, a single patch doused with J&A Accragard was run downbore a few times. A light coating of Accragard was left in the bore, but removed with a dry patch prior to loading the rifle the next time.

Part of the success with this shortcut cleaning method was based, I'm sure, on the fact that rather than allowing the bore to build with crud in the field, fouling was removed between shots with a cleaning patch and rubbing alcohol or moose milk. This is good practice because caked on fouling is hard to get rid of, plus a dirty bore raises pressures and can shoot to a different point of impact.

The outside of the firearm was wiped down with an alcohol-soaked patch on the metalwork, followed by a light application of oil. The wood was wiped down with a clean rag which had been doused with boiled inedible linseed oil. That was it. And once again, a little testing had gone a long way in providing for better black powder shooting, at least for one busy shooter who did not have time to thoroughly clean his firearms after each and every shoot. I still think the total clean-up is more conducive to the long life of the firearm. But the alternate method, with occasional dedicated cleaning, should allow for a clean muzzleloader.

That is the thrust of this book, then—testing and the results of such testing. And the aim is to give the black powder shooter more for his time and investment, not less. As we said at the beginning of this opening chapter, black powder shooting is right for the times, and there are several reasons why. First, there is the sense of *time* involved. We live in a rushed society where we have to do everything, it seems, at breakneck speed. But the muzzleloader gives us, even if only for a short while, a sense of time that is more relaxing and slower-paced. If a shooter is in a hurry to "toss lead," he'd best forget the muzzleloader.

Second, there is the *challenge.* There is no doubt that the challenge is increased with black powder arms. Actually, it's not just the idea of getting closer to game, and then having

Packing into the high country, the author totes a muzzleloader, but uses some modern hiking gear on his hunt. Other hunters prefer "going old-style" all the way and will dress in buckskins and wear moccasins on the trail. Both means of hunting employ the smokepole, and therein lies the real challenge and reward.

The author prepares for a backpack in the riverbottoms for deer. Here, the old and the new are combined—the thrill and challenge of using the old-time firearm coupled with the convenience of a modern packframe and supplies. A combination of such old and new gear leads to a lot of outdoor success, not only in terms of filling the bag, but also in terms of plain old-fashioned enjoyment.

only one shot when you do close the gap in the stalk, but it is also a matter of understanding fully the effects of the atmosphere on the black powder missile so that the shooter can help direct that projectile into the target. It's also a matter of understanding the multitude of variables that surround the black powder arm, variables that do not exist with modern guns. So, the challenge is greater. But that is an attraction that has its own reward.

Third, there are many places where the black powder fire-

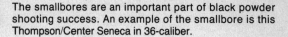
The smallbores are an important part of black powder shooting success. An example of the smallbore is this Thompson/Center Seneca in 36-caliber.

This scene shows another side of the black powder hunting—the use of smallbores. The rifle is a 36-caliber Mowrey, which is available in 32 as well. Shown with the rifle are a handmade powder horn, scrimshawed and constructed by hornmaker Vince Poulin, as well as some .350″ round balls, a short starter made by Melville "Chuck" French, a few Navy Arms No. 11 percussion caps and the beard from a wild tom turkey which was harvested with the 36-caliber rifle.

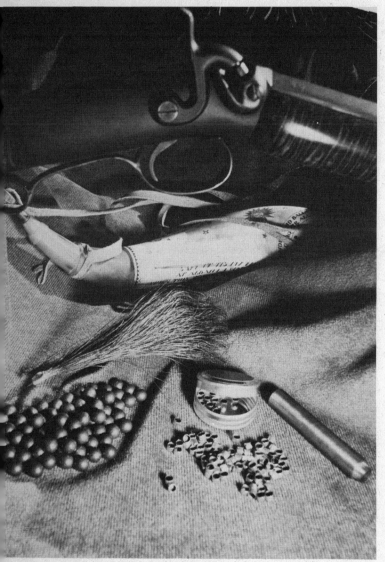

arm fits in better than the modern smokeless does. While the ultimate range of a black powder arm is still great, it does not reach as far as a modern big bore, especially when the round ball is used, and shooting can sometimes be allowed in an area that would not be suitable for today's high-power rifle. This fact can allow more man-hours in the field, and a modest harvest of game in areas where that game is often left to suffer the normal cycle of "boom and bust" that we call "the balance of nature."

Fourth, I have noticed that muzzleloader fans are often allowed in places where modern arms users would not be welcomed. This is not a black mark against modern arms users. After all, the sport of black powder is an *addition* to the general modern shooting activity. Most black powder shooters are also modern arms shooters—usually one and the same people. However, I've noticed that some farmers and ranchers have felt a bit more inclined to let us hunt or set up a shoot when we showed them our smokepoles. They simply felt that such slow-loading, modest-ranged arms were more welcome on their property.

Fifth, black powder shooting is right for the times because it gives us a feeling of relaxation and rejuvenation that is almost forced on us from the fact that these old-style arms require such hands-on patience. Our involvement is one of recreation in the best sense of the word. While we are stepping back in history, using these outdated firearms, we are actually offering ourselves a kind of therapy that fits in with *today*.

Some shooters still look at black powder as a fad. If it is, it certainly has taken a long, long time to disappear. Black powder never did die in the first place. A look into copies of *The American Rifleman* for the 1940s and 1950s, for example, will show a black powder interest, and *Foxfire 5*, the fifth book in that series, discusses the modern day muzzleloader handcrafter, who took over from his forefathers, in many cases, with the trade of making frontloaders by hand never dying out.

Those who think that there is nothing to the sport that makes it any different from firing modern firearms should have been in my boots one fall afternoon. The sun had already fallen behind a dense hillside of black timber, and in the bottom of a huge canyon in the western Rockies, a bull elk was bugling. My friend and I slowly closed ground between the bull and us on feet as quiet as owl wings. Then our environments merged, the bull elk standing at only 70 paces from the end of my muzzle, framed between two big pine trees.

The episode would have been a thrill no matter the arms used; however, I don't think the entire excitement and consequent rewards would have been quite the same if I had not held in my hands a Lancaster styled longrifle whose basic design went back into the 1700s. I eased the hammer back, lined up the iron sights, and then touched off the delicate "hair" trigger. The elk was veiled in a blue smoke haze, cleanly harvested with one shot.

When dedicated shooters tell me they have no interest in the old-time arms, I wonder first if they ever truly tried shooting this type of tool and just how successful in the game of smokethrowing they were if they did give it a try. A shooter having no interest in a replica of a plains rifle or an example of a Kentucky/Pennsylvania longrifle is the same as a car lover who shows no interest in a 1937 Lincoln Continental.

But when success is lacking, then I can understand sticking the smokepole in a closet. Hopefully, some of the hints in this book will help the shooter with his muzzleloader, answer some of his questions and appease his curiosity. We hope so.

chapter 2

How the Loads Were Derived

YOUR BLACK POWDER RIFLE, shotgun or handgun, or one very much like it, is in this book. The only exception would be with custom arms, of course, and even then, there will be some transfer value of data to firearms that have similar bores, barrel lengths and widths. The ballistics, including the all-important optimum loads, soon to be discussed, were all taken in standard firearms like yours and mine, and not in test barrels mounted to benches. Naturally, every given black powder firearm could not be included; however, we did attempt to test a tremendously broad array of available models. If a specific arm is not shown, chances are there will be one in the text which comes close enough in caliber and other vital statistics to at least give the reader a ball park knowledge of his own firearm's ballistics.

This important chapter talks about the standards which were upheld throughout the book's compilation. The reader has to sift through each category in order to understand how the data were gathered, and why we feel that the figures are valid. No two loading manuals will be the same, of course, since data will vary according to a number of factors. However, in most cases, the loads presented here are going to come quite close to matching those obtainable in the reader's guns. We have tried to keep the variables constant so that this would hold true.

Of course, changes in the "load chain," that is, powder, both brand and charge as well as granulation, projectile, lube and patch, will change the resulting ballistics. Here is an example to show the reader how this can happen:

TEST ONE
Rifle: Mowrey Squirrel Rifle 36-caliber
Projectile: Speer .350″ swaged round ball, 65 grs.
Patch: .013″ Irish linen patch, RIG lubed
Ignition: CCI No. 11 percussion cap

Powder Charge	Muzzle Velocity
20 grs. volume GOI FFFg	1,322 fps
30 grs. volume GOI FFFg	1,564 fps
40 grs. volume GOI FFFg	1,799 fps
50 grs. volume GOI FFFg	2,075 fps

Here is the very same Mowrey Squirrel Rifle tested 2 years later with a slightly different load chain.

TEST TWO
Rifle: Mowrey Squirrel Rifle 36-caliber
Projectile: Denver Bullet Co., .350″ cast round ball, 65 grs.
Patch: .015″ Ox-Yoke Precision Blue-Striped patch, RIG lubed
Ignition: CCI No. 11 percussion cap

Powder Charge	Muzzle Velocity
20 grs. volume GOI FFFg	1,416 fps
30 grs. volume GOI FFFg	1,681 fps
40 grs. volume GOI FFFg	1,826 fps
50 grs. volume GOI FFFg	1,981 fps

In both cases the Uncle Mike powder measure was used for volumetric charges; however, as seen in the figures, the resulting muzzle velocities of Test Two do not match those in Test One. They are not so very far apart as to be suspect. That's for certain, but why are they not the same? Powder temperature and elevation of the test site were the same. Let's take a look: The ball is different to begin with. Both of these projectiles are of top quality. Though both were .350″, the Denver ball "miked" at a little larger diameter on the *average* than the superb Speer ball. This is not to cast an aspersion on the Denver ball either. As we said, both are super in quality and consistency, but not identical in diameter, hence they fit the bore slightly differently.

Also the patching was not the same. In Test Two, a heavier patch was used. This usually does *not* result in much velocity change, except for very loose ball/patch fits (as will be shown clearly later on). While tight patch/ball fits (especially tight ball to the bore) did render top accuracy, those tight fits do not always not insure higher velocity. However, the .015″ patch was another variable as was the powder "lot" in the second load chain, and we did arrive at different velocities, albeit not *that* different, in the two tests.

The reader is assured that there is tremendous transfer value between the loads given in this book and his own personal firearm, as long as he is at least close to an approximation of the load chains outlined. Our tests showed conclusively that

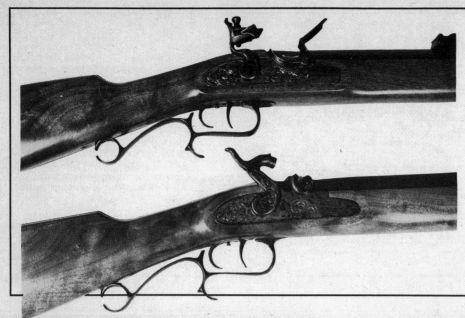

These two Thompson/Center Renegades, one in flint, the other in percussion, were tested side by side. No differences were detected. Due, no doubt, to chance alone, a few of the flinters in identical barrel lengths obtained a very slightly higher velocity than the caplocks. We felt this was not a conclusive situation and was related to chance, though further investigation might prove interesting.

The Optimum Load

A single most important factor in the load data could be the optimum load, which is presented in each case. In smokeless loading data, the idea of an optimum load is often expressed in a latent manner, but seldom expressed with a figure. In this volume, the optimum load or loads—sometimes we cannot name just one—are given as a raw figure in each test. The optimum load is based upon two criteria:

1. Ballistic dictates
2. Testing experience (and field experience)

(Left) Barrel lengths made a difference in our testing. We do not believe that black powder is a fuel which consumes itself in one burst of fire, and time/pressure curves bear this out. Therefore, barrel lengths did show some degree of velocity change. However, in *no* case was this difference enough to give the nod to one rifle over another. The shooter is urged to pick his firearm based upon his own needs and desires. Featured here are the longer-barreled Armsport Tryon Trailblazer and the more modest barrel length of the T/C Renegade, both good choices.

minor changes in the load chain produced only minor ballistic differences. For example, patch thickness, with the exception of very loose or misaligned patches, altered muzzle velocity very slightly, although a number of rifles did show higher velocity with thicker patches than without (see chapter on patching). The reader also has an opportunity to create his own pet load by using the data presented in the data section of this book, and we urge him to do so, using care and caution to remain within safe operating limits. The optimum loads given in each test are highly valuable, we feel, as starting points toward a pet load for the reader's rifle.

By combining the data revealed in the chapters on twist, patch and other loading information, along with the obtained velocities in the data section, the reader can build toward a supreme custom load for his own firearm, starting with an optimum load and going *down*, first, to test for accuracy, and then adjusting his load until the finest accuracy is obtained.

We need both, because one alone will not serve us very well. For example, we may have a firearm whose ballistic optimum is 50 grains of GOI FFFg for a resulting velocity of 1,981 fps at the muzzle. However, in the practical use of this particular firearm, that load may be of much less value than another load. To be precise, the figures just mentioned belong to the interesting little Mowrey Squirrel Rifle in 36-caliber. Since a squirrel rifle is intended for squirrel, rabbit and other small game hunting as well as modest-range target work (the atmosphere plays hob with the small ball at long-range), then surely we can see how the little 20-grain volume charge would suffice for most of this rifle's intended duty. You don't need a boat oar to swat a fly, and you don't need almost 2,000 fps to bag a bunny at 30 paces. (Small game and large amounts of black powder only serve to ruin meat.)

Furthermore, with the 30-grain volume charge I have cleanly harvested wild turkeys, though I think perhaps the 40-grain

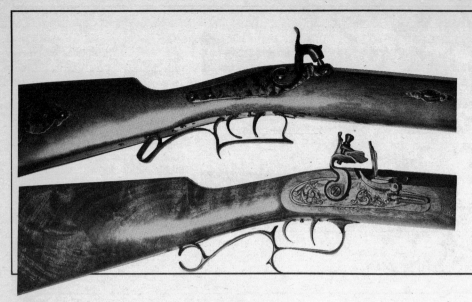

Lock styles themselves did not matter, either, in our tests as they played no roll in ballistics. However, many interesting lock styles were tried, including the once popular and excellent "backaction lock" (above), which now appears on the Tryon Trailblazer, shown here by Armsport Company. The T/C Renegade flinter is shown below for comparison—it has a more conventional (bar-action) lock system.

volume charge might give just a bit more *oomph* to that type of hunting. The true optimum load, in this case, is going to depend upon the accuracy obtained with the various powder charges and patch/ball combinations. In the test rifles, 40 grains volume was highly accurate, but 30- and even 20-grain volume charges were not far behind.

Ballistic Optimum

Basically, as you add more powder, the velocity goes up. However, over 15 years ago when I began to chronograph black powder arms, I found that there was not a definite 1 to 1 correlation between the powder charge and the resulting velocity. Nothing new, this find, since the same is true with smokeless loads. However, in a few cases, the "point of diminishing returns" was absolutely blatant. For example, in a custom 45-caliber rifle with a fine handmade barrel, we used a 300-grain bullet backed up by 70 grains weight of duPont FFFg. With that charge, the average velocity was consistently 1,292 fps at the muzzle. We did a little soul searching and decided to try some heavier charges in this well made custom rifle.

Going up to 80 grains of duPont FFFg, the velocity changed from 1,292 fps to 1,301, hardly worth the bother. But more curious were the next two loads. With 90 grains of FFFg, the velocity only increased to 1,312 fps, and with a full 100 grains of the same fuel we hovered around 1,310 fps, statistically no real difference. Very obviously, going past 70 grains of FFFg in this target rifle would be a waste of powder.

Another example of a ballistic optimum is shown in my own personal 54-caliber rifle. Looking at the figures below, one can see that there is indeed an increase in velocity commensurate with an increase in powder charge. However, a look at the actual "improvements" in velocity with the added powder shows another story.

Powder Charge*	Muzzle Velocity
110 grs. weight (not volume)	1,871 fps
120 grs. weight	1,943 fps
130 grs. weight	1,970 fps
135 grs. weight	2,020 fps

*GOI FFg only powder used

Yes, velocity did increase with added powder. But let's take a look at those increases. At 120 grains, the ball is leaving the muzzle at 1,943 fps. The 130-grain charge only gains 27 fps, and the 135-grain charge picks up 77 fps over the 120. In terms of trajectory, the increase in velocity from the 120 charge to the 135 charge is too small to bother with. Because kinetic energy figures are based on the square of the velocity, there will be slight gains in muzzle energy with the 2,020 fps load over the 1,943 fps load; however, at 50 yards or 75 yards the few remaining fps advantage in favor of the 135-grain charge becomes about as significant as the difference felt between 20 and 22 below zero.

The hunting load for this rifle, then, was gauged at 120 grains of FFg black powder, not 135 grains. The added powder would increase the recoil a bit, and increase the pressure, but without significant advances in velocity. That is a case not so much of "field experience" dictating the optimum load, but rather of ballistics doing the talking.

Maximum Load

The loading data section includes a maximum load for each load data entry. In spite of some views, black powder does develop pressures which are capable of causing trouble when safety is abandoned. Therefore, in the interest of good safe loads, a maximum has been established, often, by the manufacturer of the firearm. In some cases, we have worked our charges up to this maximum. However, in no case have we gone beyond this figure. In many other instances, the maximum was attempted in the trial runs, but not published because it was a case of the law of diminishing returns rendering that maximum an uneconomical load.

Taking the little squirrel rifle already mentioned as an example, the manufacturer has placed a maximum safe limit for everyday use at 75 grains of FFFg black powder. In fact, almost 2,000 fps was reached with only 50 grains of FFFg, and

Rifle: Custom 54-caliber rifle, 34" barrel
Projectile: Speer .530" swaged round ball
Patch: .013" Irish linen patch, w/.015" backer patch on powder
Lube: RIG lube
Ignition: CCI No. 11 Percussion Cap

loads beyond that level did not seem to drastically improve the ability of this fine little rifle in either field use or target use. Therefore, we did not print our findings beyond 50 grains of GOI FFFg black powder.

Optimum vs. Efficient

In this book, optimum load and efficient load are *not* the same thing. In smokeless powder language, the efficient cartridge is the one which delivers the most velocity per powder charge. A good example of a so-called efficient smokeless powder cartridge is the wildcat 270/300 Savage (the 300 Savage case having been necked down to accept bullets of .277″ diameter). For only 37 grains of IMR 3031 smokeless powder, the 270/300 Savage delivers a muzzle velocity of 2,701 fps with the 130-grain bullet (Ackley). Meanwhile, the standard 270 Winchester using 40 grains of the same powder, IMR 3031, renders a muzzle velocity of 2,762 fps. I have never cared for the "efficiency" approach, and the 270/300 Savage is a good example. Yes, it delivers a lot of punch from a small case, and no doubt the standard 270 Winchester is slightly overbore capacity. But the final proof of this pudding is in the shooting. While the 270 Winchester can obtain 270/300 Savage ballistics, the reverse is not true. The wildcat Savage cartridge cannot earn over 3100 fps muzzle velocity with the 130-grain bullet, but the 270 Winchester can.

So we have not attempted to use efficiency in our data. By optimum, we mean the load which delivers a *reasonable* velocity for a reasonable powder charge, but we are *not* concerned with a ratio that tells us how efficient a charge is in terms of pressure per velocity or weight of powder charge per velocity. We want to observe levels of *safety* first and foremost, and working from that platform, we hope to find the load that delivers a good velocity with a nominal powder charge.

Test Procedures

Two Oehler Model 33 Chronotachs were used to compile the data for this book. Initially, I decided to use only one machine, since the Oehler model is renowned for its uncanny accuracy and reliability. However, I decided that the reader would be more confident in the data if a firearm were tested not only in two sessions, but with two machines and two sets of screens. I not only cross-checked velocity readings with the two machines, but also against my own ballistic log files if a reading seemed out of the ordinary. At no time, however, did I obtain a velocity reading which was out of whack. Both machines correlated in all cases.

All data were taken with the screens of the chronograph highly baffled. That is, there was a wall, in this case ¾-inch marine grade plywood, with a notch to shoot through. This prevented erroneous readings which could result from shock waves or other phenomena starting or stopping a screen falsely. Also, the guns were tested twice on two different test days, which further boosted our confidence in the numbers. Five-shot strings were used. Testing was done at 5700 feet above sea level. (In black powder shooting, the difference in muzzle velocity between sea level and 5700 feet is modest.)

Reliability

The reader should also know that any load with a Standard Deviation readout of over 30 was not entered into our data section. We tend to erroneously think of black powder loads as haphazzard. In fact, a standard deviation of 15 was very common, with 10s and even 5s not at all out of the ordinary. The variables were held constant, and the components were

reliable. Hence, our standard deviations were quite superior throughout testing. Naturally, a standard deviation of 5 or 6 was considered almost as suspect as high figures. However, in cases where tests were re-run because of such low and almost unbelievable ratings, those ratings appeared again on *both* test machines, as well as in tests conducted for the author by associates.

Loosely stated, Sd (standard deviation) is a term used in statistics to determine how much variation the individual "scores" have away from the average or mean. We can also call it the standard deviation from the mean. If a load had a very high standard deviation from the mean, it's probably not reliable as a load. Therefore, we did not record it. In the past, we figured Sd "by hand," mathematically, and we will give the formula here for the curious. It is:

$$Sd = \sqrt{\frac{\Sigma X^2}{N}}$$

where: Sd = standard deviation
  ΣX^2 = the sum of all squared deviations from the mean
  N = number of shots in the string

We must add the individual deviations from the mean in the string of shots or scores; however, if we do add them simply together, then the result is zero, since the minus factors and plus factors cancel out. Therefore, we must square each deviation, since, as we know from algebra, a minus times a minus is a plus and a plus times a plus is a plus. Now we can add the deviations, come up with a working figure, and then take the square root later to arrive at our final figure.

All of this, however, has changed today. The Chronotach makes Sd a simple matter. You just push a button and the machine reads out the figure. But it is nice to have an idea of what the figure means. The number (the square root of the mean of the squared deviation) says much about reliability. Here is an example in which Sd is derived, along with the Es (extreme spread):

Low Velocity in the String:	1,182 fps
High Velocity in the String:	1,194 fps
Es (extreme variation):	12
Average Velocity for 5 Shots:	1,188 fps
Sd (standard deviation)	5 (remarkably good)

The Es figure is also nice because we can see just how much difference there was between the highest velocity registered in the string and the lowest velocity registered in the string. But wouldn't a plain ordinary *average* do it all? Actually, no. The average has a way of being misleading. Without the Es, for example, we do not know if the high and low velocities were quite close to each other, or far apart. Without the Sd, we do not have an accurate measure of the reliability, that is, the average deviation of shots from the mean (average) velocity.

Here is what can happen with an average used by itself. As an example, let's create a small custom gunshop with only 10 personnel. There is a president who earns $100,000 a year, but his employees, all 9 of them, earn $20,000 a year each. So, if we ask what the average wage is at this little shop, it comes to $28,000 per person. But the 9 workers do not make nearly that much. The average wage is not a lie. But is it really accurate without further clarification? Let's look at another shop of only 10 persons. In this shop, the president again makes

$100,000 a year. Two vice presidents each make $50,000 annually. Two foremen earn $15,000 each, and the remaining five workmen only get $10,000 each.

We come up with the same average, $28,000 per man per year. But this time we are even more off the mark. The five workmen do not make anything like $28,000 a year and the president and two vice presidents make much more than that figure. It is obvious that we need more than an average to tell us about our velocities, and this is why we have relied on the Sd and Es figures.

How Charges Were Measured

All loads in this book, with the few exceptions in the text which are cited otherwise, are tossed by *volume* and not by weight. An adjustable black powder measure* was used, and not a powder/bullet scale which weighs in "grains" (1-ounce weight equals 437.5 grains). Is this a reliable way to go? You bet it is, and it was deemed the most intelligent means of throwing charges for our book. There are three good reasons:

1. Accuracy is excellent in terms of a powder charge being thrown from a volumetric measure. Of course, the same process for tossing the charge has to be observed. In using measures for this book, the black powder or Pyrodex was loaded into the body of the measure to the overfull mark. The barrel of the measure was tapped 10 times and then the funnel portion was swung into place to level off the powder supply.

Here are actual figures with an Uncle Mike (Michaels of Oregon) adjustable powder measure set at 40 grains. Naturally, the actual charge in grains weight (as measured by a powder/bullet scale) will not be exactly 40 grains; however, the charges from one to another are very close.

Uncle Mike Powder Measure

FFg GOI	FFFFg GOI
1. 38.6 grs. weight	1. 42.7 grs. weight
2. 39.0 grs. weight	2. 43.2 grs. weight
3. 38.2 grs. weight	3. 43.5 grs. weight
4. 38.8 grs. weight	4. 43.1 grs. weight
5. 39.0 grs. weight	5. 43.7 grs. weight

FFFg GOI	PYRODEX P (for pistols)
1. 38.5 grs. weight	1. 36.6 grs. weight
2. 38.6 grs. weight	2. 36.1 grs. weight
3. 38.4 grs. weight	3. 36.7 grs. weight
4. 39.2 grs. weight	4. 37.1 grs. weight
5. 38.9 grs. weight	5. 36.8 grs. weight

2. Not only is the accuracy of the tossed charge reliable, but in black powder we have found *no increase* in accuracy in the rifle tests between carefully thrown volumetric charges of powder and charges weighed to .1 grains weight on a powder/bullet scale.

3. The third reason we have used the volumetric load is that this is the standard practice in black powder loading, and it corresponds with the responsible way to use Pyrodex. Pyrodex is less dense than black powder; therefore, used in a volumetric measure, the actual weight of the charge is less than that of black powder, which is the prescribed method of using Pyrodex according to the manufacturer. See the charts for the two powder measures used for the rifle and handgun data in *(continued page 18)*

---

*Under *no* circumstance should a powder measure designed for *smokeless powder* be used for tossing charges of black powder.

The Uncle Mike 120 and

The reader will find a grains weight listing along with our volumetric charge in the load data. However, we are also including our own "calibration" run of the two powder measures used for the rifle and handgun data in the book. By "calibration," a word we admit abusing here, we do not mean "adjustment." We merely mean checking the actual grains weight tossed at the various settings of the measures. We recommend that shooters test their own powder measures just to be certain of the grains weight charge being tossed; however, our exhaustive tests showed no better standard deviations when using weighed *vs* bulk black powder loads, nor was accuracy improved when weighed instead of volumetric charges were used. Therefore, we continue to insist that black powder loads be thrown by volume, not randomly, but with as much *consistency* as possible.

All charges below are unweighted averages of ten (10) throws.

We used the unweighted average because we felt that this was more fair and more "true to life" than a weighted average would have been. An unweighted average includes *all* samples, of course, whereas a weighted average, which is often a wise choice, *excludes* any samples which are unduly high or low according to the tester's judgement.

Naturally, the shooter will find that his powder measures will not weigh out precisely as ours did. Nor did we get identical results from powder lot to powder lot. There are many variables at work, such as humidity, variations in inner barrel dimensions of different powder measures, actual powder density, number of "taps" against the powder measure barrel, and so forth. However, in further tests of many different measures we did not find any measure which was so far off that it tossed loads that were not reliable and safe. Remember, even in the smaller calibers and especially in the larger calibers, when using black powder, very small differences in actual grains weight do not deliver important changes in velocity, accuracy or pressure. In other words, 100.0 grains weight of FFg in a 50-caliber muzzleloader and 101.5 grains FFg in the same 50-caliber rifle will not give a tremendous difference in performance levels. In fact, even the keenest observer will not be able to see a difference on the target, even with a rifle of high accuracy potential.

(Opposite page) The two powder measures used in gathering our load data for the rifle and handgun sections are Tresco, left, and Uncle Mike, right. The Tresco is an extra-capacity measure, holding up to 200-grains volume of fuel. The Uncle Mike is a twist-stem model holding up to 120-grains volume. ▶

Tresco 200 Adjustable Powder Measures

Uncle Mike 120 Adjustable Powder Measure

A. Fg GOI Black Powder*

1. 40 setting: 40.3 grs.
2. 50 setting: 50.8 grs.
3. 60 setting: 61.5 grs.
4. 70 setting: 71.4 grs.
5. 80 setting: 81.2 grs.
6. 90 setting: 91.5 grs.
7. 100 setting: 102.0 grs.
8. 110 setting: 111.2 grs.
9. 120 setting: 120.5 grs.

B. FFg GOI Black Powder

1. 30 setting: 29.6 grs.
2. 40 setting: 39.5 grs.
3. 50 setting: 49.5 grs.
4. 60 setting: 59.5 grs.
5. 70 setting: 70.1 grs.
6. 80 setting: 81.0 grs.
7. 90 setting: 90.2 grs.
8. 100 setting: 99.3 grs.
9. 110 setting: 110.3 grs.
10. 120 setting: 121.5 grs.

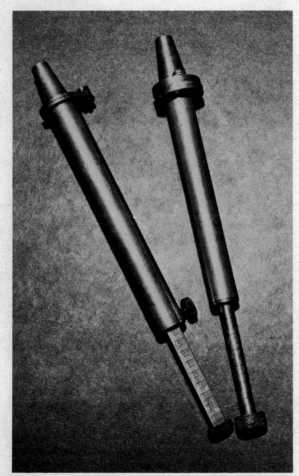

C. FFFg GOI Black Powder

1. 10 setting: 10.5 grs.
2. 20 setting: 20.7 grs.
3. 30 setting: 30.9 grs.
4. 40 setting: 41.2 grs.
5. 50 setting: 51.8 grs.
6. 60 setting: 62.5 grs.
7. 70 setting: 72.1 grs.
8. 80 setting: 82.0 grs.
9. 90 setting: 92.0 grs.
10. 100 setting: 102.3 grs.
11. 110 setting: 110.3 grs.
12. 120 setting: 121.5 grs.

D. FFFFg GOI Black Powder†

1. 20 setting: 21.0 grs.
2. 30 setting: 31.5 grs.
3. 40 setting: 41.7 grs.

E. Pyrodex RS (for rifles & shotguns)

1. 20 setting: 14.0 grs.
2. 30 setting: 21.0 grs.
3. 40 setting: 28.0 grs.
4. 50 setting: 36.1 grs.
5. 60 setting: 44.5 grs/
6. 70 setting: 52.2 grs.
7. 80 setting: 60.0 grs.
8. 90 setting: 68.2 grs.
9. 100 setting: 76.0 grs.
10. 110 setting: 82.1 grs.
11. 120 setting: 88.0 grs.

F. Pyrodex P (for pistols)

1. 10 setting: 7.7 grs.
2. 20 setting: 15.3 grs.
3. 30 setting: 24.0 grs.
4. 40 setting: 31.0 grs.
5. 50 setting   38.7 grs.
6. 60 setting   46.5 grs.

G. Pyrodex CTG (for cartridges)

1. 50 setting: 42.0 grs.
2. 60 setting: 51.1 grs.
3. 70 setting: 60.0 grs.
4. 80 setting: 68.5 grs.
5. 90 setting: 72.8 grs.
6. 100 setting: 85.0 grs.
7. 110 setting: 92.2 grs.
8. 120 setting: 99.2 grs.

---

*Usually, Fg weighs "light;" however, the density of this Fg run was somewhat on the high side, yet velocities with this same Fg did show normal trends.

†Not for a main charge in the breech. FFFFg is pan powder.

(continued on page 16)

Tresco 200 Adjustable Measure

A. Fg GOI Black Powder

1. Unit Closed: 31.7 grs.
2. 40 setting: 40.4 grs.
3. 50 setting: 50.2 grs.
4. 60 setting: 60.0 grs.
5. 70 setting: 69.9 grs.
6. 80 setting: 79.9 grs.
7. 90 setting: 89.8 grs.
8. 100 setting: 99.8 grs.
9. 110 setting: 109.7 grs.
10. 120 setting: 119.8 grs.
11. 130 setting: 129.7 grs.
12. 140 setting: 139.6 grs.
13. 150 setting: 149.5 grs.

B. FFg GOI Black Powder

1. Unit Closed: 32.4 grs.
2. 40 setting: 40.8 grs.
3. 50 setting: 50.2 grs.
4. 60 setting: 60.2 grs.
5. 70 setting: 70.1 grs.
6. 80 setting: 80.1 grs.
7. 90 setting: 90.0 grs.
8. 100 setting: 99.7 grs.
9. 110 setting: 109.7 grs.
10. 120 setting: 119.6 grs.
11. 130 setting: 129.6 grs.*
12. 140 setting: 139.5 grs.
13. 150 setting: 149.6 grs.

C. FFFg GOI Black Powder

1. Unit Closed: 33.0 grs.
2. 40 setting: 41.5 grs.
3. 50 setting: 51.6 grs.
4. 60 setting: 61.4 grs.
5. 70 setting: 71.6 grs.
6. 80 setting: 81.5 grs.
7. 90 setting: 91.4 grs.
8. 100 setting: 101.0 grs.
9. 110 setting: 111.2 grs.
10. 120 setting: 121.0 grs.
11. 130 setting: 131.1 grs.
12. 140 setting: 141.3 grs.
13. 150 setting: 149.8 grs.*

D. FFFFg GOI Black Powder†

1. Unit Closed: 33.3 grs.
2. 40 setting: 42.0 grs.
3. 100 setting: 101.6 grs.
4. 150 setting: 153.0 grs.

E. Pyrodex RS Powder‡

1. Unit Closed: 24.2 grs.
2. 40 setting: 30.5 grs.
3. 50 setting: 37.2 grs.
4. 60 setting: 44.3 grs.
5. 70 setting: 51.8 grs.
6. 80 setting: 58.1 grs.
7. 90 setting: 66.7 grs.

---

*Although we used the best possible care and consistency in our test run, there was not an exact continuity in our figures due to the slight variables inherent in any volumetric unit. This is why we might have the measure show 129.6 FFg at the 130 setting and then 139.5 at the 140 setting.

†This information is for the reader's interest only. We do not recommend nor condone the use of FFFFg pan powder in the breech for main loads.

‡Fresh Pyrodex.

This is the Dixie Gun Works powder tester. It works on the principle of placing a small fixed-volume measure of powder in the chamber and then rotating the indicator wheel into place. The blast from the powder charge will move the indicator a certain number of notches. When set prior to firing, the indicator reads "1" and then it changes from "1" up to "12." The higher the number, the stronger the powder. While a beautiful decorative item, the tester is excellent for showing the different thrusts among various powder brands, but especially among different granulations. It is enlightening to watch, perhaps, a "3" registered with a larger granulation and perhaps an "8" with a finer granulation, and newcomers especially can learn graphically how much granulation means in terms of powder strength.

8. 100 setting: 72.5 grs.
9. 110 setting: 79.3 grs.
10. 120 setting: 87.5 grs.
11. 130 setting: 94.0 grs.
12. 140 setting: 103.6 grs.
13. 150 setting: 108.0 grs.

F. Pyrodex P Powder (for handguns)§

1. Unit Closed: 25.9 grs.
2. 40 setting: 33.3 grs.
3. 50 setting: 40.5 grs.
4. 60 setting: 47.9 grs.
5. 70 setting: 56.9 grs.
6. 80 setting: 64.6 grs.
7. 90 setting: 72.7 grs.
8. 100 setting: 81.7 grs.
9. 110 setting: 90.0 grs.
10. 120 setting: 96.3 grs.
11. 130 setting: 105.2 grs.
12. 140 setting: 113.1 grs.
13. 150 setting: 118.0 grs.

G. Pyrodex Cartridge Powder (CTG)

1. Unit Closed: 26.7 grs.
2. 40 setting: 34.0 grs.
3. 50 setting: 41.6 grs.
4. 60 setting: 51.0 grs.
5. 70 setting: 58.2 grs.
6. 80 setting: 66.6 grs.
7. 90 setting: 74.9 grs.
8. 100 setting: 83.5 grs.
9. 110 setting: 90.9 grs.
10. 120 setting: 99.7 grs.

§Hodgdon has gone on record stating that Pyrodex P may be used in rifles; however, this is only in appropriately reduced charges and in our book we used P only in the handgun loads.

11. 130 setting: 107.8 grs.
12. 140 setting: 116.1 grs.
13. 150 setting: 125.2 grs.

Author's Note: The reader may notice that the figures shown in this consistency run for the Uncle Mike Powder measure do not exactly correspond with the figures given for the same Uncle Mike powder measure in our calibration tests. This is correct. The figures are accurate. There is no error. Why, then, could there be this variation? As far as the GOI powder figures are concerned, the slight variations are due to a different powder LOT. A "lot" of powder is one given run. We used the newest GOI black powder available straight from the factory for our test runs and figures.

We did find that our Pyrodex batch, also straight from the factory and very fresh, was less dense than our older Pyrodex had been. Moisture content was also slightly high, mainly for an added margin of safety in shipping, even though Pyrodex is already considered so safe to ship that U.P.S. (United Parcel Service) allows this powder to be shipped via their carriers.

The reader will see that the fresh Pyrodex charges did not render as high a velocity as we have been used to getting. However, we hasten to add that as the cans of new, fresh Pyrodex "cured," that is, dried to a degree, the fuel performed just as we had expected it to perform and velocities were again up to par.

In summary, although we did use the same Uncle Mike measure in our calibration run and our consistency run, the two tests were conducted far enough apart in time so that different powder lots were used and we therefore experienced a normal and expected small variation in actual grains weight from one test to the other.

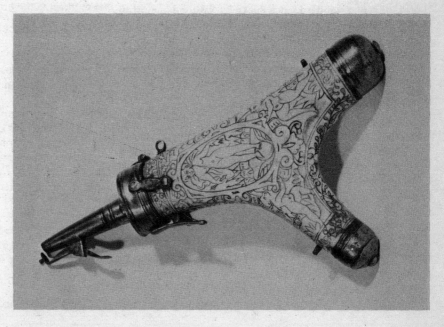

An original powder flask from out of the past is shown here courtesy Gene Ball and the Buffalo Bill Historical Society of Cody, Wyoming, home of the Winchester Collection. The powder container is made from a section of antler, fitted with metal caps and funnel dispenser. Measuring black powder by volume is a perfectly fine way to load our muzzle-loading arms.

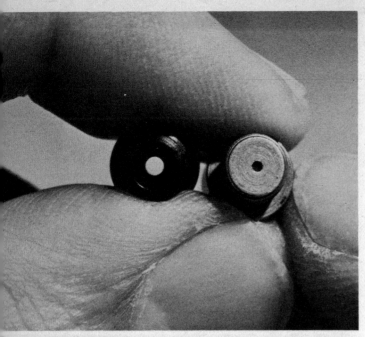

This illustration graphically shows the differences possible in the base hole of the nipple. The larger hole in the base is less desirable than the smaller hole due to blowback. Note that the larger-holed base is simply a "straight-through" cut.

this book. For the shotgun loads presented in the data section we used a Lee powder measure.

The individual shooter should scale his own personal powder measure to see just how much it throws in grains weight. It should not throw *more* than the number it is set on. Of course, measures set up for FFg will throw heavier charges of FFFg and FFFFg, since there is less air space around these smaller kernels of powder.

Patches

Since there is so little variation in velocity between a heavy and medium patch (as long as the ball fits reasonably to the bore), only one standard patch thickness was used in most of our testing with the round ball in obtaining the velocity figures. The important chapter on patching explains these points and serves to help you make the best patch selection possible.

We try to save the patch from destruction mainly for *accuracy* reasons— more so than velocity reasons.

Lubes

The lubes used for the loads in our data section are fully identified. Since a grease is credited with *slightly* higher velocities than a liquid, RIG was an often-used patch lube and sometimes used as a Maxi or Minie lube as well. In some cases the Ox-Yoke Wonder Patch was used, since this self-lubed patch contains agents which keep fouling very soft. Also used was Young Country No. 103 lube, which is known for its ability to allow shot after shot without heavy bore clean up. Lastly, we used sperm whale oil in some of our testing. (A suitable substitute for natural whale oil is J&A Old Slickum.)

Nipples

One of the first things accomplished on a test firearm was to check the nipple. In all cases where the standard factory nip-

ple was of the "straight-through" variety, that nipple was removed and replaced with an Uncle Mike Hot Shot Nipple. The "straight-through" design, as can be proved by chronographing, can sometimes cause a loss in velocity. Plus, there is a chance for more blowback and cap debris from a nipple with the large hole in the base. The Hot Shot, with its small hole in the base of the nipple, plus a tiny hole through the cone of the nipple, has proved more reliable than those nipples with the large orifice at the base.

On many rifles, of course, where a flat-based nipple was already in use, with a pinhole sized orifice in the base, the standard nipple was retained.

Cleaning Between Shots

Except with a few lubes and the use of Pyrodex, the build-up of fouling totally destroys accurate chronographing. As a matter of fact, even with some of the miracle lubes, the tester could see velocities going *up* shot after shot because the fouling build-up in the bore is raising pressures. Young Country No. 103 lube seemed to maintain a constant in velocity without laborious cleanup between shots. However, for the sake of consistency in the testing cycle, *all* arms were cleaned between each chronographed shot.

The cleaning was accomplished with an Ox-Yoke cleaning patch saturated with rubbing alcohol. Such alcohol dries quickly and does not tend to innundate the nipple area with moisture. It is easily wiped free with a follow-up dry patch.

Ramrod Pressure

This aspect of the loading cycle was not held to a scientific level. However, a scale was used to determine pressure applied to the ramrod and the average pressure applied was 40 pounds. Black powder is supposed to burn better when mildy compressed, and the 40 pounds pressure proved to be a useful aspect of the loading cycle, for a brief test of very lightly compacted charges did show more spread in individual velocities in the shot string and a less reliable Sd. Under no circumstances was any gun fired with the load loosely packed into the chamber area. Separated charges mean *trouble*. The author has blown up three black powder guns using black powder with the charge separated from the projectile. Whether or not this is a case of detonation, I do not know. But all loads were kept intact in the breech.

Miscellaneous Data Variables

Air Temperature

Most of the atmospheric temperatures during the testing cycle were in the 60-degree F. to 70-degree F. range.

Powder Temperature

The powder was kept warm during the entire test period. A photographic thermometer was used to determine the temperature of the powder immediately prior to loading and firing. The temperature is probably off a few degrees, but it does give the reader a general idea.

Ignition

Mainly, CCI No. 11 percussion caps were used for the tests, with other caps mentioned when they were employed. For the muskets, the Navy Arms Musket Cap was used.

Altitude

Testing took place at an elevation of about 5,700 feet.

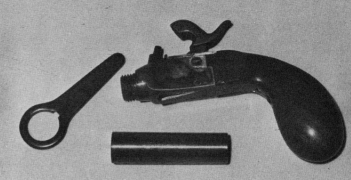

The Dixie Gun Works Screwbarrel Pistol is shown (left) fully assembled and (below) dismantled. With barrel removed, the Screwbarrel Pistol can be fitted with a percussion cap and fired in a darkened area. The shooter will be able to see, first-hand, the length of the spark, the consistency of spark from one cap to the next out of the same box, the shape of the spark and so forth. The Screwbarrel, in this instance, becomes a percussion cap *tester*.

A good percussion cap is a *consistent* one, such as these made by CCI. A cap need not necessarily be the strongest in order to be the best, though there are some firearms which indeed do seem to need a "hot" cap for good ignition. Today, percussion cap size No. 11 is the most popular.

The musket cap is a larger unit than the standard run of percussion caps. It fits, obviously, those rifles which employ a large-coned nipple. These are quite often of military or target type, or the Sharps arms of percussion ignition.

The SAECO lead-hardness tester is very useful, especially for those interested in casting alloy bullets for the black powder cartridge guns, including the big Sharps number and the 50-140 class case (not a Sharps invention, by the way). The tester comes with full instructions and is a quality instrument.

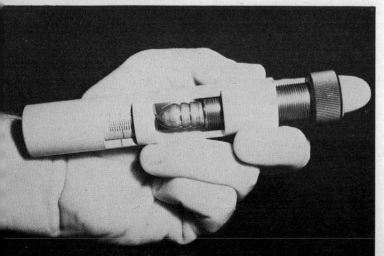

Twist

The chapter on this important subject explains why we have included the twist of each firearm in the data.

Projectiles

In the main, three commercial missile brands were used: These are the Speer swaged round balls, Hornady swaged round balls and Denver Bullet Company cast round balls and Maxis. Each projectile is labeled in the data. We also used projectiles thrown from Lee, Lyman and Shiloh moulds.

Remaining Velocities

There is no doubt that remaining velocities, not only in this book, but in other manuals, are an approximation only. The derived remaining velocites are usually computed from a standard C (ballistic coefficient) using a model coefficient of form and computed for a theoretical perfect or "normal" atmospheric condition with a barometer reading calibrated for sea level. I was going to test at 50 yards or even 100 yards by actually firing over the chronograph screens, until I determined that the screens were worth more to me than the satisfaction of my curiosity.

I did get a few sample shots off before I lost my nerve, and in fact the actual remaining velocities obtained were quite close to derived remaining velocities. In short, the reader can use the figures knowing that they are valuable and they can be instrumental in determining how to sight a firearm in and also they are useful in deciding just how much "punch" a load has at a distance from the muzzle.

That's how the loading data were put together. The following chapters on loading designs and patch data and twist, and other related loading subjects, should be digested by the dedicated black powder fan because, as it turns out, the process for making truly accurate and authoritative loads is no haphazard process in the world of the smokepole. The fascination lies with mastering this great sport and ending up with custom pet loads that safely strain every ounce of potential from that favorite frontloader. The black powder cartridges are somewhat simpler to deal with, with fewer variables to observe. And we will devote a little space to their loading idiosyncracies, too.

19

chapter 3

Basic Loading Procedures

THE DYED-IN-THE-BUCKSKINS veteran black powder shooter might want to flit through this chapter like a quail through the short grass, but there might be a point or two here worthy of consideration, and even argument. We hope the knowledgeable smokepole artist will stick with us for a look at basic loading procedures, especially flintlock methods.

This chapter has to do with the frontloaders only, the caplock rifle, flintlock rifle, handguns of the same ignition style and the frontfeeder shotgun. (Loading black powder metallic cartridges is discussed in Chapter 11, and in Chapter 12 we deal with the black powder shotshell.) While the very basics of the black powder load chain are quite simple, there are a few wrinkles presented below which could be of vital interest to the shooter who wants to prepare more than simply a "good load." He wants a custom load.

Also, the modern black powder shooter might consider, as he walks the path of frontloader methodology, that this aspect of the shooting sports is among the best of teachers for the beginning shooter. As we study the basics in loading the older-style guns, it becomes evident that a newcomer to the sport of shooting has a chance to truly see the *function* of the firearm. Instead of a loaded cartridge inserted into the firearm, the shooter is building, one at a time, a total charge for himself. He can see where everything goes in relation to each component part of the load. One could do worse than start a new shooter with a smokepole, teaching all the tenets of safety.

Loading the Caplock Rifle

The most popular firearm in black powder shooting is the muzzle-loading caplock rifle, or percussion rifle. Loading this type of charcoal burner is no problem, but in order to gain a *consistent* performance from this rifle, there are a few procedures that have to be observed. The steps below, with explanations, are geared to give the percussion rifle enthusiast a trustworthy load every time.

1. Wipe the Rifle Dry

The first thing a percussion rifleman does is see that the bore is dry before loading. Remember, when we closet the smokepole, we like to leave a trace of oil or grease in the bore to inhibit rust. However, now, before loading, that oil or grease has to be removed. Also, it's a good idea to run a pipe cleaner into the nipple to insure no lubricant is present which might cause a hangfire or misfire.

2. Pop a Cap

A percussion cap is mounted on the nipple; the muzzle of the rifle is aimed at a light object on the ground in a safe direction away from anyone and the rifle is fired. The thrust of the cap alone, if the nipple vent and the bore are truly clear, will blow small objects out of the way. For example, on the range a small leaf will be moved aside from the blast of the cap. This proves to the shooter that his bore and nipple vent are clear and he can proceed with loading. If there is a *crack!* at the nipple, and if the object on the ground does not budge, the shooter must check his bore and nipple vent to see if something is clogged. Sometimes it is wise to fire more than one cap when the rifle is getting its first load of the day.

3. Charge It

Pour a measured amount of the appropriate black powder or Pyrodex straight down the bore. It's not a bad idea to smack the sides of the barrel to settle the powder charge into the breech below. Naturally, the muzzle of the firearm is pointed away from any person during this and all other loading procedures.

4. Patching the Powder Charge

If the shooter is firing the popular "patched round ball," he must now have a patch ready. Often, especially with hunting charges, or with any charge that happens to harm the standard patch that goes around the ball, it is wise to protect the main patch by first putting down a single patch directly on top of the powder charge. If there is any fear of a smoldering patch causing trouble, the shooter may wish to place a piece of hornet nest downbore on top of the powder charge. The nest will protect the main patch on the ball from harm in terms of the powder charge eating it. Sometimes, a poorly fitted patch, however, will still become damaged by the rifling, or in some cases, sharp lands will cut a patch even though the patch is safe-

LOADING THE CAPLOCK RIFLE

(Photos by Bill Fadala)

(Left) Before loading, be sure to wipe the bore dry. This serves to remove any oil or grease that might retard ignition.

Fill your powder measure with an appropriate charge of powder (above) and drop that charge directly down the bore (left).

Using a short-starter, the patched ball (above) is placed on the muzzle and forced into the bore a short distance. The longest portion of the short starter is then used (right) to force the patched ball further into the bore.

LOADING THE CAPLOCK RIFLE

At this point, a standard ramrod is used to *firmly* seat the patched ball on the powder charge.

guarded from the onslaught of the powder charge. In severe cases, a gunsmith will have to lap the bore to prevent this problem.

5. The Ball Patch

Centered directly on the muzzle is a pre-cut, and pre-lubed patch. Naturally, the old-style of centering a hunk of cloth on the bore, pre-lubed, is equally good. In this case, a sharp patch knife is used to slice off the cloth after the ball has been seated below the crown of the muzzle with the stub end of the short starter. However, today, we usually use the pre-cut patch, and this is simply centered over the muzzle's bore and the ball is placed directly in the center of the patch.

As for lubes, these are discussed elsewhere, but we generally prefer a grease lube for field use and a liquid lube for range use, the grease being more rust-prohibitive, the liquid attacking black powder fouling better where quite a number of shots will be fired.

6. Short Starting

Still speaking of the round ball, of course, we need to get

that ball sunk below the lip of the muzzle crown. This can be accomplished in several ways. But the normal method is to use the short starter. The ball should fit to the bore quite well for accuracy (though it should not have to be beaten into a shapeless hunk to get it downbore). The patch will not affect a true gasket, but its amazing properties are outlined in the chapter on patching.

With the stub end of the short starter, the ball is seated below the crown of the muzzle with one sharp whack from the palm of the hand on the handle of the short starter. My favorite short starters have leather padding on the tip of the stub so that the ball is not disfigured here. Slight damage to the nose of the ball does *not* affect accuracy; however, some of us prefer, for cosmetic reasons mostly, to maintain the shape of the ball as best as possible. Also, our tests on ball deformity were not run at long-range, and it could be that severe deformity does affect accuracy at the longer ranges.

7. Seating the Ball

Now, with the longer rod on the short starter, the ball is forced down the bore a few inches. This gives the wiping stick

Lastly, using a capper like the Hawken Shop model (right), you carefully seat a percussion cap on the nipple (below).

You are now ready to fire.

or loading rod a chance to work. The loading rod is used to push the ball all the way downbore and seat the patched ball firmly at the breech. We do not want any separation at all between the ball and the powder charge. The longer stem on the short starter will have pushed the ball far enough downbore so that the loading rod is now capable of fully seating that ball. This should be done with pressure. The shooter can use his bathroom scale to initially determine how much pressure he is using when seating the ball.

With the standard loading rod placed directly on the scale, the shooter can push down and "get the feel" of the pressure he is exerting on the ball and powder charge down in the breech. In this book, I tried to stay with about 40 pounds of pressure, roughly. Shot-to-shot variation was so small in testing that we can be rest assured the pressure used here was adequate and at the same time, not too strong. The loads were very uniform in velocity readings.

Notice we mention a loading rod here and not a ramrod. The ramrod that rests in the pipes underneath the barrel of the rifle is highly useful and necessary for the field; however, it is an expedient on the range. A good loading rod, such as the Uncle Mike or the Durango, or Excellent N and W Rod— especially those rods fitted with a muzzle protector—is far better than the wooden ramrod. Naturally, in the field the ramrod is used for second shots. With a squirrel rifle, for example, I keep my patching material thin enough so that I will not break a ramrod in the field, since shooting for squirrels and rabbits can mean a lot of loading in a day, and I often use a liquid lube, even though I am in the field and not on the range, so that fouling is cleared away more thoroughly.

8. Cap It

The rifle is loaded. Now we need to place a cap on the nipple. I like to use a capper, such as the Hawken Shop model, as this is fast and handy, and it also prevents the fingers from having to squeeze a cap onto the nipple, though if done carefully the cap should certainly not be so sensitive as to go off from merely forcing it on the cone of the nipple. We maintain the position of the muzzle always in a safe direction, and now that the piece is capped, this is even more vital to safety.

9. Shoot It

First step in loading the Hatfield 36-caliber Squirrel Rifle in flintlock ignition system is to block the touchhole. The author uses a tapered pipe cleaner to block the touchhole here. However, a well-fitted metal rod is even better for this task.

With the touchhole blocked, the powder charge is poured downbarrel. Naturally, with a caplock, we do not worry about a touchhole. We leave the hammer on halfcock and pour the powder. In both firearm types, we must have a bore free of oil, and it's wise to swab the bore dry before loading. With the caplock, we also fire a few caps to clear the nipple of oil.

10. Clean It

In the field or on the range, I like to clean between shots if possible. This is so simple. All I do is swab the bore very quickly with one pass of a cleaning patch mildly saturated with rubbing alcohol, followed by one or two dry patches. Why clean the bore? First, I have seen changes in accuracy when bores were not cleaned. The first thing we want from shooting is accuracy, and cleaned bores deliver better accuracy. Pyrodex does not foul as much as black powder and many shooters find that they do *not* need to clean between shots as often when using Pyrodex.

With Pyrodex, I usually fire a string of up to five shots and then wipe the bore down. Another problem with a dirty bore, and we are speaking of black powder fouling now, is the fact that it raises pressures. I have fired several shots in succession over the chronograph screens without cleaning between shots and the velocity keeps going up, indicating a rise in pressures. Accuracy goes down the drain when velocity continues to rise, since the ball or bullet will no longer strike the target in the same place.

There are some miracle lubes on the market today, however, which do allow for several shots in a row without cleaning, and one of these is Young Country No. 103. Here, for example, is a test run using No. 103 with a Denver Bullet Company 220-grain Maxi ball in a 45-caliber H&A Buggy Rifle underhammer. The charge was 70-grains volume, GOI FFg black powder:

Shot Number
1. 1,317 fps
2. 1,323 fps
3. 1,325 fps
4. not recorded
5. not recorded
6. 1,373 fps
7. not recorded
8. not recorded
9. not recorded
10. 1,375 fps
11. through 19. not recorded
20. 1,322

With the stub end of the short starter, in this case the Tresco short starter, the ball is forced below the crown of the muzzle. Of course, it rests in its lubricated patch. With heavier loads that will eat the patch from the expanding gases of the ignited charge, you may wish to insert a patch down upon the powder charge *before* entering the patched ball. A piece of hornet's nest may also be used very effectively for the same purpose.

Out of the ball bag, the shooter removes one .350″ round ball. Remember, the powder charge is in the barrel at this point. The same process applies to both flinter and caplock.

These were consecutive shots with no cleaning between shots whatsoever. Directions on the Young Country No. 103 jar were followed to the letter. One can see that the difference between shot No.1 and shot No. 20 is insignificant. On the other hand, with standard lubes, I have seen marked increases in velocity when the bore was not swabbed. It is wise, therefore, to swab between shots or use a lube which allows for various numbers of shots to be fired before cleaning is required. The shooter, of course, must choose a lube as part of his load chain in terms of individual rifle accuracy and other factors.

The Caplock Rifle with the Maxi or Minie

Here, we follow the same procedures as above; however, we do not place a patch of any kind on the conical. The conical is run downbore pre-greased. All other factors are the same.

Loading the Flintlock Rifle

Many of the steps here are like those above; however, there are some major differences and we will target in on those differences.

1. Wipe the Rifle Dry

Same procedure as before for the same reasons

2. Try for a Spark

The flintlock can be "dry-fired." We simply ear the hammer back and close the cover on the pan, putting the frizzen into place, and pull the trigger. A shower of sparks should rain down upon the pan as the frizzen flies open from the hammer blow. Incidentally, there are different names for flintlock parts, and we are using those currently popular. Often, the hammer was called a cock and the frizzen could be called a hammer or even a frizzle.

3. Charge It (after blocking the vent hole)

Provided that a spark shower has occurred, we can charge the rifle as we did above. We should make sure before loading that the vent is clear and blocked before we pour down our powder charge. Naturally, we want to have a clear vent so the the spark from the pan powder can jump into the main charge in the breech and set it off. However, why "block the vent?"

25

The longer stem on the short starter is now used to drive the patched ball farther into the bore. One swift smack of the hand is enough to seat the ball to this depth. Again, the same process applies to the caplock rifle and to the single shot pistol.

Now, preferably with a loading rod, such as the N&W rod shown, the load is fully seated, with the ball firmly pressed down upon the powder charge. Remember, we are looking for consistent pressure upon the loading rod, and, a strong, stable rod, such as this N&W model, will easily bear up under the kind of modest pressure demanded here. Remember, the *process* remains the same for caplock and pistol. With a Minie or Maxi, we do not use a patch, but simply seat the projectile directly upon the powder charge.

What we are after is a clean *pathway* for the spark to take from the pan powder to the main charge in the breech. If the vent is filled with powder, then the powder has to burn out of the way before the spark can ignite the main charge in the breech. This is a fuse. We do not want a fuse. We want the rifle to go off with the best possible lock time. In fact, well constructed flinters with the touchhole rather high on the wall of the flat facing the pan, often have a very fast lock time that closely rivals the lock time on a percussion rifle. We want the touchhole to be high so that it will not be invaded by powder from the pan.

I was speaking with Bucky Malson, world famous expert black powder shooter, and I mentioned that I blocked the vent or touchhole on the muzzleloader *before* dropping the charge downbore. I waited for his reaction when I said I used a pipe cleaner. "You are wrong, Sam," he began, and I was pretty downhearted because I knew I was speaking with a voice of authority on the subject. "Don't use a pipe cleaner,"

he continued, "Use a small metal rod instead. That works better."

Don "Bucky" Malson was right, of course. The little metal rod truly filled the vent hole with precision, and it was extended easily into the vent or touchhole (same thing) as far as it would go.

Now, with the touchhole blocked, the main charge is dropped downbore and compacted into place with pressure, just as we described above. When the little metal rod is carefully removed from the touchhole, it leaves the touchhole clear and the packed powder in the breech has a small "tunnel" in it from the position of the metal rod. Now, the flash from the pan powder can fly through the clear touchhole and into the main charge.

4. Prime the Pan After the Ball Has Been Seated As Above

Since the metal rod was left in the touchhole during the loading, we now have a charge in the breech and a clean

At this point, the charge is seated firmly in the breech. If shooting a caplock, the percussion cap is placed upon the cone of the nipple. In shooting our Hatfield flinter, we push the frizzen forward, carefully extract the little rod or pipe cleaner from the touchhole and then we prime the pan. Priming the pan is accomplished here with a pan priming tool from Navy Arms Company. The tool holds a quantity of FFFFg pan powder and dispenses a small amount as the nose of the tool is forced inward.

With frizzen snapped back to cover the pan, the Hatfield is ready to fire. With careful loading, a good flinter will "go off" with top regularity. In a test of this rifle, we got 29 out of 30 ignitions. A chipped flint accounted, we believe, for the one misfire.

touchhole. But we must prime the pan with the fuel that will ignite the main charge in the breech. Naturally, FFFFg is used for this operation. The pan is *not* filled. The pan is given a modest amount of priming powder only, from one-third to a bit over one-half full. The shooter should test his own flinter to see which is best.

5. Fire

After closing the pan, the hammer is cocked back, and we are ready to shoot. Naturally, the patching and seating of the ball follow the same procedure as above, and we need not go into that again. There are no differences there. Also, we might point out that we have discovered *no* differences between the same barrel lengths and calibers in flintlock velocities and caplock velocities. Here's an example:

Renegade Flintlock *vs* Renegade Percussion

Renegade 54-caliber rifle in flintlock *vs* a Renegade 54-caliber rifle in percussion. With the Denver Bullet Company 54-caliber Maxi in 400-grain weight, here are three test velocities for these two rifles:

Renegade Percussion			Renegade Flintlock		
		Muzzle			Muzzle
Charge	Powder	Velocity	Charge	Powder	Velocity
80 vol.	FFg, GOI	1219 fps	80 vol.	FFg, GOI	1222
100 vol.	FFg, GOI	1375 fps	100 vol.	FFg, GOI	1381
120 vol.	FFg, GOI	1499 fps	120 vol.	FFg, GOI	1508

Considering that these are two different rifles, even though both come from the same company and the barrels are virtually identical, it was a surprise to me when I saw how extremely close the tested figures were. Other rifles of similar barrel length and caliber in flint and percussion were also close in ballistics.

6. Clean (same as described before)

LOADING THE BLACK POWDER REVOLVER

The first step in loading the black powder revolver is to insure that the gun is clean and free of oil in the chambers. We fire one or two percussion caps on each nipple to blow any minor deposit of oil out of the vents. Then, as shown here, the powder can be introduced to the chambers. We are using a CVA flask with a short 24-grain spout. The flask generally comes with a 30-grain spout. Remember, there are *no caps* on the nipples at this point.

Directly on top of the powder, we can insert a corn meal filler if we wish to. In this case, we have elected to omit the filler and we are using a single Wonder Wad (Ox-Yoke Co.) on the powder charge. This will prevent a chain fire and no grease need be put over the balls after loading.

Now the ball is introduced to the mouth of the cylinder's chamber, one ball for each, one at a time and seated one at a time of course. The ball merely rests upon the loaded chamber at this point. Remember, the powder and Wonder Wad are already in the chamber.

Loading the Caplock and Flintlock Pistol

The caplock pistol follows along the same loading procedures as established with the caplock rifle. For the flintlock pistol, again, follow the basic procedures outlined in the steps for loading the flintlock rifle.

Loading the Black Powder Revolver

Here, we have another story. The black powder revolver is entirely unlike its modern cousin in loading, and it is also different from the other muzzle-loading arms we have discussed or will discuss. (For a complete rundown on black powder handguns, the reader may wish to consult *The Black Powder Handgun*, DBI Books, Inc.)

1. Clean It

Once again, we must wipe away any preservative oils so that we have a clean bore and clean nipple vents. The pipe cleaner, especially the tapered model, will work well to clear the nipple vents of any oil.

2. Fire Caps

One or two caps can be fired on each nipple to insure that all the lubricant is dried up. The muzzle can again be pointed in a safe direction toward some light object that when the trigger is pulled will be moved aside from the thrust of the cap in the empty revolver.

3. Charge It

The chambers, with the exception of one, are loaded with powder. A handy device is the flask, such as the CVA model, which can dump the correct charge quickly. The empty cham-

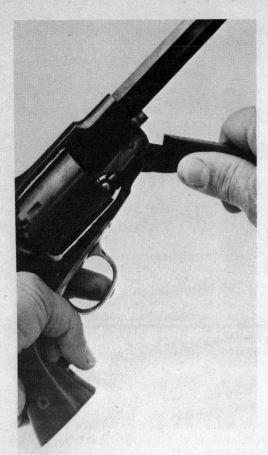

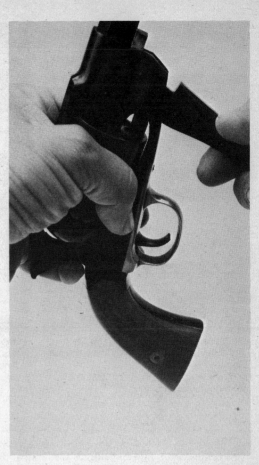

(Left) With the ball resting on the mouth of the chamber, the loading rod is pushed downward to drive the ball down into the chamber. We found accuracy somewhat improved by filling dead air space in the chamber with an inert substance such as corn meal.

(Right) The ball is driven all the way down on top of the powder charge using the loading rod.

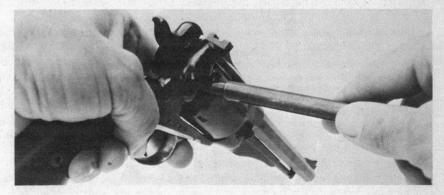

With a Hawken Shop capper, each nipple of this Navy Arms Remington '58 revolver is capped. We are now ready to shoot.

ber is aligned with the barrel for safety in carrying the handgun. Of course, the Remington '58 style safety notch may be used in which case the shooter may load all six chambers at his own discretion.

4. Ram the Ball or Bullet Home

A dry, unlubed ball or bullet may now be inserted into the mouth of each chamber and rammed home using the ramrod that is provided on most revolvers. In some cases, the shooter may wish to position a felt greased wad *between* the powder and the ball. This precludes having to place lube on top of the ball later. Ox-Yoke Company offers their Wonder Wad for this purpose. The ball or bullet is firmly rammed home. In an unchamfered chamber mouth, a slight ring of lead will be cut away from the round ball during loading, which is all right.

5. Grease Cylinder Mouths

If no wad has been used between the powder and ball, it is wise to grease the chamber mouth so that fire from one detonated chamber will not chainfire other loaded chambers.

Note: Just as in other black powder firearms, we do not recommend a space between the powder charge and the projectile in the handgun. When light charges are used, the space in the chamber not taken up by powder can be filled with something inert, such as cornmeal. Usually, this provides better accuracy than leaving the space empty, and we recommend this procedure.

6. Cap and Fire

Naturally, we must position a percussion cap on the nipple of each loaded chamber for ignition purposes, and the revolver is ready to shoot.

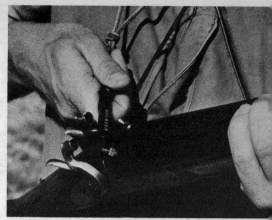

After seating the over-shot wad, which is merely a case of inserting the wad into the muzzle by hand and forcing the wad down-bore with the ramrod, the gun is capped and ready to fire. By leaving the hammers on halfcock, the charge is better seated because air is more easily driven out through the vent in the nipple.

Wads are inserted into the muzzles by hand and with the ramrod the wads are seated on the powder charge. Of course, a one-piece plastic wad can also be used. And it, too, is seated with the ramrod.

On top of the over-powder wad(s), a dose of shot is poured. Here we again use a horn, a shot horn, with the spout correctly calibrated to toss a specific amount of shot.

Loading the Caplock Shotgun

The joys of the muzzle-loading shotgun are many. It is an obedient servant, and its ballistics are not that far behind the modern scattergun. All the caplock shotgun asks is to be loaded correctly. While this is a rundown on the basics, we have a chapter on loading fine points which will help the reader create truly effective loads.

1. Wipe the Shotgun Dry

This is the same old advice. We need a clean gun in order to insure proper function.

2. Pop a Cap

Once again, we pop caps on the nipples to insure that the bore and nipple vents are clear. The shotgun, because of its big bores, makes a hollow *thump! thump!* when the vents on the nipples are clear. When the vents are not clear, the sound is more like a *crack!*

3. Charge It

There is nothing mysterious about charging the shotgun. As we discuss in a later chapter, we keep a balance between powder and shot in a *volumetric* way for standard shooting, and we vary the balance in favor of powder or shot when we want to affect a different type of pattern. See the chapter on shotgun loads and patterns for the fine points.

4. Over-Powder Wad

On top of the powder, we need an over-powder wad. If we are going to use a one-piece plastic wad, this can usually, but not always, be omitted. With a felt wad, the over-powder wad is useful because it aids in keeping the felt wad from having a hole burned through it by the powder. By leaving the hammers on half-cock, the air can be expelled through the vent of the nipples as the wad(s) are being seated.

Again, we leave the exact type of wads to be used for our shotgun chapter. We can use standard strong cardboard wads for closer shooting and the fine modern components for longer range shooting if we want to.

5. After the Over-Powder Wad

On top of the over-powder wad we can insert a one-piece plastic wad or we can use a felt wad.

6. Shot Charge

The shot is poured home from a dipper, a shot flask or some other means as long as we stick to a definite volume and weight of shot for safety.

7. Over-Shot Wad

Some form of wad over the shot is necessary. There are some very good over-shot wads available from Dixie, Circle Fly and Ballistics Products, Inc. These wads should fit tightly so that the load is held intact in the bore. Naturally, when one barrel is fired a few times without the opposite barrel being fired, it's wise to check the unfired barrel to make certain that the charge is still intact in the breech and *not* moved up the bore!

8. Cap and Fire

This is self-explanatory. We simply set our caps on the nipples (I like using the capper) and then fire the gun.

The reader will gain insight into several little loading tips and tricks as he winds his way over the path provided by our book. These have been only the basics, of course. However, we will provide more than the basics in other chapters. Black powder loading is simple, not difficult, but it is at the same time a precise maneuver, not a haphazard one. The shooter who takes care in putting his loads together is in for more enjoyment and success.

chapter 4

Propellants for Muzzleloaders

PYRODEX AND BLACK POWDER *are the only two fuels recommended in this book for our loads.* The simple reason for this is the fact that there are no other generally available propellants which we can safely recommend. While there are some well-built firearms with barrels of gun-quality steel in the muzzleloader world, and while these barrels can often take out-and-out abusive and rather pointless overloads of black powder, believe me, other types of powder will smash even this class of frontloader. Although this warning goes out almost daily, if not daily, in our black powder press, we have cases each year of damages caused by a shooter using smokeless powder.

Someday, an enterprising chemist is going to come up with a new "black powder." It will be just as safe as black powder, and it will produce the same or even better ballistics. It might even make smoke and smell bad, but it is going to be non-corrosive. The person or company to come up with this fuel is going to make millions on it. After all, and it's too bad to admit this, there are thousands upon thousands of shooters who would take up the sport of muzzle-loading, but for one thing—they do not want to clean the guns after and during shooting. In my opinion, the cleanup is a minimal chore. But I can understand an aversion to pouring hot soapy water down barrels and running cleaning patches down the bore.

Pyrodex

The story on Pyrodex is both interesting and of course sad in that its inventor was killed by a flash-off. No one has shown Pyrodex to be anything but safe, however, and the January 27, 1977 tragedy which killed Dan Pawlak near Seattle, Washington, was no doubt one of those incalculable events of life. Pyrodex was, in my opinion, somewhat misunderstood from the start, and it was also misrepresented by some of us who wrote on the subject. Hodgdon's Powder Company made no outlandish claims for the fuel. They simply wanted to provide the shooter with a safe product, and one which would not require clean-up between shots.

Merits of Pyrodex
1. Easier to Transport
Pyrodex is gauged as safer by some experts, which is shown

in the fact that it can be shipped by U.P.S. (United Parcel Service), while black powder cannot. I have never taken possession of a can of black powder other than from my dealer or via truck.

2. Consistent Pressures
Pyrodex has a good record for giving consistent pressures shot after shot.

3. Consistent Velocity
Linked, of course, with item No. 2 above, the use of Pyrodex gives very consistent velocities. The Sd (Standard deviation) computed for Pyrodex loads proved to be low, which of course, is good.

4. More Shots per Pound
The bulk of Pyrodex is quite different from the bulk of regular black powder, and the shooter will get more shots from a pound of Pyrodex than he will from a can of black powder equaling the same pound weight. We are looking at something like 20+ percent difference in this respect, so that when the shooter burns 100 grains of black powder, the equivalent load in Pyrodex will be about 75-85 grains. This is not exact, but it's a fair approximation.

5. No Swabbing Between Shots
This is true. One need not swab between shots with Pyrodex; however, I do not care to shoot indefinitely with any fuel without paying some attention to the bore. Remember, however, when we use Pyrodex, we find that the velocity will not continually rise shot after shot. Using large volumes of black powder, for example, will show a rise in pressures from shot to shot unless the bore is cleaned after each shot. Beginners in black powder chronographing often ignore this fact, and they find the data in test books do not coincide with their own readings. As the fouling in the bore builds up, pressure rises. As pressure increases, so does velocity.

Pyrodex Clean-Up
Hodgdon has never, to the best of my knowledge, so much as suggested that you simply tote your smokepole home and

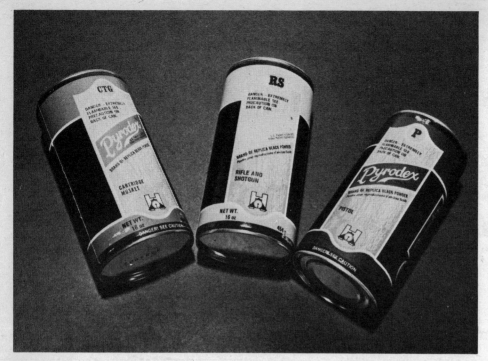

The Pyrodex granulations are "CTG", or Cartridge, far left in the photo, "RS" in the middle and "P" on the right. CTG is useful in the cartridge case as well as in heavy shotgun gauges, such as the 10. It is not recommended for standard charges in the muzzle-loading rifle. RS (Rifle-Shotgun) is suited for shotgun and rifle loads, while P (Pistol) is best suited for the revolver and some pistols.

forget it after a shooting session with Pyrodex. It is true that Pyrodex is hygroscopic. That means it will "attract" moisture and hold it. Naturally, we end up with some compounds such as ferric hydroxide $Fe(OH)_3$ plus ferric oxide Fe_2O_3, or *rust*.

Pyrodex is cleaned up just as black powder is cleaned up, and that means using some form of solvent. Water, the universal solvent, is often as good as any when a complete cleanup is called for, and there are some indications which suggest that soap in the water helps out. Others think soap is not helpful. But the idea is to break down the residue left by Pyrodex and flush/wipe it from the bore. So clean-up *after shooting* is not only a good idea, it is absolutely essential with both black powder and Pyrodex. Some trusted shooters do not use water cleanup, but rather moose milk and other agents.

Pyrodex in Flintlocks

Mainly, Pyrodex was intended as a fuel for caplocks, and it is not at home in the flinter. Some shooters do use a duplex load with Pyrodex, and it does work. This means first putting a small *measured* amount of standard black powder downbore into the breech area, followed by the remainder of the bulk load in Pyrodex. The starter load of black powder *and* Pyrodex *together* make up the total load. It is *not* a matter of tossing in *extra* black powder for the kicker and going over the recommended charge. As will be seen in this chapter, I am not a duplex load lover for black powder. I can tell the reader that I did try Pyrodex in flintlocks with and without the duplex load method. Simply stated, it worked well in the first method, but it did not work in the second. I used a charge of 10 grains of FFFg with 40 grains of Pyrodex RS in a 45-caliber flinter with satisfactory results. Regular FFFFg pan powder is used in the priming pan for ignition only.

Pyrodex Ballistics

Pyrodex can vary slightly, lot-to-lot, just as modern black powder (or even smokeless) varies from lot-to-lot. There is nothing new about this phenomenon. I have found that my test lot coupled with the specific measures I have used for my tests produced weight-for-weight differences of up to 24 percent (roughly) between Pyrodex and regular black powder. In other words, a 100-grain volume of black powder in the Uncle Mike measure for FFFg produced about 100 grains weight of that fuel (actually a shade more), but the same measure at the same 100 setting averaged out at about 76.0 grains of Pyrodex by weight.

However, in keeping with the laws of using Pyrodex, this is as it should be. The shooter must *not* load by weight with Pyrodex. *He must load by volume.* Simply set the measure for the stated *standard black powder load* and then use that measure at that setting for Pyrodex. The weight of Pyrodex will be less than the black powder weight, which is correct.

Peak Pressures for Pyrodex

As with black powder, Pyrodex can continually rise in pressure. Yes, the same laws of diminishing returns apply, and it is foolish (unsafe) to pour in more Pyrodex than the maximum calls for because this can result in problems of high pressures, often with little value in velocity gains.

Ignition with Pyrodex

The use of the Hot Shot nipple aided Pyrodex ignition in our tests. Since Pyrodex is harder to ignite than black powder, the concentrated spark and larger orifice at the cone of the Hot Shot did aid ignition qualities with Pyrodex. This is not to suggest that there are no other good nipples on the market for Pyrodex. I also found success with the Ampco nipple, such as sold by Tresco. Finally, it is suggested that the shooter who wants added information on Pyrodex turn to the *Hodgdon Pyrodex/Black Powder Shooters Handbook,* which is an 83-page booklet on the subject. (It's available from Hodgdon for $2.95, postpaid.)

There *are* differences among various black powders. This is not to suggest that this makes one black powder necessarily better than another, only different. We detected great differences in velocity among various brands. In fact, one brand of FFg gave velocities similar to another brand's FFFg.

Black Powder

The first thing we should know is that our current black powder is of very good manufacture, quite consistent and powerful. We are lucky to have it. I refer in the main to GOI, which stands for Gearhart-Owens Industries. This is the brand of propellant most of us will find at the local gunshop, and it is the only brand referred to in this book with some minor exceptions as noted.

Differences Among Brands

Black powder has *always* varied from one brand to another, and those variations have always been rather great, with the exception of du Pont black powder of not very long ago, and the current GOI black powder, which are very similar in nature. However, just for the sheer learning value, let's look at some figures which compare two black powders. These are from my own tests:

TEST ONE
**58-caliber test rifle,
32″ barrel with 460-grain Lyman Minie**

Charge	Powder	Muzzle Velocity
150 grains volume	GOI FFg	1,612 fps
150 grains volume	Nobel FFg	1,411 fps

TEST TWO
Same Test Rifle but with 600-grain Lyman Minie

Charge	Powder	Muzzle Velocity
125 grains volume	GOI FFg	1,371 fps
125 grains volume	Nobel FFg	998 fps

This is not to put down Nobel black powder at all. We must hasten to point out that Nobel got good velocity per pressure, and that it did use larger doses of fuel to get its velocity, but it got top drawer velocities within reasonable pressure limits. However, one can see at a glance that the two different brands of powder are indeed different in performance. The reader *must* know this. A load listed in here for GOI *cannot* be switched to another brand of black powder. More importantly, the modern GOI fuel *cannot* be used in the same proportions of milder black powders.

When a reader sees a load out of the past, he must immediately assume that this load is too much for our more efficient GOI propellant. Therefore, those old prescriptions that we might run across out of olden day manuscripts are to be shunned as a reference. I once saw a load of 200 grains of FFg for a 53-caliber rifle—this load was taken from old data. I'd say that the powder was of the milder sort. Certainly, 200 grains of FFg behind a .520″ ball today with GOI would be considered imprudent. Enough said on the subject. But let the reader always remind himself that not all black powder is created equal.

Granulations

There is also a very large difference among granulations and how they perform. These differences are tremendous, not minor. The granulation of a powder (in black powder terms) corresponds to the shape and coating used on modern smokeless powders. We all know that there are vast differences among smokeless powders, and yet some shooters want to treat black powders, no matter the brand or the "cut," as the same. It won't work that way. Basically, the different granulations of black powder are gauged by a type of sieve and the finer cut will go through the finer mesh, of course, and give us our FFFFg and FFFg granulations.

There is not exact precision in any given granulation as labeled on any particular can of black powder. However, one can be rest assured that FFFFg is very fine of grain, while FFFg is a bit less fine, and so forth.

Here are the four basic black powder granulations available and most popular today. Upper left we have FFFFg, a pan powder. While some revolver manufacturers recommend FFFFg in their products, this fuel's main use is in the pan of the flintlock firearm, where it creates a flash which ignites the main charge in the breech by passing through a touchhole. FFFFg is the *finest* granulation. To the right of FFFFg is, FFFg. FFFg, or Three-F, is a highly useful fuel. It is recommended for many pistols and revolvers, is excellent in the small caliber rifle (under 45 caliber), as a main charge, and is highly useful as a plinking charge in the big bores. Lower left, we have FFg. FFg is more coarse than FFFg and less coarse than Fg. It is the choice for hunting charges in 45s and up. On the lower right is Fg, best used in the big bore shotguns, such as the 10-gauge and in some muskets. Also useful in the 12-gauge with round ball.

As an interesting side note, we find that some black powder out of the past, in this case we think the 19th century in America, came in rather odd-sized containers, such as this one shown here. The container shows that this was FFFg granulation black powder, and the small can may indicate that handgunners or sub-bore shooters bought their fuel this way.

FFFFg: The 4-F granulation is for priming pans, and that is about it, with the exception of some modern black powder revolver manufacturers who say that it is OK to use FFFFg as the main charge in their handguns. These are generally stoutly built firearms, and no shooter should ever use FFFFg as the main charge in the breech of any black powder gun unless the manufacturer has expressly allowed him to do so *in writing*. I have but one gripe with the famous red and white can of black powder we are so familiar with today, which is as fine a fuel as any shooter could ever ask for. That one complaint has to do with the statement on the can. When we read the label, we find out that even in FFFFg granulation the back of the can reads, "SUITABLE FOR MUSKETS, PISTOLS & SHOT-GUNS." Well, it isn't. I don't even like FFFg in muskets or shotguns, let alone FFFFg. I think the wording should be changed to, "SUITABLE FOR PRIMING FLINTLOCKS" on the FFFFg can. Then the owners of the few revolvers which allow FFFFg as main charges can make a note of this use, while the general shooting public will be told to leave FFFFg out of the breech.

FFFg: This is a highly useful granulation. It is enough coarser than FFFFg to burn safely in the small bores, and it is also useful in *small* doses for target work in the larger bores. The reader will note that we often show a low-end load of

The excellent GOEX black powder makes certain statements on the back of the can which require interpretation. For example, the writing at the top of the can states "Black Rifle Powder," however the fuel may be useful for pistol or shotgun or revolver as well as rifle, or it may be suitable for none, as in the case of FFFFg in the rifle. Below that statement are the words "suitable for muskets, pistols & shot-guns;" however, a charge of FFFFg, again, would not be necessarily suitable for pistols, nor muskets nor shotguns. We consider FFFFg primarily a pan powder, with the exception that some revolver makers allow FFFFg as the main charge in the chambers of their products. The remainder of the information on this excellent product is self-explanatory and important.

FFFg on the left and FFFFg on the right show how markedly different these two granulations are.

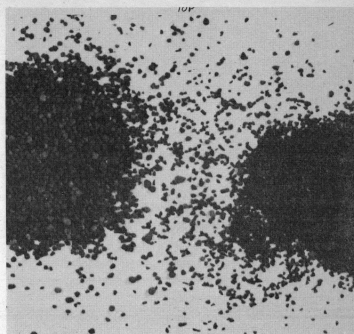

Pyrodex CTG shown on the left compared with GOEX FFg clearly indicates the differences one can expect among granulations in black powder fuels.

A Comparison of FFg and FFFg in Rifles
Data compiled and prepared by Edward M. Yard

Caliber	Charge	Muzzle Velocity	Pressure
45 caliber	80 grs. FFFg	1970 fps	10,500 LUP
45 caliber	80 grs. FFg	1910 fps	8,000 LUP
50 caliber	70 grs. FFFg	1700 fps	8,600 LUP
50 caliber	80 grs. FFFg	1850 fps	10,000 LUP
50 caliber	100 grs. FFg	1850 fps	8,800 LUP

FFFg for the big bores, but we never use FFFg for big hunting loads in calibers of 45 and up. Naturally, FFFg is good for the sub-calibers such as the 32 and 36, also revolvers, small bore pistols and main charges in calibers up to 40 or 44.

FFFg burns clean. It has become the darling child of most black powder shooters, but I am not in favor of its use in the 45s and up for *hunting* loads. I think FFg is better here. We can often get as much velocity out of FFg as FFFg with *less* pressure for those hunting loads. Yes, we will use more FFg than FFFg to get that velocity, but the fact remains that we will do so with *less* pressure.

FFg: For shotguns, this kernel size along with Fg is best, and it is best, in my own opinion, for the heavy hunting charges in 45-caliber and up. A note in the *Lyman Black Powder Handbook* on page 85 of the copy I have shows why FFg is my preferred fuel for the larger bores. In a test using the pressure rig, Lyman got 1,779 fps with a charge of 140 grains of FFg, GOI brand. The pressure was rated at 8500 LUP (Lead Units of Pressure, not the same as PSI). Meanwhile, with only 100 grains of FFFg in the same 54-caliber firearm shooting the same projectile, the velocity was 1,740 fps, almost as high as the FFg charge of 140 grains. But, the pressure for the 100

grains of FFFg was 11,700 LUP, appreciably higher than the FFg charge of 140 grains.

This was not an isolated test. In further tests that I have been privy to, the same results showed up. Naturally, and we have to keep hammering at this, there are dozens of variables when we try to test any of these things, and we cannot expect to have data repeat itself exactly in other rifles. In fact, in some cases, especially in calibers of 58, 60 and up, FFg seemed to offer a velocity much closer to FFFg charge for charge. This is in *some* firearms.

However, I'll stick my neck out a short distance and suggest that for hunting loads, FFg be used in 45-caliber and up, saving FFFg for target work and for the smaller bore arms.

Fg: The useful 1-F powder is at home in the big bore arms that we call muskets. It burns well behind the heavy ball or Minie used in these big bores. In fact, some of the very best shotgun patterns which I have gotten from the 12-gauge (and especially the 10-gauge) resulted from Fg loads. So, with round ball or shot in the shotgun, and in firing muskets of 75-caliber and that range, Fg fuel is very much at home.

Fg is not very useful in the small bore arms. And I mean from 54-caliber on down. In some of the 54s, with Maxis, Fg was not without merit. But let's look at what happens in a 54-caliber custom rifle when Fg is used:

54-caliber rifle, 1:79 twist, 34″ barrel
RIG lube, Irish linen .013″ patch

Charge	Powder	Projectile	Muzzle Velocity
120 weight (Not volume)	GOI FG	225-ball	1,515 fps
140 weight (Not volume)	GOI FG	225-ball	1,682 fps

Now let's compare the velocity in the exact same rifle using FFg GOI black powder. Where 120 grains weight of Fg had earned 1,515 fps at the muzzle, a charge of 120 grains by weight (not volume) of FFg GOI gave the same ball a muzzle velocity of about 1,943 fps. (Later, in this same rifle, the average was closer to 1,975 fps.) And with the 140-grain weight charge of Fg the 225-grain ball obtained a muzzle velocity of 1,682 fps, while that very same charge weight in the same rifle with the same ball earned 2,084 with FFg GOI. In short, Fg was not the medicine for this ball-shooting, 54-caliber rifle.

A Few Black Powder Facts

We will show in a moment that black powder ignites very swiftly and easily; however, untrue to the data from the past, it does not go *whoosh!* in one big boom. It indeed, in the Winchester test we will be referring to, took about 3.75 milliseconds to totally burn in the bore. So, black powder does ignite quickly, but it does not simply "blow up" in the bore and burn itself out in the first couple inches of breech area.

Black powder, depending of course on brand, lot, granulation, and so forth, requires about 600 degrees F. *(roughly)* to ignite. One measurement of the temperature of the burning gases was 4,000 degrees F. In a lower atmospheric pressure, rate of "explosion" or burning can be altered. (See "Muzzle Loading Chemistry," *Muzzle Blasts Magazine,* Joe W. Craig, page 9, October, 1972.) We do not have last minute data on black powder burning with full details explained, but chemists who are interested in black powder, such as chemist Bill Ihm, who is also a superb muzzleloader custom builder, can help us learn about the burning characteristics of this fuel.

The data I have, both from Ihm and the Craig article, confirms that the deposits left by the burning of black powder are mainly salts. This means that a polar solvent, such as water, will best dissolve these salts. Below is a list of residue remaining after a charge of black powder has been ignited in the bore. And remember that over 50 percent of the black powder charge is left behind as solids. It is not turned from solids into a gas. Therefore, black powder is very different from smokeless powder. Here are the agents, most of them, left behind after a charge of black powder has been ignited:

Potassium carbonate	K_2CO_3
Potassium sulfate	K_2SO_4
Potassium sulfide	K_2S
Potassium thiosulfate	$K_2S_2O_3$
Potassium thiocynate	$KNCS$
Carbon	C
Sulfur	S

(This data from Joe W. Craig's "Muzzle Loading Chemistry," *Muzzle Blasts Magazine,* Oct. 1972, p. 9)

We can immediately see that all of the solids above are salts except for C and S, carbon and sulfur. Oils would have very little effect upon these solids. This is why we suggest a patch lube that is "watery" for the range. But we like a grease for the field because we are not interested in immediately loading numerous times while big game hunting. We are interested in bore protection and a good lube quality. Sometimes when the rabbit hunting or squirrel hunting is fast-paced, a liquid lube in the field is acceptable and preferable.

In higher humidity, according to Craig, there is more smoke because the moisture in the air actually retards the oxidation process and more carbon stays in the bore, hangs in the air and in short, is "retained" rather than burned up.

These are the gases left in the air from black powder oxidation:

Carbon dioxide	CO_2
Carbon monoxide	CO
Methane	CH_4
Hydrogen sulfide	H_2S
Hydrogen	H
Nitrogen	N_2

These are the properties of black powder in terms of its combustion, and according to the data worked up by Joe W. Craig and printed in *Muzzle Blasts Magazine* for October of 1972, as well as data discussed with chemist Bill Ihm. The important factors are clear—we see *how* our fuel behaves and we better understand that behavior. We can also see why it is imperative to clean black powder residue out of the bore. However, there is one more important point.

In effect, the black powder charge is in part the projectile, is it not? The expanding gases not only have to push the ball or conical out of the bore, but they must also push on all that "ejecta," the sum total of projectile *plus* all the unburned solids of the charge. And this is why, in part, we cannot simply load more and more fuel into the black powder arm and expect the results to be higher and higher velocity ad infinitum. We can in fact get more pressure without more velocity.

That is worth repeating. We can get more pressure without getting more velocity, at least not an important increase in velocity. Now the reader can see why we suggest optimum loads and why we speak of a law of diminishing returns in regard to the powder charge which is dropped down the bore. Also, we might add that shooting a black powder rifle without any ball or conical will still develop considerable pressure in the bore, because the black powder itself acts as a missile in part. It has to push itself out of the bore, requiring energy and costing in terms of pressure.

The Black Powder Curve

During the latter part of the 1960s, Winchester ran a time/pressure curve using both black powder and smokeless powder, and while this testing needs further interpretation, there are many interesting lessons learned. The data were printed in the good book by David E. Butler entitled *The American Shotgun.* Among the points made by the Winchester test, and we will offer a diagram of the time/pressure curve for examination, we have the following:

1. Ignition proved to be very rapid and facile. Black powder was *not* hard to ignite at all.

2. The black powder charge did not consume itself in the first few inches of bore. Bore time showed that the black powder charge did not erupt as one blast.

3. The immediate pressure rise was very rapid, because of the easy ignition quality of the black powder; however, the pressure *fell back* after the first rise. To supply figures here, the pressure rose from zero to 2200 PSI (pounds per square inch) in less than .1 (one-tenth) of one millisecond. But the pressure fell back to 1800 PSI almost immediately, and peaked out at 4,900 PSI.

4. The pressure/time curve characteristics proved to be

much smoother in profile for black powder than for the particular smokeless ball powder used in the test. The peak pressure was low and it had a much slower pressure decline than the smokeless powder.

5. The bore time of the black powder load was slower than the bore time for the smokeless load. The projectile, in this case a charge of shot, since the test was conducted within modern shotgun hulls, was not accelerated up the bore as rapidly during the early phase of burning; therefore, it took the shot longer to reach the muzzle when propelled by black powder than when it was propelled by smokeless powder. The black powder bore time was 3.75 milliseconds, while the smokeless powder bore time was 3 milliseconds. In other words, the black powder load was in the barrel .75 milliseconds longer than the smokeless.

It would be well to take a look at the Winchester time/pressure curve now, as it shows a rather interesting burning characteristic for black powder. First, however, let's establish the details of the loads:

A. **Black powder load**
   12-gauge hull, 1⅛ ounces of No. 7½ shot
   82.0 grains of du Pont FFFg black powder by weight
B. **Smokeless powder load**
   12-gauge hull, 1⅛ ounces of No. 7½ shot
   18.5 grains of W.C. 441 ball powder (a Winchester propellant only used by the factory)

Duplex Loads

We must concern ourselves with this topic in our discussion of powders, for duplex loading means mixing various granulations of powder in the breech, one type or granulation on top of another. *I am against the practice.* I find it of no value. However, as with the other aspects of our discussion, we need to talk about the *why* here, rather than dictating to the reader. Here is a load chart to ponder:

Duplex Loads With the H&A Deerstalker
(58-caliber, 32-inch barrel, Lyman 525-grain Minie, Hodgdon Minnie [*sic*] lube, du Pont powder)
1. 10 FFFg + 100 FFg = 1164 fps muzzle velocity
2. 20 FFFg + 90 FFg = 1258 fps muzzle velocity

Of course, the velocity increased a bit with the second load. We already know that FFFg delivers more energy, more pressure and hence more velocity (in most cases) than FFg, so there is nothing earth-shaking about the data above. But there is something else we know: Black powder ignites very, very easily. Therefore, the duplex load is of little to no value to us. If FFg were harder to ignite than FFFg to such a level that ignition were a problem, then we might consider using a duplex load to "kick" FFg off. But FFg does not require a hotshot boost from FFFg. The shooter should stay with one granulation of powder in black powder shooting. I am aware that there are those who do not agree. I am aware that to this day, some shooters, very few, actually mix various powders to boost their velocities. The little bit of gain is not worth the bother.

Other Powders

1. du Pont Bulk Smokeless

Somewhere along the line, there has been a mild confusion on this powder. It was on the market from 1893 into the early

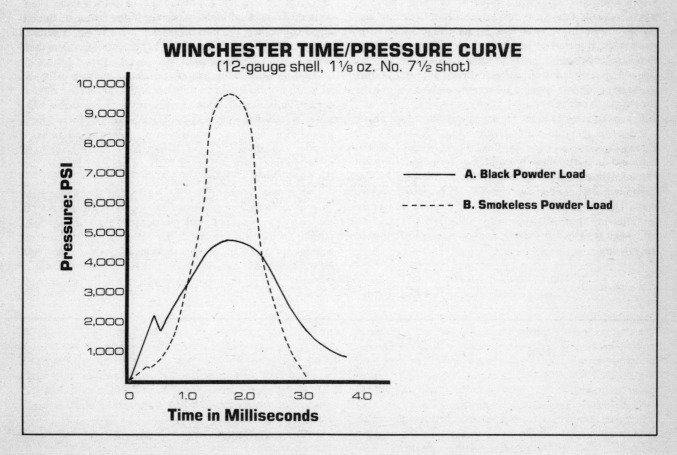

1960s. And du Pont strictly warned, and I quote: "Warning: While it [Bulk Smokeless] is intended for volumetric loading by drams it is not suitable for use as a replacement for black powder in older guns." In spite of this warning, I still receive queries from shooters concerned with Bulk Smokeless. They want to know if they can't use it in their muzzleloaders. They want to mix it with black powder. The answer to these queries is short and it is simple—NO! The powder was designed to be used inside of shotgun hulls, but it was never intended for use in any muzzleloader. It was introduced when smokeless powder was new. Shooters have always been handloaders and du Pont felt that this powder would be useful in shotshells because it could be loaded (in shotshells only) bulk-for-bulk with black powder volumetric dram measurements. But if some Bulk Smokeless is encountered today (and some is still no doubt to be found in someone's loading cabinet), it should be kept entirely away from muzzleloaders of any sort.

2. Dense Powder

I also had queries about Dense Powder. To quote from *Gun Week,* Friday, December 22, 1978, " 'Dense powder' is a modern smokeless powder, frequently combined with nitroglycerine, that gives ballistics results identical to those obtained with black powder." But *Gun Week* does not for a moment imply that this fuel should be used in muzzleloaders. The paper does not tell the shooter he can use the powder in frontloaders of any sort. It is, in fact, not suitable for use in muzzleloaders of any kind and there is no recommendation to the contrary that I know of.

3. King's Semi-Smokeless Powder

One would think that this stuff would be as defunct as last year's newspaper; however, I still hear about it, and in two ways I actually ran across small quantities of the powder. I was given a can for test purposes, in fact, and to the best of my knowledge, it proved to be black powder. My strong suggestion is to implore the reader to leave King's alone. It's old, real old, and while my test sample worked out all right under *strict* test conditions, I would not recommend the use of King's for any reason whatsoever.

For the curious, I will list the ballistics obtained with King's and we will also quote an advertisement for this product, again to appease our curiosity. But I repeat—if any is located, it should be consummately avoided as far as loads are concerned. Using No. 103 lube in a 45-caliber rifle with a 20-inch barrel, we arrived at an average of 1,425 fps muzzle velocity with 70 grains volume and a 45-caliber, 220-grain Denver Bullet Company Maxi ball. The average velocity for 70 grains volume of GOI FFFg with the same projectile was 1,429 fps muzzle velocity.

Black Powder Storage

In the closing passages of this chapter, let's remind ourselves to store black powder safely. This means keeping it away from the inquisitive fingers of young Einsteins who want to make loud noises with various concoctions of substances they find lying around. That safe place away from children should be a dry spot, of course, and not a damp one. The powder is best kept in its own container, with the lid screwed on tightly. The less air getting to the powder, the better.

Black powder will last a very long time in top condition and strength if it is not exposed to dampness and to air. Also, it should never be stored in glass, for the obvious reasons of breakage, but also because light can attack the powder. The powder should be kept in the dark. Full containers are better than partially filled containers, for more air is excluded when powder takes up the volume of the can.

Composition

This is a loading book, not a history book, and we have avoided going into drawn out details of where black powder comes from, as if anyone knew for sure (nobody does). However, the dedicated and interested muzzle-loading fan should know at least what black powder is, and we will spend only a few moments talking about that before we leave the subject of the fuel that propels our Minies and round balls downrange.

According to W.W. Greener, from his book *The Gun and Its Development,* beginning on page 553, black powder was actually carried into the field of battle unmixed prior to the 16th century. Then it was mixed right there in the field just before use. Black powder was then, and is now, a mechanical mixture of three things: These are Saltpeter (Potassium nitrate), sulfur and a "body" of charcoal (carbon). There have been countless variations on the theme, to include mixing refined sugar with the powder (maybe that made it smell sweeter?). But the shooters kept coming back to the basics. There were differences, all right, especially in the charcoal. But we could count then and now on black powder being 75 percent saltpeter, 15 percent charcoal and 10 percent sulfur. And that, as they say, is the whole show.

Black powder, while still a mechanical mixture of Potassium nitrate, charcoal and sulfur, is also a varying fuel dependent upon its manufacture. This is why we have such a wide range of ballistics from very old black powder of early America to this point in time, and why even modern brands of black powder can differ widely in performance. I think we have shown in this chapter that the fuels we have for our modern day muzzleloaders are serious propellants.

Unfortunately, there is always a faction which wants to sway away from the established rules, and we have accidents caused by the misuse of black powder or the use of the wrong powder in the muzzleloader. The entire fascinating and rewarding sport of black powder shooting is a lot more fun when we treat the basic fuel with respect. Black powder is as safe as we make it. It is, however, an explosive and it does demand respect.

chapter 5

Black Powder Pressure

IMPORTANT! No shooter can rest assured that his loading methods are truly safe and reliable unless he considers the pressures that he is developing. A "working pressure" is that which is well within the metallurgical, structural and design capabilities of the firearm in question, and this is the type of pressure we are concerned with when we build an "optimum load." Pressure is not a dirty word. *Excessive* pressure, however, is just about the nastiest term in the shooter's vocabulary. Without pressure, we could not shoot. With excessive pressure, we may not be shooting because of possible damage to the firearm or ourselves.

Unfortunately, as with so many false black powder concepts handed down and repeated by all of us over the years, there is a very wrong "rule of thumb" pertaining to black powder pressures. Often, I have been told that under no circumstances can a black powder load generate more than 25,000 PSI (pounds per square inch) of pressure. Primarily, PSI is established with some source of electrical machinery. Today, PSI is very often replaced in shooting tests by LUP and CUP. LUP stands for *Lead Units of Pressure* and CUP represents *Copper Units of Pressure*.

The latter two are derived from a pressure gun in which a piston smashes a specific mass of lead or copper. When the pressure is too high for lead, then copper is put into the crusher instead so that a reading can be taken. The more the pellet is smashed by the pressure operating the piston, the higher the reading. The higher the reading, the higher the pressure. Neither LUP nor CUP is a perfect means of deriving exact pressure; however, both indicate sufficiently what is going on in that breech area, and we should believe strongly when they tell us that a level too high for safety has been reached. Naturally, the shooter does not carry a pressure gun to the range with him.

This is why it is so vital that a modern black powder shooter know something about black powder pressures in general, and it is also why it is very upsetting when a "law" is laid down, only to be disproved later on by test machinery. Getting back to our "law" concerning 25,000 PSI as a black powder maximum, that is a faulty one. Nobel and Abel, in the England of the 1880s, got readings up to 96,000 PSI with black powder. We must recognize a fact—their test machinery was not primitive. It was reliable.

Today, pressures of over 25,000 PSI have been generated. Granted, loads within the specified recommended maximums are generally well below the 15,000 CUP range. However, we need to know that *it is* possible to generate more than 25,000 PSI, in spite of the fact that our black powder firearm is not normally designed for that type of pressure. I have, on several

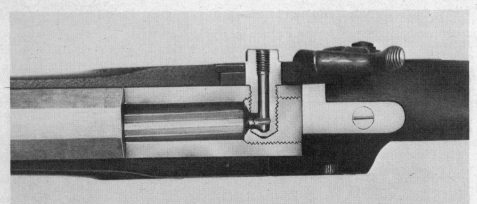

The reason we are often concerned about black powder pressures is the fact that our muzzleloaders, even the best of construction with good design, are an "open" system. Gas can escape back through the nipple itself. Therefore, we use black powder or Pyrodex *only* and *never* smokeless powder of *any* kind— ever! The muzzleloader design is perfectly safe and millions of shots have been fired with this system. All that is required is sensible loading with black powder or Pyrodex *only*.

occasions, purposely destroyed black powder firearms under test conditions, *using only black powder*. Therefore, if the reader will understand that it *can* be done, he should be perfectly safe in all his black powder shooting.

Frankly, it takes some effort to destroy a well made modern smokepole with black powder. Black powder shooting is *very safe*. All that is required is to follow the rules of loading practices. We will find that over 50 percent of black powder remains as a solid after firing. (See Chapter 4 on propellants) These solids end up being driven from the bore, or caked onto the walls of the bore, and they significantly change the dimensions of the "breech" and bore itself. When you have up to 57 percent of a charge remaining as a solid instead of becoming a gas, you have something to deal with.

Black powder is a rather amazing substance in that it gets a lot of work done. It is actually very effective. In fact, in *isolated cases*, a black powder charge may propel a missile with a reasonable velocity better than a smokeless charge can do within the framework of the same pressure. The Winchester time/pressure curve in Chapter 4 demonstrated this. Of course, smokeless powder is much more efficient, getting far more work done for the actual mass of the charge. But the shooter has to understand that black powder is not a sooty charcoal that makes a lot of noise and smoke and pushes a ball downrange in the process. It is a real gunpowder. It can develop some strong pressures.

We have also spoken of the Law of Diminishing Returns in regard to black powder shooting. This is so vital I want to touch upon it briefly once more. In some tests—tests run under *strict* safety structures—the velocity actually *dropped* after extremely heavy charges were developed, making them grossly beyond anything any manufacturer or responsible "expert" would recommend. So, we had a case of getting more pressure with less velocity. Of course, velocity normally goes up as powder is added, to be sure, and this trend continues well past suggested or recommended charges in most arms. Even in these normal cases, however, the actual increase is often miniscule compared with the dose of added powder required for that tiny gain in velocity.

I am told by an independent tester that he believes black powder can generate at least 100,000 PSI, this based upon the tests run in his lab. At the same time, he had to work to get that kind of pressure. Let's now agree that we have established two facts: first, black powder can generate pressures which would be harmful to firearms if black powder loads are abused in terms of both amount and manner of loading. We will speak of "amount and manner of loading" in a moment. Second, we are absolutely certain (through testing) that black powder is a viable, useful and effective fuel.

When Pressure Is a Problem

In testing for problems arising from the *misuse* of black powder, one associate of mine turned to conduit to which he fitted a patched ball load and ignited the powder in the makeshift "breech" (one end of the tube merely sealed with lead). Amazingly, the conduit held nominal charges of black powder using a patched lead ball. Now, in the same breath I can tell the reader that by loading incorrectly, I have, without a horrendous charge of black powder (about twice max) blown a 1-inch, 50-caliber barrel to smithereens.

The only thing I did wrong was to fail in seating the ball firmly upon the powder charge, aside from the fact that I had deliberately used double the maximum charge recommended for the rifle. In other tests, using more than double the amount of maximum powder charge, but with the charge seated, barrels did not blow up. *This does not mean that we can put a lot of powder downbore as long as we firmly seat the charge.* I am only pointing out what occurred in those few tests.

The upshot of the whole thing is that I believe unseated charges do something very nasty (at times) to gun barrels when firing black powder loads. I am aware that others do not agree. I am aware that some actual tests show less breech pressure with unseated charges. And yet, it seems that there is a condition which *can* exist with unseated charges that turns good barrels into junk. Some suggest that a particular "harmonic" is set up in the bore during these mishaps.

Others suggest that the black powder detonates. I do not know if this is the answer either. When we burn black powder

Black powder guns can be made to explode using black powder. The old rule which said something about black powder peaking out at 25,000 PSI was false. Here, we have a black powder test gun being blown up with black powder. Note that the barrel (in the midst of the smokey explosion) has broken free from the remainder of the apparatus. Note, too, that a long sliver of steel barrel is ascending skyward. The testers were far too close to this barrel failure, for one hunk of steel was found a full 40 yards from the gun, while the hunk going up (marked by arrow) was never recovered at all. (Anybody see a new satellite lately?)

(Left) Here is the remainder of the test firearm which exploded. Note that the barrel has truly burst. This is not a simple fracture.

(Below) We found that the short-started Minie ball had remained in the bore and was not blown free when the barrel ruptured. In 100 percent of our test cases so far, we have found that the rupture of the barrel takes place precisely at the base of the short-started projectile, where that projectile rests in the bore. In the case of the bulge in the barrel, or "walnut," we have discovered that in 100 percent of the test cases so far the bulge has also occurred at the base of the short-started projectile.

(Left) Here is the bulge in the barrel referred to as a "walnut." This particular barrel was short-started. That is, a ball was rammed part way down the bore, but the ball and patch were *not* seated firmly on the powder charge. The barrel bulged precisely at the base of the unseated projectile. It is the opinion of the author that *all* loads should be firmly seated down upon the powder charge and never left partway downbore. *Ram that load home!*

unconfined, it seems to erupt all at once. It is one big *Pooffff* and it is gone. But we know for certain that even though all black powder, FFFg, FFFFg or Fg for that matter, seems to go up in one poof of smoke upon being ignited in a pile in the open, this does not seem to be the case when the powder is confined within the walls of a gun barrel's bore. Therefore, we cannot judge the burning rates of black powder by pouring little heaps on the ground and touching long matches to them.

We do know that granulation size matters significantly in both the velocity that we get and the pressures that we get in a bore. This is why I recommend FFg over FFFg in larger bores (for stout hunting charges). So, if all black powder simply went *Poof!* we would not have to be concerned about kernel sizes. In an interesting document from France, translated by the United States Navy, and written before smokeless powder was highly in use, the authors state that:

8. To suppose that the combustion is instantaneous, is not however permissible. If it were so, the gases being sud-

denly formed in a volume very nearly equal to that of the powder, would produce enormous pressures which the gun could not withstand. It is only by the use of *progressive powder* that the high velocities and low pressures of recent times have been attained." (p. 39, *Researches on the Effects of Powder* [1874-1988]

What the researchers were saying is that by going to slower burning powders, be they smokeless due to coatings and kernel configurations or even if black powder due to kernel configurations (Fg through FFFFg), if we got the powder to burn some at a time, rather than in one big *boom!,* velocity per pressure would be better. Now, if we did have a situation of black powder strung out on the "floor" of the bore/chamber area, and it did go off all at once, we might (conjecture) be seeing the root of the problem when we separate charges and projectiles.

This is speculation. We present it not as fact, but rather as part of our discussion on black powder pressures, and it is stated because we have blown up black powder arms using black powder. In every case so far, the eruption has taken place precisely where the base of the projectile was separated

(Right) A shooter should check for any sign of leakage in his rifle. Here, a leak has shown up at the breech plug, indicated by allowing a solvent to rest in the bore until the solvent itself actually found its way through the gap in the threads. Later, the same rifle was tested with a white thin paper shield taped over the suspected leaking area and escaping gas marked the paper at this point.

(Below) The Hot Shot nipple was designed to relieve pressure through the holes in the cone of the nipple itself. One will also see that the upper end of the cone is very large. However, the chamber orifice is limited in size and the base hole is of a very tiny proportion. In this way, the flat base with the tiny hole helps in retaining the normal backpressure found in the muzzleloader caplock system.

A can of black powder exploded. The can did not rupture. And yet a rifle can be destroyed *with black powder*. This shows, we think, that *abuse* of the fuel is the cause of most trouble, and that black powder, properly handled, is a viable substance for *safe* shooting as long as it is treated with *respect*.

from the charge of black powder. Again, we can only speculate, however, upon blowing up a rifle with a separated charge. W.W. Greener concluded that a particular gun barrel was ruined by a separated charge. We quote from p. 572 of *The Gun, 9th Edition*. "One only was bulged; the other burst at the rear of the impediment, but without moving it [the bullet] or affecting the breech mechanism."

We know that with certain "slow-burning" modern smokeless powders, burst arms have occurred when half-charges of powder were used. In one case, a 270 was blown up with a charge of slow-burning powder that amounted to only 30 grains, when that rifle had been found fine with a charge of the same powder at 60 grains weight. Again, we can only speculate. But those who feel that the black powder charge is indeed ignited easily and it does indeed gain pressure rapidly, but that it does *not* consume itself instantly, have a point that seems to be backed up by time/pressure tests. The pressure does not peak out toward the "detonation" posture.

We saw that the black powder pressure rose very rapidly upon ignition in the Winchester test (Chapter 4), but then it actually falls back slightly, and then produces a rather smooth curve during the remainder of the bore time. Until we have proof, which can only arise from more tests with sophisticated test equipment, let's do the practical thing—let's assume, just for safety's sake, that one of the ways to get black powder to behave badly in the breech is to separate it away from the projectile. Let's go ahead and make certain that the bullets, balls or shot charges used are seated firmly on a safe quantity of black powder. The firmly seated projectile has been the norm in black powder shooting for just about as long as that propellant has been around. Again, play it safe; firmly seat *all* projectiles or shot charges on the black powder load you select.

Black Powder Pressures and Bore Size

It is very easy to see that a tiny bit of powder "goes a long way" in the sub-bores, but that larger doses of increased powder charge do not gain spectacular results in the big bores. For example, in our own 36-caliber tests we have:

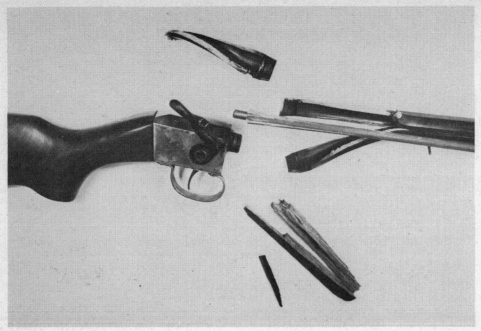

This Navy Arms Morse rifle did not succumb to many overloads of black powder. However, a smokeless powder load did finally destroy this strongly-constructed barrel. This is strong visual evidence and a warning to those who wish to use the improper powder in muzzleloaders. While this tough barrel stood up to foolish overloads of black powder, it did not hold the smokeless powder charge. DO NOT USE SMOKELESS POWDER IN MUZZLELOADERS.

Ozark Mountain Muskrat Rifle
(36-caliber/.350″ ball)

Charge	Powder	Muzzle Velocity
20 FFFg	GOI	1477 fps
30 FFFg	GOI	1721 fps
40 FFFg	GOI	2015 fps

So, for an increase of FFFg powder of only 20 grains, we gained in velocity by 538 fps raw average. We went up over 36 percent in our velocity, which is another way to look at it. Now let's look at a 54-caliber rifle:

Thompson/Center Renegade
(54-caliber/.530″ ball)

Charge	Powder	Muzzle Velocity
60 FFg	GOI	1260 fps
120 FFg	GOI	1748 fps

In this case, an increase of 60 grains of powder—albeit FFg in this case, and not FFFg as with the Muskrat—increased the velocity by 488 fps. Looking at the percentage increase, the two are not that far apart. But when looking at the raw increase in velocity for the additional powder, it's obvious that the little added powder in the 36 had much more effect than the additional powder in the 54. We are not suggesting that a shooter can pour plenty of powder down a rifle barrel just because it is a big bore. Not at all. After all, with a safe and reasonable load in my own 54 firing the .530″ round ball, I have shot totally through a bull elk at close range. So safety and "power" can go together.

Of course, we are dealing with FFFg and FFg above, and we know these two burn differently, so let's turn to some data as supplied by Lyman in their *Black Powder Handbook*. On page 89 we see a 36-caliber rifle tested with a 37-inch barrel. A 25-grain charge of FFFg GOI earns an LUP rating of 4,150. Now, turning to page 116 of the same volume, we see a 54-caliber rifle with a 28-inch barrel, also firing a ball and also using FFFg GOI powder (140 grains), rating a pressure of 8,870 LUP. This supports, I think, the idea of black powder pressures and variations in bore size.

Pressures in the Cartridge and Shotshell

Black powder is also used in shotgun hulls and in cartridge cases, and we have supplied data for both of these in our book. Naturally, we will run into one major difference here: in either the shotgun case or the brass case, the amount of space for powder is limited. This is not the case in the muzzleloader, except for the revolver in which the chambers limit how much fuel can be poured in. With the shotshell, space must be occupied by the shot and by the wad column. In the rifle case, space must be occupied by a portion of the bullet.

The shotgun shell can often be more of a problem than the cartridge case for the rifle or handgun because a shooter can vary the wad thicknesses and contrive a means of getting in more powder than perhaps he should. Let's talk about the shotgun hull for a moment. Based upon the information disseminated by Ballistics Products, Inc., we can bend the general rulings for smokeless powder only slightly and apply them to the loading of a charge of black powder propellant in the shotgun hull:

Causes of Pressure Problems in the Shotgun Shell

1. Too Much Powder

Here, we have simply a situation whereby the shooter has managed to get in more powder than is necessary. With FFg granulation of black powder, there should not be a great problem with an overcharge, since we still need room for wads and only so much powder can get into the case. All the same, the shooter should bear in mind that a *safe charge* is called for, usually in a volumetric way, and that he should stay with that charge, *not* going over it.

2. The Wrong Powder

In the shotgun, FFg and Fg seem to be the best in terms of pattern, and certainly FFFg is not called for in any of the shotgun sizes of 20-gauge or up. In fact, in one 24-gauge tested, FFg was still the better powder. Let's stick to FFg or Fg in the shotguns.

3. Wrong Shot/Powder Ratio

In smokeless powder shooting this can be a very serious problem, and there are shooters who load quite safely with *some* smokeless powders using a hand-held volumetric measure. After all, the measuring device on the fine shotshell reloading units are volumetric in nature and safe. All that is called for is keeping the components *agreeable*. If a tested load calls for a "volume-for-volume" measurement of shot/powder *with black powder,* then this *balance* should be maintained. If more powder is to be used, the shot charge will have to be cut back in the shell.

4. No Yield in the Wad Column

What this implies is that someone has applied a series of wads in the shell which were not called for in the load. A wad column certainly has to yield to pressure and move up the bore. If it is restricted in some way, this can cause pressure retentions that are unwanted. The shooter should stick with tried wad columns, or at least vary his wad columns using standardized wads. The use of wads which might bind up in the bore is not wise.

5. Sloppy Loading Technique

Just because we are now using Fg black powder in the shotshell does not mean we can simply toss the load together any way we want to with no respect for balance. We still have to use correct wads, correct wad columns, correct powders, correct powder charges all in the right shell and with *uniformity*. Every shell should be prepared with caution and respect. Take your time, fellow shooters. It's bad enough that we all have to rush around trying to get our business done without making the fantastic sport of loading and shooting a race, too.

6. Avoid High Pressures

A. Use the correct measuring devices so that the proper volume of black powder is loaded into the shotshell case (or the muzzleloader for that matter).

B. Do not use FFFg in shotguns. Use Fg or FFg black powder or Pyrodex, in the CTG kernal size.

C. Do not fire doubtful loads. I have seen shooters staring at a shotshell load and wondering where it came from. It was not labeled. It somehow simply got into the box. These loads are best avoided.

Causes of Pressure Problems in the Rifle

1. Poor Rifle

This applies equally to any firearm, shooting any kind of powder, but especially applies to some of the original old-time arms which may have been in Old Uncle Fred's barn for the past 50 years. I know there are many useful and strong old-time original firearms around, but the shooter owes it to himself to have any newly acquired original firearm checked by a competent gunsmith before he fires the piece with *any* load.

2. Powder Charge

In this case, we can say that too little might be worse than too much, because the case itself will limit the amount of black powder which can be dropped into it. However, there have been indications of problems with some black powder ri-

fles when underloads of black powder have been used. It is best to load the prescribed amount. In this book, we have given only *one* recommended load for most of the grand old rifles and handguns of black-powder style. The load will be one which fills the case, but which is not compressed unduly by the bullet.

Shooters will find that modern cases in the original black powder cartridges simply do not hold as much powder as did the old-time "balloon head" cases. Therefore, our loads will not correspond to the actual number of grains weight suggested by the very name of the round. For example, the 45-70 was so named because it was/is 45-caliber and because 70 grains of Fg black powder was its usual load. Today, with a modern 45-70 round, a charge of 67 grains of FFg was about all I could get down using any reasonable means of pouring powder into the case. The little 25-20, as another example, would be a projectile of 25-caliber backed by 20 grains of black powder. We found that 17 grains of black powder was right in the modern case.

General Black Powder Pressure Comments

Obviously, some of the same rules mentioned above apply as well to the muzzleloaders. A poorly constructed or a damaged firearm is a menace whether it shoots shotgun hulls, cartridges or is a muzzleloader. And sloppy loading is dangerous with any firearm of any type. Mainly, we have wanted to show the reader that the data proves black powder to be a strong fuel, a potent and useful gunpowder. It is not a toy. But it is safe when used *safely*.

We are not able to prove as much as we would like to be able to prove concerning black powder pressures or how black powder actually burns in the bore. Sometimes we are forced to rely on conjecture or we could say nothing at all if we had to wait for true proof to surface. But if we do speak (based upon an opinion), two things will be true: First, the opinion will be based upon many tests, sometimes dozens of repeated tests, and while proof may not be as yet possible, the "guess," we hope, will be an educated one. Second, we will always lean toward the safe practice. If only two guns burst and we believe separated charges were the cause, even though we can't for a moment *prove* that it was the separation, rather than an extraneous variable we simply have not isolated, then we'll still warn against separated charge/projectile loads. We might be laughed at later when another reason shows itself to be the cause of the burst barrels, but that's OK—*safety* is our goals.

One thing is sure—overloads are uncalled for. There is plenty of ballistic force contained in the safe load. Overloads cost in powder and pressure, and give back very little in useful velocity.

In closing our black powder pressure chapter, just to show that conjecture was sometimes all the greats in gun design and function also had, along with us peons, here is how W.W. Greener, the genius gunmaker, felt about the burning rate of black powder when it was confined. It was not a powder which detonated. In fact, Greener said, on p. 573 of his Ninth Edition, "Unfortunately, all these nitro-compounds are more prone to 'detonate' than is black gunpowder; their combustion is accompanied by greater heat, and they are more susceptible to slight changes in the method or intensity of the ignition."

Greener wanted the shooter to have good loads, but with *safety*. That is the same goal this book strives for.

chapter 6

The Importance of the Patch

AUNT FANNY'S PAJAMAS, Uncle Elmer's discarded socks and the baby's old diapers do not make patching material for black powder ball-shooting pistols and rifles. Unfortunately, the patch has been touted for what it is not, and neglected for what it is. It is not a true gasket, but writers and loading pamphlets keep calling it one in spite of mountains of proof to the contrary. It is a very important component part of the load chain, and it must be uniform and strong, but we often see illustrations of the intrepid loader who is out of patches cutting one off his shirttail to win the big shooting match.

The patch serves several *vital* shooting functions. It is one of the most important aspects of the load. Here are a few of its services:

1. Safety: The patch holds the ball down upon the powder charge where it belongs. Separated ball/charges can be trouble, and I have samples of firearms with a "walnut" or bulge in the barrel from "short-started" projectiles. I also have firearms which have blown up after having been short-started. In fact, in 100 percent of the cases so far, and it's nice to have something consistent to work with, the bulge in the barrel or the walnut has occurred precisely where the short-started ball rested in the bore and nowhere else but at the *base* of this projectile. So the patch is for safety. It holds the ball and charge together as a unit. Furthermore, although many muzzleloaders have held together fine during short-started tests, sometimes, even with lighter loads, a black powder gun has blown.

We do not have proof of a definite reason for short-started problems. However, one theory which may end up holding water is the thought that there is harmonic disruption when the ball is started down the barrel part way, left there and then hit by the expanding gases from a powder charge that was strung out just right (or just wrong) along the bottom of the bore. A rapidly oscillating pressure wave strikes, and the barrel steel cannot hold up to this pressure. It's only a question mark right now, but we do know that there has been trouble with short-started loads, loads where the ball is not seated upon the powder charge. A well-fitted patch can prevent this problem.

2. Accuracy: The patch is vital to accuracy. Before going a

step further, I admit that I have, *under experimental conditions,* obtained accuracy with a tightly fitted ball and no patch. However, for all practical purposes, it is the patch which translates the rotational value of the rifling to the ball in order to spin it, which in turn averages out the imperfections in the ball around a common axis, making the sphere of lead "fly true."

3. Pressure on Powder Charge: The patch, in the process of retaining the round ball down upon the powder charge firmly, also acts to maintain a pressure upon the powder charge itself. Black powder, it is believed, burns better under pressure. In our tests, we used a scale to develop a means of putting *about* 40 pounds of pressure on the loading rod. A patch holds the ball down on the charge with such pressure at least partially maintained.

4. Windage: That space between the bare ball and the interior of the bore is called the "windage." This space is taken up by the patch. When a ball is rather loose, the patch can act to detain that ball, to some degree, aiding its inertia. As the gases from the powder overcome the inertia, the ball "obturates," or upsets in the bore better, thus "fattening out" to fill the bore better. In some cases, though rarely, such a condition will aid in velocity. In most cases, if the ball fits fairly well to the bore, the ball will get *about* the same velocity with or without a patch, as we shall show.

5. Leading: While leading with a lower velocity ball is not a real problem, it is conceivable that some leading could occur, especially in some loads which send the round ball out of the muzzle at 2000 fps or even a bit more. The patch, of course, is between the rifling and the ball, so it will prevent any leading. Also, the patch may save the base of the ball from some mild harm from the powder charge, though this is not a big possibility. High-speed projectiles such as the Nosler Partition work fine with lead exposed to the gas of the powder charge. However, the soft lead of the ball might be protected to a small degree by the patch. It is a possibility, though certainly not much of a factor.

6. Lube: The patch holds the lube, as it were. Naturally, the lubed patch can also damage the powder charge, so we might wish to put a hunk of hornet nest or perhaps a dry patch down

Here is a very fine combination of patching: We have on the left the standard pillow ticking patch. This patch, somewhat smaller than the patch on the right, is going to be put down upon the powder charge *prior* to loading the main patch. Then, on the right, we have our main patch. In this case, it is a .013″ thick pure Irish linen patch—note the tight weave. No patch is a true gasket. Even the pure Irish linen patch exhibits a few gaps in the material, which can be seen as black spots due to the black background of the photo.

upon the powder charge before we run the ball downbore. Then the lube on the patched ball will not leak out into the powder charge. What little excess lube does escape will be caught by the first patch sent down. But the patch does serve to contain any running lube.

The Patch Is Not a Gasket

We might as well get this out of the way, because it will cause no end of trouble for us and we know it. However, the patch is not, in spite of the tons of commentary to the contrary, a gasket. But who cares? Frankly, it's not that big an issue. The patch does so many good things, that if a shooter believes it is a gasket, let him. But a knowledgeable modern black powder shooter wants to know the truth, or at least he wants to try to know it, and we would be cowards to shun this argument just to remain popular.

As a friend of mine said when he found out, by testing his own firearms, that his patches weren't gaskets, "If you were setting out to make a gasket, you sure wouldn't make one out of cloth, would you?" I guess you wouldn't. Of course, many years ago, patches were made of things other than cloth, too. Were they better as gaskets? I am not sure. But a look into the interesting book *Espingarda Perfeyta (The Perfect Gun)*, printed in Portugal in the year 1718, tells us, "Others made barrels with rifling inside, some with more, and others with less rifling, all of them deep and twisted in the form of a spiral. These were loaded by putting the bullet in a little piece of leather of a thin glove, folded only once, dipped in oil, and thus it was pushed down to the bottom in such a manner that the bullet may not lose its roundness." (p.341)

I did test a rifle with leather patching. The results will be given in a moment. But first, we need to establish what a gas-

ket is before we say a patch isn't one. *The Standard College Dictionary* gives this definition of a gasket: "A ring, disk, or plate of packing to make a joint or closure watertight or gastight." The last word is the clue —"gastight." The patch is not gastight. Therefore, by our definition, it is not a gasket. Here are three strong pieces of evidence which support our statement:

1. Mr. Ed Yard, a well known expert in the field of ballistics, tested for the ability of a round ball cloth patch in the area of being a gasket. His work appears in the 1980 *Gun Digest* in a manuscript entitled, "The Round Patched Ball and Why They Used It." The findings of Mr. Yard are based upon tests with a pressure gun. In other words, this is seeking out data by going directly to the source. We are talking about leaks, and Mr. Yard was testing for pressure leaks.

His conclusions are perfectly straightforward. On page 237 of the above book, Mr. Yard says, "The inherent inefficiency of the patch as a bore seal was the big factor and the basis of the loss [in pressure]." On the same page, Mr. Yard states, "It [the patch] does not really seal the bore." And again on the same page, Mr. Yard concludes that, "Even the tightest most thoroughly greased patch that can just barely be gotten down a clean barrel without hammering does not seal the bore."

2. My own chronograph tests aroused suspicions about the patch as a gasket. I was testing a big 58-caliber rifle and using different patch thicknesses. With one specific load, I obtained a muzzle velocity of 1,210 fps with a very heavy patch/ball combo that I could scarcely get downbore without a mallet.

One will note here that the patch has holes where the ball rested in the bore, and the holes correspond to the location of the grooves of the rifling. This is a very typical "blown" patch. It is not a torn or cut patch. Nor is it a true blown patch in terms of a big hole existing where the ball had rested. The dedicated shooter always reads his patches to see what they are trying to tell him. Sometimes, they shout "trouble!" A hunk of hornet nest would have prevented this damage.

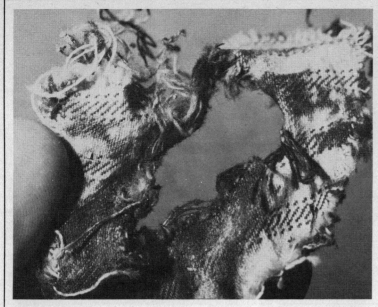

Here are examples of blown patches. One can see that in each case the center of the patch is literally blown away. Again, we recommend a backer of some sort. At the range, another patch on the powder charge will help this situation. Some prefer a piece of cork cut into a circle. Others might prefer the hornet nest so often mentioned in the text.

(Right) A shooter should hold the spent patch up to the light to inspect it. In this case, if a shooter did hold this patch up to the light, he would find a hole in every spot occupied by a groove in the rifling. A wise shooter always checks his patches.

Then, just for fun, I tried a rather thin patch of about .010″ instead of the heavy patch I had been using and the velocity went up, not down. Now the rise is not that significant, so let's just call it about the same velocity. However, for the records, after two different chronographing sessions, I did arrive at 1,210 fps with the heavy patch, and with just as much testing, I arrived at 1,260 fps with the light patch.

Being bothered, I put the rifle away and got another rifle out. That first rifle, constructed mainly for conicals, had a very shallow groove. Maybe that was the problem, I thought. So, I grabbed up another 58, one made to shoot round ball, with .012″ depth of groove and a twist of 1:72. It did do better with the heavy patch, but not significantly better. With the heavy patch it earned a starting velocity of 1,653 fps and with the light patch the velocity fell to 1,596 fps.

Later, I chronographed, under *test* conditions (DO NOT REPEAT THESE TESTS!) a bare ball in a rifle. I was shocked. I achieved the same velocity—give or take a modest few fps—without a patch that I had obtained with a patch! If the patch were sealing gases behind the ball, it had a funny way of showing it. Of course, part of the reason for velocity with a decently fitted ball and no patch was the "obturation," already mentioned. The ball was fattening out to fill up the bore to at least some degree.

3. Mr. Hugh Awalt, NMLRA field representative from Maine, was on the line one day. He introduced himself and then he said something like, "I hear you are getting some flak about your patch-and-gasket theory." He proceded to relate information he had concerning a high-speed filming of a muzzleloader going off. Well, if the patch were a gasket, we should see the nose of the ball, still wrapped in the patch of course, and then smoke and flame behind it. The film did not show that. It showed smoke, flame and then the patched ball.

And now, after dozens and dozens of tests, we still have a mild mystery on our hands as to the exact situation going on down there in the deep dark recesses of the breech as far as patches are concerned. But finding out that patches were not truly good gaskets has helped us a lot in determining how to best treat the patch, and how to best load the patched round ball in the rifle. Even barrels which come out of the same shop or plant exhibit some difference in how they handle a patch and ball. And heaven knows that two barrels from two different makers can be many light years apart in performance. Therefore, we set out to test many different firearms, getting a lot of raw data to work with.

Some of these tests should interest the reader, and he has a right to see the raw figures anyway. After all, we are not suggesting that all of the answers on patching are contained herein. My own studies (along with interested friends and business associates—the "we" part of my story), have a long way to go. But the results, so far, are more than a little interesting.

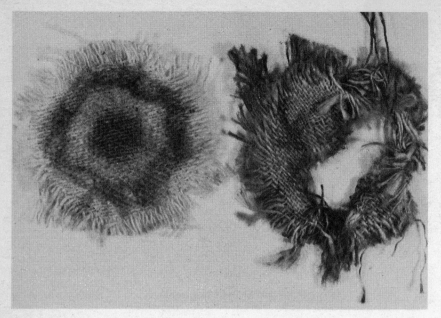

Using a .445″ ball in the 45-caliber Patriot, we found that only 30 grains of Pyrodex P or FFFg would sometimes blow the patch. When a backer patch was added this ceased immediately. The good news is that this interesting and accurate pistol produced far better groups after the backer patch was installed. The patch on the left was used with the same 30 volume charge of Pyrodex P, but with a backer patch.

TEST ONE
Rifle: Custom, 54-caliber, 1:79 twist, .008″ groove, 34″ barrel, .530″ Speer round ball

Powder Charge	Patching	Average
110 Vol. FFg, GOI	.005″ Ox-Yoke, RIG lube	1,223
110 Vol. FFg, GOI	.010″ Ox-Yoke, RIG lube	1,628
110 Vol. FFg, GOI	.015″ Ox-Yoke, RIG lube	1,600
110 Vol. FFg, GOI	*no patch at all*	1,647
110 Vol. FFg, GOI	one patch on powder, one .010″ on ball, per normal	1,790

I related these findings to a fellow shooter and friend, Jim O'Meara, after having tested several rifles. In some cases, the double patching gave higher velocities. In other cases, the double patching did not. But in most rifles, *at that time,* that I had tested, two patches seemed to average higher in velocity, and Jim was interested in chronographing his own rifle.

TEST TWO
Rifle: 54-Caliber CVA (Jim O'Meara's), standard .530″ Speer round ball

Powder Charge	Patching	Muzzle Velocity
115* FFg, GOI	.015″ sail cloth, saliva lubed	1,852 fps
115 FFg, GOI	*no patch whatever*	1,854 fps
115 FFg, GOI	double patched	1,842 fps

*approximate charge tossed by custom measure

We see right away that Jim's 54 did not gain one jot with double patches. The velocity is insignificantly lower, in fact, with two patches. However, this witnessed chronographing revealed that the CVA 54 got the same velocity without a patch as it did with a strong sail cloth patch. All of the above tests were with a Speer .530″ round ball. When we went to a Speer .535″ ball in this rifle, which seemed a bit better fit, we got 1,895 fps MV using No. 103 lube on the leather patch. Yes, we did try a leather patch here, a tanned piece of deer hide. With the same .535″ ball and *no* patch, the velocity was 1,874, no significant difference.

TEST THREE
Mowrey Squirrel Rifle, 36-caliber, Speer .350″ round ball

Charge	Patching	Muzzle Velocity
40 volume FFFg, GOI	.015″ pillow ticking patch	1,730 fps
40 volume FFFg, GOI	*no patch at all*	1,741 fps
40 volume FFFg, GOI	double patching	1,865 fps

This witnessed test was conducted right after we had run Mr. O'Meara's rifle through the chronograph. I had already obtained higher velocity in the Mowrey using two patches, and I wanted to see if the data would repeat itself. It did as Mr. O'Meara looked on. It is also very interesting to note that when this rifle was tested 2 years later, using the same RIG lube, but with a different lot of powder and ball from a different company, the velocity with a single patched load was changed from an average of 1,730 fps to 1,826 fps. This shows us what a change in components can do, a point we discuss in Chapter 7 on accuracy.

There were many other tests conducted; however, we must rapidly admit that the results were quite generally much the same as already stated above, with a few exceptions. We did run across one rifle, and only one, which got higher velocity with a single patch than without any patch at all. This was the 50-Caliber Navy Arms Ithaca Hawken, using a .490″ Speer ball and .013″ Irish linen patching, RIG lubed. With one patch, the velocity was 1,993 fps with 110 grains of GOI FFg behind the ball. But with no patch at all (and the same load and ball), velocity dropped to an average of 1,852 fps. With a patch down on the powder charge, plus the standard .013″ patch around the ball, velocity averaged 1,988 fps. In other words, the one-patch load and two-patch load were virtually the same, but without a patch, this rifle earned *less* velocity.

We also found several rifles in which a single patch earned the lowest velocity. In fact, no-patch was always higher in muzzle velocity than a single patch in these arms, with two patches sometimes giving the same velocity as one patch, and sometimes beating both the no-patch velocity and the single-patch velocity. All of this, of course, would be of no value in a

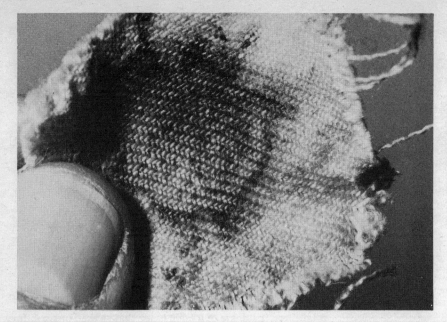

A good tight-weave patch is the Ox-Yoke Precision Blue-Striped ticking patch. Here we can see the close weave. Also note that the patch was not burned through. It was however, backed up by a hunk of hornet nest down upon the powder charge prior to loading the patched ball. The hornet nest is a natural "asbestos" which prevents patch burnout. The nest material itself will not burn up in the bore and there will also be no smouldering patch lying around.

practical sense if we did not apply our findings. When we do apply our findings, then the reader can use these notes to help him build better loads, especially in the accuracy department.

Loading with Two Patches

When we use two-patch loads, we do not, *ever*, mean two patches wrapped around the ball. We do mean putting a patch down on the powder charge first and then loading the patched ball in the standard way. We also recommend the use of hornet's nest on the powder charge if a shooter can talk a hornet out of his house. The hornet nest material *will* prevent patch burnout. So, there will be no danger of a burning patch on the range nor in the woods. While I have never heard of a documented case of a fire started with a smoldering patch, we should let the reader know that hornet's nest will prevent any such problem.

While two patches did give a little higher velocity in *some* rifles, this factor does not interest us very much. It was not sufficiently higher to get all that excited about. However, in some rifles, and again we must qualify our statements, we most certainly did get *better* accuracy by using two patches. In fact, whenever I found that a patch was burning out, I used double patching and very often obtained better accuracy. We can recommend right now that a shooter pick up his patches at the range and examine them. Patch reading is no trick. It's simple. If the patch is "blown," that is, if the patch has a hole in the center, or if the edges are badly frayed and appear burned, then a double patching job is certainly worth a try.

Barrel Longevity

If the reader will allow it, I'd like to toss in a surmise, a guess, a possibility about round ball barrel life. The whole problem of round-ball shooters eating up barrels is an interesting one because there is, as usual in black powder shooting, a large body of examples which do not agree with each other. I tested some 50-caliber barrels, and to the best of my ability found that after 1,000 shots, accuracy was markedly affected.

Others tell me they have shot rifles 4,000 times, and the bores still look good. It is a puzzle. But I wonder if ball/patch fit has anything to do with this conundrum? At first, I figured

the patch was simply lapping the bore. In fact, in one rifle I kept track of, a .535″ ball would not fit down the bore, not even with a .010″ patch. The best accuracy was obtained with a .530″ ball and a .015″ patch. However, in only 500 shots a .535″ ball with a .015″ patch fit the bore fine.

The rifle remain highly accurate with the .535″ ball and .015″ patch and at the 1,000-shot mark, the bore was *not* noticeably worn, nor had accuracy dropped off. The ball/patch fit is tight with the .015″ patch and the .535″ ball. Could it be that the first 500 shots lapped the bore in, and now the fit with the .015″ patch and .535″ ball is going to last a long time? I don't know.

But what about this: we know the patch is *not* a gasket. If we insist that it is a gasket, at least we have to admit that it is a darn leaky one. So, gas is rushing past the patch/ball and cutting, I should imagine, right through the grooves. In all that I have been led to believe, when gas rushes by the projectile in a jet, this cuts the bore metal. If this is true, then it follows that a loose patch/ball fit might encourage more bore wear than a tighter patch/ball fit. In speaking with owners of older rifles that are still shooting well, they all say that they used a ball that fit well to the bore, coupled with a fairly tight patch. But in all cases, it was the ball that was the first concern.

I think often that we have turned something around in our quest for the right patch/ball fit. We usually say we need a tight patch. It seems to me, from the data we have gathered both from the chronograph and the pressure gun, as well as the high speed picture, that maybe what we should say is that we want a tight *ball* fit. The ball should be close to the land-to-land size of the bore.

Patch Thickness

We must remember that when we are talking patch thicknesses, the dimensions that we use refer to the *uncompressed* patch. For example, when I am measuring a patch with a micrometer, I turn the handle until the jaws make contact firmly with the material, and not as far as I can turn them into the material itself. Therefore, we have, in fact, a measurement which shows a very *slightly* compressed condition only. Often, we will find that a patch of .015″, for example, will compress

This patch seems to be blown. However, it is not. We discovered that the patch was being cut upon entry into the muzzle. We found this out by loading a patched ball and then extracting the patched ball unfired by using a screw. The patch was pre-cut on the sides, and then even a modest powder charge ripped the patch the rest of the way, as indicated here. By going to a thinner patch, actually, the cutting ceased. This was a case of trying to ram home a patch too thick for the job.

down profoundly from that thickness. When we buy a .015″ patch, we are buying a thickness gauged not at full compression, but at a very modest compression to almost no compression at all. Therefore, while our mathematics may show a patch thickness of .010″ as perfect to take up the windage in the bore, we may indeed use a .015″ patch, since the .010″ dimension refers to an uncompressed patch thickness. However, we still believe that we should look for a well-fitted ball size *first*, and then worry about the patch. The continued urging to "use a tight patch" might better be stated "use a well-fitted ball, and then a patch that fits to the bore."

Patch Compression

Staying with the above line of thinking, let me relate a story about a rifle that was supposed to have a fine handmade barrel that was going to deliver wonderful round-ball accuracy. The barrel was a 40-caliber. The groove depth was .010″. And the bore from the bottom of one groove to the bottom of the other groove miked out at .420″ size. The barrel, with .395″ balls was blowing patches. It did not blow every patch. But what was really interesting was the fact that it would group two or three shots beautifully, then throw a ball 3 or 4 inches out of an otherwise magnificent group.

The shooter decided to check a patch every time he fired a shot. Shot number one was in the group, and the patch was *not* blown. Shot number two was in the group, and the recovered patch was just fine. Shot number three was *out* of the group, and you guessed it, the retrieved patch looked like the torn pants of a circus clown after a bulldog got through with them. Staying with this trend, the shooter continued to check and sure enough, when a shot was out of the group, the patch was damaged.

He did not try double patching. However, he did go to a ball that was .400″ size. In other words, the same dimensions as the bore, land-to-land. Patches were no longer a problem,

and accuracy was maintained. I wonder if the same thing would have been affected by simply putting a patch down on the powder charge and then using the patched ball? This would be worth looking into. The problem with getting those larger round balls down the bore is often the crown of the muzzle and the design of the rifling. But some rifle barrels are made to accept a ball that is very close to "bore size."

We must bear in mind that patches do compress. In fact, when we give the size of a patch, we are talking about its uncompressed thickness. Some patching materials are useless, I think, because they compress too readily and they often tear. But we have to think in terms of patch compression when we select a patch, because we might be able to use a larger round ball with a heavy patch after all, if we will give it a try. The 40-caliber barrel mentioned above ended up using a patch of .017″ uncompressed thickness.

Patching Material Factors

Ned Roberts, who is mentioned more than once in this book, had a great deal of experience with muzzleloaders and wrote a fine book on the subject, which is now available in reprint. I was fortunate to to able to purchase a used original. In his book, *The Muzzle-Loading Cap Lock Rifle*, on page 27, Roberts is speaking of barrel wear in round ball shooting guns. He related the fact that some black powder rifles fired 20,000 to 30,000 rounds before being worn. Roberts felt that the patching itself caused bore wear, for the rifles firing 20,000 and 30,000 times with continued accuracy were *all* bullet-shooters, not ball-shooters.

Roberts said, still on page 27, "The linen, cloth or paper patch used with the other types of muzzle-loading rifles [other than conical shooters] is the chief cause of the wearing out, or 'shooting out,' of the bore after a comparatively few years' use…" However, at the same time, we have some very old original arms which used the round ball, were apparently fired a lot, and remained accurate. We should point out here, I think, that round ball shooters can last a long time. And we need to look at two factors. One we have mentioned already.

Backer patches are not always necessary. In this case a .013″ pure Irish linen patch was fired with 70 FFg in a 54-caliber rifle. Many patches were gathered and none showed a problem. The accuracy was superb, so no backer patch was added to this load chain.

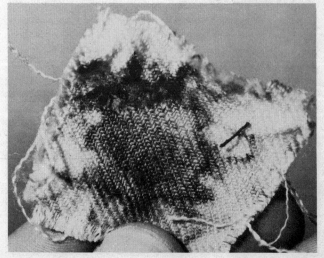

The ball should probably fit the bore fairly closely, not so tightly that a mallet is necessary to load it, but not loose either. Secondly, I feel we should talk about the materials we use for patches. The patch, it seems to me, should have these attributes:

1. Strength (so it won't tear)
2. Uniformity of material (so uncompressed thickness is uniform)
3. Tight weave (so as not to be porous)

Irish linen, when it can be found, has these attributes, and the new materials, at least new as this is written, from Ox-Yoke, also enjoy these points. The Ox-Yoke Precision Blue Striped Pillow Ticking is 100 percent cotton, strong and uniform. In running a test on this material, the advertised .015″-.016″ size *was* .015″-.016″. There are also other good commercial materials available. But I think the shooter who scrounges in the rag bag for his patching is looking for trouble.

Patch Performance Factors

What, then, are the factors which govern patch performance? I think they run like this, and I'm sure I have not included all of the many factors which do surround the simple hunk of cloth that attends the round ball:

1. The material the patch is made of.
2. The thickness of the material.
3. The uniformity of the thickness.
4. The powder charge used in the load.
5. The size of the ball.
6. The length of the barrel.
7. The configuration and design of the bore's rifling.
8. The crown of the muzzle.

If the shooter will look at these factors, and do what he can to control them, I believe the end result will be increased accuracy and even a chance at longer barrel life (maybe). Naturally, the latter is also enhanced by using clean patches. If the material is new, then the sizing must be washed out. I wash my patch material in laundry detergent, then sack it up in a plastic bag. The sizing is a starch-like substance put into the fabric to make it look better in the store. It is not good for the interior of the bore when it burns. To make the patching material manageable, I like to use a fabric softner in the rinse water. (For more basic hints on patching, see *The Complete Black Powder Handbook*, DBI Books, Inc.)

During the course of testing for this book, I had a chance to do an extensive run with a newly manufactured 50-caliber rifle. It was the Navy Arms Company Ithaca Hawken in the flintlock version. Using .013″ Irish linen, RIG lubed, and one patch, with 110-grain volume of FFg GOI, the average velocity was 1,902 fps. In this rifle two patches made a difference, for the velocity (all aspects of the load remaining the same of course), rose to an average of 2,002 fps. With no patch at all, the velocity was 1,963 fps average, or higher than the one-patch load.

I also had a chance to test another new rifle, the Tryon Trailblazer from Armsport. This interesting back action lock 54-caliber rifle was patched with an Ox-Yoke Wonder Patch, which is impregnated with a solution that makes fouling very soft and easy to remove, hence a lot of shots can be fired. I still cleaned between each and every shot for my test uniformity, of course. At one point in the test, I decided to run a no-patch reading. With 90 grains of FFg GOI, and no patch, the average velocity was 1,599 fps. The average with one patch and 90 grains volume of FFg GOI was 1,562. Had I run across those figures a few years ago, I would have repaired to the funny farm and stayed there.

After dozens of such tests, however, it was no shocker to learn that the patch was not affecting a gasket in the bore, or at least not delivering any more velocity than a no-patch load was capable of. It was also not alarming to learn that with the 100-grain load the velocities of no-patch and one-patch loads were about the same, with neither truly winning out. Patches are simply interesting bits of cloth calculated to give black powder shooters fits.

The patch is so vital to the load chain that it certainly has deserved this entire chapter's devotion. The more I shoot the wonderful black powder ball-tossers, the more I believe that we give too little credit to the piece of cloth around that missile. If a shooter does not pay attention to his patching, he's leaving out a vital link in the load chain, and he's likely to pay for his sin of omission in a loss of potential accuracy.

As Mike Belle told me as we visited one afternoon in Atlanta, Georgia, "To me, the patching material is the most critical thing in the world (for accuracy). It is also the weakest link in the load chain." Coming from a man who has been instrumental in the wonderfully accurate barrels from H&H, the barrel-making people, that statement is a very important summary of the status of the round ball cloth patch.

This patch was fired with 90 FFg in a 50-caliber rifle. It does not indicate any major or severe holes when held up to the light. Each rifle is different, dependent upon the sharpness of the lands, rate of twist, depth of groove and many other factors. Hence, the shooter must check his own patches in his own rifle in order to determine any change in loading practice that might be indicated.

chapter 7

Loading for Accuracy

ACCURACY means many things to many people. I've told the story before of a day on the range when a couple men were shooting a muzzleloader at the 100-yard butts. The rifle was well supported on the bench, and I noticed that during a misfire the shooter did not flinch an eyelash, so I had every reason to believe that a reasonable group was coming together on the other end. A few moments later, the pair walked up to my bench with target in hand.

"Finally have it shooting," one of the men said, and the other fellow nodded his head in agreement with a smile on his face that showed more pride than pleasure. They held the face of the target in my direction, and it looked like it had been hit by buckshot from a cylinder-bored shotgun at 40 yards. Instead of what we'd call a group, there was more of a scattered peppering of holes all over the paper. I tried to smile as I was thinking of something to say about the target.

"She used to shoot all over the place," the man holding the target assured me, "but we finally got the right combination of Minie ball and lube to fix that." In the course of our conversation, it became apparent that these fellows expected nothing from a black powder firearm in the accuracy department, and if a few holes appeared somewhere on the target, that was good enough. Their level of expectation was low, indeed.

What should we expect from a muzzleloader in terms of accuracy? Of course, it depends upon the firearm. Some of the fine target rifles and handguns of the day will print groups that rival the best smokeless powder arms. And then there are other muzzleloaders that simply were not intended for high degrees of accuracy, but their owners carry these tools into the riverbottoms every year and come out packing good venison. When we talk accuracy here, we are mainly concerned with the "average" black powder firearm, the one a shooter can buy off the shelf. The benchrest boys with their muzzleloaders that resemble steel girders for bridges do not need me to tell them about accuracy.

What They Used to Get

In the classic book, *The Kentucky Rifle,* by Captain John G.W. Dillin, NRA, 1924, the author shows verified targets fired with an original flintlock in which a half dollar will touch upon the edges of the holes in the target, the range being 100 yards. There is a 3-shot group fired in 1922 from this same original flintlock, a hunting rifle, which allows a nickel to touch the holes, and this, too, from 100 yards. Another target dated 3/23/23 shows a 100-yard group for 5 shots which spans 2.10 inches.

Mainly, our problem is one of sights when we are trying to decipher the true accuracy ability of a muzzleloader. Equipped with iron sights, our tests usually tell us more about our eyesight than they do about our firearms. I have, however, attained some 1-inch, 5-shot groups with a muzzleloader at 100 yards, benchrested, using a telescopic sight. This was from a hunting rifle, not a target rifle, showing me first-hand that a patched round ball is indeed capable of accuracy, even accuracy by modern standards.

However, we get into immediate trouble when we start talking about what a rifle "averages" at so many yards. My most accurate ball-shooter (in my hands, and with its iron sights) will print 1½-inch groups at 50 yards. I can say that without having to worry about being embarrassed when a fellow shooter says "prove it." But I have shot 1-inch groups at 50 yards with this rifle, not all the time, however, but rather only when everything was "right." The rifle does not *average* an inch at 50 yards in my hands. I can get away with saying it averages 1½ inches, and even then I'm really speaking of a "mode," not a true "mean" or average.

Mr. William "Bill" Large, who has been handmaking superbly accurate muzzleloader barrels for more than a half century, has many witnessed groups that would put my 1-inch to 1½-inch 50-yard groups to utter shame. Mostly, these groups were made from Bill's fine target-grade barrels, of course. But they prove that the *capability* for fine accuracy is there. The benchresters with those stove-pipe wide shooting irons that weigh more than a hunk of railroad track produce astounding groups, too.

Bill Large has witnessed groups of 1½ inches center to center for 5 shots at 200 yards, using a scope sight fitted to the rifle so that he could determine the actual accuracy potential of the firearm. So, we say these things to tell the reader that the old-time rifles in both original as well as modern form, can shoot. The Whitworth rifle, again being sold in this country, won long-range shooting matches in its day and will shoot with superior accuracy now. The ball-shooters can do it, too. And even when we are not getting target accuracy, we should be able to expect an over-the-counter muzzleloader to give us "hunting accuracy." Some call this 4 inches at 100 yards. I won't argue. But I personally would like to have at least that kind of grouping potential in my own hunting rifle and hopefully even a bit better—realistically, day in, day out.

The famous Ned Roberts, author of *Muzzle-Loading Cap Lock Rifle,* began his black powder shooting career by aiming at a 2-inch black bull's-eye at 10 rods, or 55 yards. When young, Ned could keep 5 shots in a row inside of this bull's-eye, and his teacher, "Uncle Alvaro," reduced the target size later to a dimension of the standard percussion cap box or about 1⅜ inches. Ned could at least touch this target from a rest with all 5 shots. At 20 rods, or 110 yards, a 4-inch bull was used, and Ned could hit it 5 times for five or 4 out of 5 from the sitting position. From a rest, Ned Roberts was satisfied when he could hit a 6-inch bull from 30 rods, or 165 yards.

Our heritage for black powder accuracy is a strong one, and I think we often settle for far too little, thinking that just because the style of the firearm is old, that accuracy is best described as wishful thinking. In 1876, during our own Centennial celebration, American shooters won the International Rifle Match at Long Island at ranges of 800, 900, 1,000 yards using the "Old Reliable" Sharps in 45-120-500 with a paper-patched bullet as well as the 45-caliber Ballard with similar bullet. The event was reported in both *Forest and Stream* and *Harper's Weekly* at the time. Modern riflemen with rifles of similar weight intended for similar purposes will, today, find it quite difficult to outshine the groups made by those black powder rifles when using the same type of sights.

Significance of Powder Variations and Accuracy

I read not long ago in a prestigious magazine that pouring black powder from a horn or other receptacle into an adjustable powder measure was ruinous of accuracy and that nobody could get reliably accurate loads using this method. The author led the reader to believe that only those charges which are weighed on a powder/bullet scale could possibly lead to anything remotely resembling a "group."

I'm sorry to say that the writer should have tested his loads in the rifle rather than with scale only, for he may have wished to retract those words. Some of the fine groups, such as fired in the Bill Large barrels mentioned above, as well as highly accurate groups shot with barrels from Richard Hoch, and others, created those groups with charges of powder carefully dumped by volumetric measure, and not by weighing. The proof of this pudding is in the shooting.

There are two reasons for accuracy possibilities in the black powder arm using bulk loads: First, there is the fact that a *practiced* and careful shooter can toss a rather accurate measure of black powder. Second, there is the fact that a grain or two weight of black powder, especially in the Fg and FFg granulations, will not change the muzzle velocity enough to alter the point of impact on the target; therefore, if the point of impact is not changed through velocity variation by these minor trespasses in exact powder charge, accuracy remains constant.

As we know, there is quite a bit of difference in the small bore arms when we change the powder charge, and less differ-

ence in the big bore arms. For example, if the reader will look at a 36-caliber test in this book, he will see that a change of 10 grains volume FFFg will alter the velocity quite a bit. But that same 10-grain charge variation in a 50-caliber (using FFg) will not change the velocity as much. Therefore, in the small bores, we adivse the most careful of powder measurements when accuracy is sought for. But we still use volumetric measurements, not scale-weighings.

Powder Measure Accuracy

Using an Uncle Mike powder measure, and with the best technique that I knew of (*consistently* filling to slightly over full, then tapping the barrel of the measure a precise number of times), I took readings and kept records during several attempts at creating reliably similar powder charges. In one such test, my greatest spread was 2 grains, from a low of 98.0 to a high of 100, with an average of 99.5 FFFg when the measure was set on 100. With FFg, my low was 96.8 grains while my high was 97.5 grains, and so forth. I urge the shooter to get the "knack" of obtaining closely matched powder charges by being consistent in the use of the measure.

Powder Variation and Velocity Changes

With *carefully weighed* powder charges, I fired several test runs with a custom 54-caliber rifle, seeing what would happen with an FFg GOI powder charge that weighed exactly 140 grains and then another charge that weighed precisely 143 grains on the scales. The 140-grain charge averaged 2,084 fps, while the 143-grain charge averaged 2,074 fps. By shear accident of velocity reading, the 143-grain charge gave us 10 fps *less* than the 140-grain charge, Of course, this is insignificant.

It does not for a moment suggest that we were truly obtaining more velocity with the 140 charge. What it does say, however, is that there was no *statistically significant* difference registered in the 3-grain charge difference, because other variables in the load chain were accounting for more than 10 fps velocity variation *over the long run* in so many tests. Again, in the smaller calibers, and with FFFg powder, there will be more sensitivity to such variations and the shooter must be all the more careful to use his powder measure with consistency. But accuracy with the powder measure in black powder shooting is possible, as has been proved over and over again. Nothing, of course, that we have said here pertains to loading smokeless powder in maximum charges.

Accuracy Changes and Time Factors

Time and barrel wear can make a difference in the accuracy potential of the muzzleloader. Of course, as time passes, the exact "ingredients" for the load may also change. The shooter may not find the exact patch material or lube he used to create his special load, and there could be a small change in the lot of powder used. In a rifle of mine, I noticed that after about 500 rounds the .530″ ball was not fitting to the bore the same as it had previously. I was using the same components, for I had purchased plenty of ball, powder, lube and patching material when I got the rifle. A switch to .535″ ball increased accuracy, and the rifle has been shooting very well ever since.

However, when the rifle is used for hunting more than for target work, the shooter may expect very little change in actual performance as time passes. In another 54-caliber rifle, I decided to buy new black powder, a different lot from the one used to initially chronograph the rifle, and also a new batch of

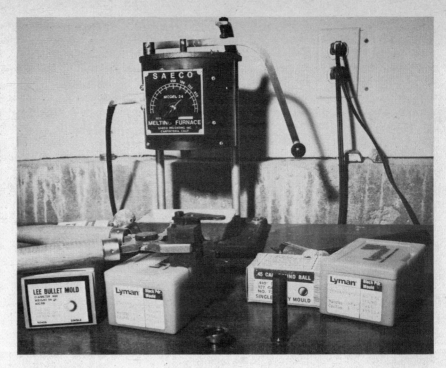

While it is true that many of the old-time black powder shooters "ran ball" (moulded projectiles) right on the trail over the campfire, it is also true that the softer brass moulds expanded and that ball to ball reliability MIGHT not always be true. Today, it is still fun to mould 'em on the campfire once in a while for the aesthetics of it all, but when we want uniform projectiles we turn to fine furances, such as this SAECO model shown here, and top grade moulds such as the Lyman, Lee, N.E.I. Thompson/Center and others. Accuracy depends first and foremost on projectiles. They must be uniform in mass, though slight out-of-round or blemished balls/bullets have proved accurate because obturation forms these in the bore.

patching and lube, though of the same type and brand. Here are the results of chronograph sessions that are 3 years apart in time:

INITIAL TEST		3 YEARS LATER	
Charge	Muzzle Velocity	Charge	Muzzle Velocity
80 FFg	1211 fps	80 FFg	1219 fps
100 FFg	1393 fps	100 FFg	1375 fps
120 FFg	1513 fps	120 FFg	1449 fps

The shooter can see that there is no truly widespread difference in the velocities earned in the first test and the second test 3 years later.

Accuracy and the Cast Projectile

We labor under many misconceptions regarding the casting of missiles. In the first place, impure lead can indeed be cleaned up, and while we have always assumed that we were indeed *creating* an alloy with our fluxing processes, we probably never were. It takes more than a spoon and some wax or fluxing agent to make a true alloy of metals. When we flux, however, we do notice a great deal of "dross" rising to the surface. This "lighter than lead" material may often be tin or antimony, or a number of other metals. However, it is very often just plain dirt as well. When we "flux" and skim this product, then we are cleaning up our lead.

I have produced cast lead round balls from "scrounged" lead which were very close in weight from one sample to another. If I were to cast projectiles for the purpose of ultimate purity, however, I'd buy the Lawrence Brand lead available from the Taracorp Company. This lead is 99.90 percent pure or better. It is the same lead as used by the companies which give us superb round ball which are factory swaged. Often, I have weighed a box of such ball to find that there is no more variance than one would find in a box of modern bullets, and we know how fine our modern projectiles have become, with jacketed bullets weighing in at tremendous closeness from one sample out of the box to the next.

Projectile Precision and Accuracy

Cast ball, or cast Minie/Maxi projectiles, can be created with a great deal of precision. We also know that the good companies supplying us with cast or swaged missiles are giving the shooter a superb degree of precision right "out of the box." But sometimes it pays for the shooter to weigh a batch of his own cast projectiles to insure that things are going well. It can also improve confidence if the shooter will weigh a few "store bought" ball and conicals as well.

Here are a few samples for the reader's own knowledge:

A. Lyman .520″ Mould
   1. 211.5 grains
   2. 211.2 grains
   3. 211.1 grains
   4. 211.2 grains
   5. 211.0 grains
B. Speer .570″ swaged ball
   1. 268.5 grains
   2. 268.5 grains
   3. 269.0 grains
   4. 269.1 grains
   5. 268.7 grains
C. Shiloh .610″ Mould
   1. 624.0 grains
   2. 621.2 grains
   3. 626.0 grains
   4. 625.5 grains
   5. 626.0 grains

Often, we will detect a bit of variation in the very large projectiles that we cast ourselves. The target shooter might indeed wish to quickly weigh a batch of missiles before using them. It only takes a few moments. I weigh all my big game hunting projectiles, partly because I want to know the recovered weights should I find them in game later, but also to insure that no ball with air pockets or other problems gets used by mistake. I think, however, that we can remain confident that our muzzleloaders will not suffer from using a haphazard projectile mass if we cast with care and if we buy good products over the counter.

Naturally, haphazard projectile weights will destroy accuracy if the variation is great enough. As Ned Roberts put it on page 2 of his book the *Muzzle-Loading Cap Lock Rifle,* "Uncle was very particular to impress upon me the fact that only perfect bullets would give real accuracy in any rifle, and it was only a waste of good powder and caps to use imperfect bullets."

Accuracy and Powder Granulation

In theory, FFg will burn better in a more rapid twist than it will in a slower twist. This has to do with the idea of barrel friction. The more rapid spiral applies more friction to the projectile, retarding it, and meanwhile allowing the larger granulation powder a better opportunity to be consumed. While I cannot argue with the principle, in actual shooting I have not been able to discern a truly remarkable difference in accuracy between FFg or FFFg in a slow-twist or a fast-twist bore.

In the first place, other factors are at play. For example, the configuration of the rifling or "rifling style" will also play a role in friction. A sharp land and a rounded land will surely "hold" a ball differently. So, we should, of course, try different granulations in terms of bench accuracy, as some bores may be more sensitive than others to this phenomenon. However, I would try FFg and FFFg both regardless of twist just to see first-hand which will give better accuracy, if indeed the shooter can actually discern a difference. For hunting, I'll still use FFg in the 45-caliber and up for power loads.

Remember, however, that there are differences in actual pressures among the various granulations of black powder and one may find that FFg may be better than FFFg or vice versa in a particular firearm with *target* loads. It is interesting to use the Dixie Gun Works Powder Tester with various granulations just to convince ourselves and new shooters how much difference there can be among black powder granulations in terms of "punch." Though the basic formula is the same, the smaller granulations propel the wheel on the powder tester much more than do the larger granulations.

Accuracy and Lead Storage

The shooter may be surprised to open a box of lead balls or conicals which has been stored for a period of time to find the contents coated white. I had some round balls in this "oxidized" condition and attempted to shoot them for accuracy, but had only the 50-yard range to work with. There was no real difference detected at that range. However, it is conceivable that enough build-up on lead missiles could cause minor changes in accuracy.

Just to be safe, or over-safe, I spray a very light mist of WD-40 over the lead projectiles that I intend to keep stored a long period of time. I also transfer them from paper cartons to tin cans, with a clean paper towel on the bottom of the can to absorb any excess spray. We know that poorly cast balls deliver low accuracy. I tested for this, and in an accurate 40-caliber rifle I obtained about 1½-inch groups at 50 yards with well cast balls, and the group opened up to 3 inches with balls that had been purposely miscast with inconsistent lead temperatures.

But after casting good balls, we should keep them that way by safeguarding them from harm.

Accuracy and Misloaded Patches

What would happen if the shooter haphazardly flopped the patch on the muzzle and miscentered the ball on it? That is what I wanted to find out. I used two rifles, both in 50-caliber, and I will report the findings on one only because both were nearly identical in results. First, I kept the powder charge consistent at 70.0 grains of GOI FFg, using a .015″ Ox-Yoke Precision patch, a .490″ Speer swaged ball and RIG as a lube, with CCI No. 11 cap.

Velocity tests were run first. With the patch laid over the bore so that the ball was centered in the middle of the patch, per normal, velocity averaged 1,487 fps with the load as prescribed above. With no patch at all, the same velocity was reached. But with the patch laid on the muzzle so that only half of the ball was touched by cloth, the velocity averaged 1,401 fps, or about 86 fps *less* than no patch at all or a properly centered patch.

We cannot draw the conclusion that we will "lose 86 fps with miscentered patches," or 150 fps, or any other such figure. That is totally unscientific because different calibers, loads and various bore factors will change the figures. However, in a second rifle, almost identical results were found and later in testing, a third rifle was fired and again the results were the same. Misloaded patching caused a loss in velocity.

There was also a loss in accuracy with the two test rifles. We can say no more than that. We cannot suggest that all rifles in the world will lose accuracy when the patch is loaded incorrectly. We can only say that accuracy was lost in two test rifles. But we do have that much to go on. The suggestion is to load the patch centered on the bore so that the ball has patching material on all sides. When I noticed the loss in velocity with the off-center patch, I had to wonder if there was any parallel between this and the fact that some of my patched, round-ball rifle loads have actually delivered a bit less velocity than no-patch loads. *NOTE: Never load a round ball without a patch—these were controlled tests.*

Accuracy and Round Ball Damage

Obturation, our old friend, has much to do with the accuracy that may be obtained with soft lead projectiles that have been damaged. While I prefer to keep the best possible missiles in the best possible condition, it is true that "bullet upset" with soft lead will often overcome minor to even somewhat major scars and damages on the ball. I'm not the only one to conclude this. Roberts, in his many years as a black powder expert, stated on page 105 of his *Muzzle-Loading Cap Lock Rifle* book, "While the commercial buckshot and round balls appear to have their surface completely covered with minute flat spots, as seen under a magnifying glass, they appear to give fully as good accuracy as the best cast round balls in the majority of rifles." I have found the same to be true, but *not always*. I think that in some cases it is not so much that the "pock marks" harm the accuracy of some buckshot used in the handgun or rifle of black powder type, but rather a problem in consistency of mass that might cause the trouble. I have achieved both good and bad accuracy from such projectiles. We must also consider the bore and the type of rifling used.

In a test which used three rifles, 40-, 50-, 54-caliber, I wanted to find out if a badly damaged round ball would fly away

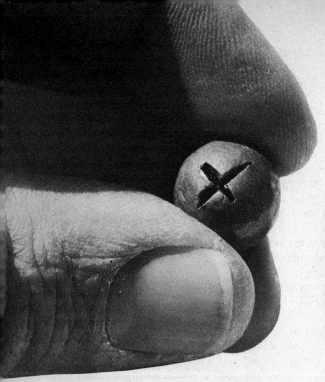

The cross indented into the round ball was used in a test to determine what would happen if damaged balls were fired for accuracy. Our tests were definitely NOT conclusive. The INDICATION was somewhat strange in several tests, however, and our tests continue and will continue until we can draw some sort of conclusion. We know that damage to the base of the bullet is very serious in impairing accuracy, while a smashed nose can often mean no loss in accuracy. However, in several successive tests, we found that base-damaged balls did not depart from the group, while nose-damaged balls did. We offer no statement as to the veracity of these findings. However, in an independent test which the author conducted with other shooters, once again the datum presented itself in the same way—base damage not bad, nose damage bad.

from the mark, or if it would create a good group. The first test was held on a somewhat windy day, and the best grouping I could get with a totally undamaged ball was 1½ inches at 50 yards. Actually, over the years I have come up with 107 good excuses for missing the target, and wind is only one of them. Other excuses are: drank too much coffee the night before and unsettled my nerves; the guy next to me sneezed just as I was about to touch 'er off; a gnat hit me in the eye as I fired; there was a mild earth tremor that nobody else felt.

At any rate, I then fired two damaged-ball groups. I had purposely damaged these with a sharp chisel by making a deep cross on one side of the ball. This is not a very scientific method, as the degree of damage could never be the same. But let's look at it this way: the balls were decidedly harmed and no mistake about it. For the first 5-shot group I loaded the ball so that the deep cross was facing out and toward the target.

There was no difference in either the point of impact upon the target, nor was there any difference in the size of the group.

The second 5-shot group was fired with the damaged portion of the ball loaded inward facing the powder charge. And again there was no difference in the point of impact upon the target nor the size of the group. I can only report what occurred. I was using 50 grains of FFFg GOI in this first rifle, a 54-caliber firing the .535″ ball with a .013″ Irish linen patch. The second rifle tested was the 50, then the 40; in all cases the data were repeated.

We have to be careful with results like these. Again, all we can say is that in three test rifles at only 50 yards the damaged balls (and we must keep in mind what kind of damage) went into the same group sizes and same placement on the target as the undamaged balls, all producing good groups. I also want to point out that this has not changed my mind about taking care of the projectiles that go into my muzzleloaders. In fact, I have a Forster short-starter which I use with my 54-caliber exclusively because the rifle has a muzzle protector, for one reason, but also because it does not damage the ball in loading it.

Severe Ball Damage

We also wanted to run a few cursory tests on severe round ball damage. No one can give blanket statements based upon a couple of test rifles and a handful of tests, and this additional information is merely to offer more data. It is not the "last word." As soon as a shooter thinks he has his hands firmly gripped on "black powder truth," he'll find to his embarrassment the "black powder truth" has slipped away after all.

In fact, our additional run of round ball with more severely damaged missiles did *not* confirm original data, therefore giving us more to ponder. As the reader will recall, our round ball with a "+" cut into the front or back did not depart from the normal group, using the three test rifles mentioned (in 40-, 50-, and 54-caliber). However, we wanted to see what would happen with a couple other rifles, and with a *deeper* indentation on the projectiles. Turning to another pair of 50- and 54-caliber rifles our data departed from the above. In other words, the damaged round balls did not group as well as the non-damaged, although, they did strike the target at the same point of impact.

Above, I called the balls "badly damaged," because I do not think a shooter (under normal conditions) would cut a "+" into the ball prior to shooting for first place at the turkey shoot. However, we'll call this run a test of "severe damage" because the "+" was cut at least twice as deeply into the soft lead ball. In the 54-caliber rifle, my best average groups were in the 1¼-inch domain. I fired 5-shot groups three times and averaged the 15 shots, with the omission of a couple fliers. This is called a weighted average, when obviously poor information is discarded.

With the 54 making 1¼-inch groups, I then loaded the severely damaged ball with the deep cross pointing outward. My groups opened to over 4 inches using center-to-center measurement. With the cross aiming back toward the powder charge, the group averaged about 2½ inches center to center for the 15 shots. The 50-caliber rifle produced a weighted average for the 15 shots of 1½ inches center-to-center from

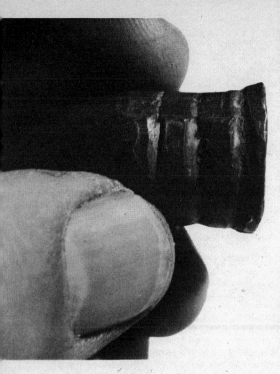

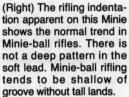

(Left) This particular Minie was fired into a good group. Note that the flare of the base did not affect accuracy at the 50-yard test setting. This much flare, we believe, is not harmful to general accuracy at black powder ranges. However, when the skirt is flared out in a fan-shaped pattern, accuracy can suffer, and split skirts or blown skirts caused accuracy problems in all cases in our own tests.

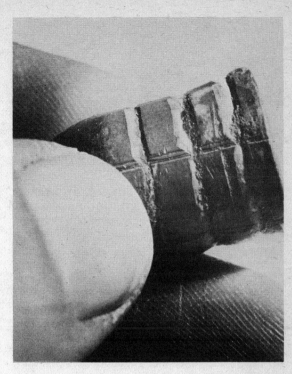

(Right) The rifling indentation apparent on this Minie shows the normal trend in Minie-ball rifles. There is not a deep pattern in the soft lead. Minie-ball rifling tends to be shallow of groove without tall lands.

the bench at 50 yards, the same distance for all of our previous ball damage tests. However, when the severely damaged ball was loaded with the cross or "+" facing outward, the group opened up to 6 inches, and when it was loaded with the ball facing down on the powder charge, the group averaged 5 inches center-to-center, not all that much difference.

Incidentally, in both of these additional test rifles, there was *no difference* in the original undamaged-ball groups and subsequent smashed-ball groups. In the 54-caliber rifle loaded, with the nose of the ball smacked flat, the group at 50 yards was 1¼ inches, and with the flat spot on the ball facing the powder charge, the group was still 1¼ inches (again in the same spot on the target). The 50-caliber rifle maintained a 1½ inch group with the flat portion of the ball facing outward (and with it facing down) on the powder charge.

Conclusions: I'd rather stick my neck in a noose than try to tell shooters that severely damaged lead projectiles will do this or not do that. In our little runs, the round ball which was not too severely cut on the nose or on the base did not depart from the group, nor did it produce a larger group. In our tests involving the firing of severely damaged round balls, with a deeper "+" in the ball, the rifles did deliver larger groups, though still at the same point of impact.

Smashed round balls did not depart from the group in any of our tests. With reservation, I'd say that the normal kind of damage a ball receives in loading will not lose a match for a fellow, while severe damage might. I'd also suggest that at long-range targets, I'd want to keep the ball as intact as possible, with as little damage done in loading as can be managed. This is stated on the basis of being very careful, rather than on the basis of the information, for the tests were conducted at only 50 yards. Furthermore, I think I now understand how the target shooters at the range get those fabulous groups when I have seen them smacking the ball downbore, to include loading with a mallet. The reason those groups are still small is related to the fact that the ball is somewhat shaped by the pres-

sure it is subjected to in the bore (obturation). The fact that it smashes into the atmosphere as it emerges from the muzzle (not to mention the trip through the bore), may also cause some changes in the original shape of the ball.

Maxi Ball Damage and Accuracy

In short, our tests indicated that harm to the rear of the Maxi ball was more injurious to accuracy than was harm to the nose of the Maxi. In fact, we could detect no difference in impact on the target nor in group size with a Maxi that had a cross cut in its nose, but with the cross cut in the base, the Maxi's group at 50 yards was almost twice as large as the undamaged Maxi group.

Minie Damage and Accuracy

Only one test was run with the Minie ball, and this was to cut a small V-slit in the skirt of the projectile. In all cases, the Minies which had the slit cut in the skirt were out of the group.

Accuracy and the Oily Bore

In three test rifles, two shooting patched round ball and one firing a Maxi ball, whale oil (in the round ball guns) and grease (in the Maxi gun) was left in the bore after recording a series of groups in which the bore had been dried with a clean patch *after* the ball or Maxi had been rammed home on the powder charge. In all three rifles, the oily or greasy bore caused a slight opening of the group *size* at 75 yards and in all three cases the point of impact was changed. The most offensive rifle, a round-ball gun, threw its missiles about 4 inches high and to the left of the normal group.

Velocity and Accuracy

In a rare few cases very small powder charges gave the best accuracy. In a rare few cases, upper end powder charges gave the best accuracy. In most cases, something between the low end and high end load was the most accurate. The reader will note that in many instances we have given a rather small load

57

with its velocity and energy ratings. The reason for this load is two-fold: First, it is possible to have a mild load for small game and plinking. Second, with this small load as a starter, the shooter can build slowly upward until he locates the most accurate "custom" load to fit his rifle or handgun.

In effect, when we speak of powder charge and accuracy, we are actually talking about velocity and accuracy, for it is the increased speed of the projectile in the bore, along with other factors, to be sure, which changes how that projectile will react to the control of the rifling and then to the atmosphere it must fly through on its way to the target. Our best advice is for the individual shooter to prepare his own custom load for accuracy. Remember that for big game hunting added velocity in a safe, but upper end charge, means flatter trajectory and in no way means less penetration, though it may not mean more penetration on some specific media.

Accuracy and Lubes

Although the tests included a great many lubes, there were only minor differences in accuracy that might *possibly* be attributed directly to the lube itself. Patches moistened with saliva shot well. Patches using fancy greases shot well. Patches using fine oils shot well. However, lubes were selected upon the basis for intended use. For target work, the watery lubes cleaned best. For hunting, a protective grease would be best. We also used Young Country Arms Number 103 and found that when directions were followed without variance, the shooter could get a great number of shots off using target and plinking loads without cleaning the bore between each shot. Also, using No. 103 with a Maxi ball gave constant velocities without cleaning between shots, which was not true of standard waxes and greases, in which case velocity increased as the bore grew dirty with residue.

Accuracy and Nipples

In the main, the nipple's work is in the area of transferring the flame from the percussion cap to the main charge in the breech and that's that. Many old-timers felt that this was best accomplished, as far as accuracy goes, by a modest spark, as long as the powder charge was consistently ignited. So, the job of the nipple remains a simple but important one—a route, as it were, from a "starting spark" to an ignited charge.

However, I did notice one type of nipple that could possibly cause a problem not only in the area of gas losses, but also in the area of accuracy. The "straight-through" nipple with its large exit hole in the base did, at least on a few occasions, give inconsistent velocities. Well, what does this have to do with accuracy? It could have a lot to do with accuracy. If the velocity fluctuates, then the point of impact is bound to change from shot to shot. In other words, the group will grow bigger.

To show the reader that small bores can have a problem with the large-hole-in-the-base nipple as well as the large bore, here are results taken from a smallbore rifle:

Charge	Muzzle Velocity	Comments
20 FFFg GOI	1,418 fps	(consistant velocity with good nipple)
20 FFFg GOI	1,214 fps	(fired with a nipple having large exit hole in base)

The reader is wise to use a good nipple at all times, not only to get his full measure of velocity for the powder used, but also for reasons of consistency.

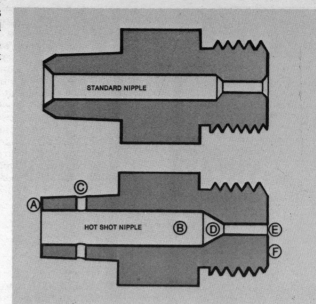

Nipples can affect accuracy because they can affect the consistency of velocity to various degrees. Here, on the bottom, we have the Hot Shot nipple, which was designed with a larger than average vent. However, the large vent tapers down to a very small orifice in the base of the nipple, a good design Looking at this schematic for the Hot Shot nipple and the standard nipple, one sees the six areas of difference. **A:** Maximum flat area; **B:** Larger primary chamber; **C:** Vent holes; **D:** A funnel area; **E:** Optimum size, gas orifice; **F:** Flat exit from the orifice.

Variations in Load Pressure and Accuracy

The Sd (standard deviation) gives us a pretty good idea of how consistently a load will perform for us. That is, we can have a very good guess as to our chances of getting the same velocity with that load over and over and over again. Remember, consistent velocity means consistent placement in the group. This is assuming that all other factors are held firmly in check—such as projectile uniformity and so forth.

I decided to haphazardly load in terms of pressure upon the loading rod. In one case, I simply touched the ball to the charge. When I could feel it touch, I stopped applying pressure to the ramrod. In another case I attempted to apply all the pressure I could muster, and in a third case I tried to use my standard loading rod pressure. While the results were not 100-percent clear, it did seem that Sd and consistency of velocity favored the constant pressure load.

Since there are several variables at work in a given load, it is difficult to single out loading rod pressure and say that this one factor gave a better Sd than some other factor. However, we can safely say that a trend seemed to favor the loads which were seated with constant pressure, and because of this, our recommendation is to stay with the medium pressure on the loading rod, neither crushing the powder charge, nor seating the ball loosely upon the charge. And, of course, in no case do we condone having the patched ball or conical bullet seated away from the powder charge and up the bore of any black powder firearm.

Load Pressure and Accuracy

DATA: These are the results of testing three rifles using a heavy to light pressure on the ramrod and then a consistent medium pressure of about 40 pounds.

RIFLE A Random pressure from light to heavy: 57 Sd
Consistent pressure: 19 Sd

This is a very interesting recovered missile, a .530" round ball reclaimed from the carcass of a mule deer buck. The portion facing the reader is the rear of the ball. The checkered marks are actually an imprint from the patch. In this case, the patch was not soft, but was somewhat stiff. Washing the same patching material made it soft and the pattern no longer appeared on recovered round ball. However, we could not conclude that the checkering effect had anything whatsoever to do with accuracy. it is the duty of the individual shooter striving for accuracy to check for himself when he finds a peculiarity in any of his shooting hardware or projectiles.

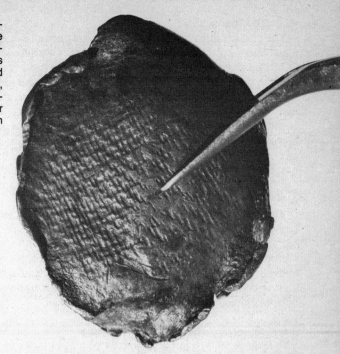

RIFLE B	Random pressure from light to heavy:	62 Sd
	Consistent pressure:	12 Sd
RIFLE C	Random pressure from light to heavy:	71 Sd
	Consistent pressure:	21 Sd

Patch Materials and Accuracy

The shooter eventually settles upon the patch material he thinks is the best in his particular firearm, and this is certainly the most useful route to patch material selection. For example, in one of my rifles I have found that pure Irish linen in .013" thickness along with a ball that fits closely to the bore size of the rifle is the most accurate combination I have tried so far, and I have tried many different ball/patch matchups in that firearm. In another rifle, a .017" patch seems better. But the shooter who wants the most from his firearm in terms of accuracy had better give patching a lot of consideration.

As Ned Roberts said on p. 2 of his famous book concerning the advice of his revered Uncle Alvaro, "He insisted that patches should be cut from 'shirt-bosom linen' only, if the best accuracy was to be obtained." You see, good old Uncle Alvaro knew that you don't get good materials for patching from the rag bag.

Patch strength is important. There is a difference between a cut patch and blown patch. I have run patched balls downbarrel, and then removed them with a screw without shooting, and I have found that the lands of the rifling had already sliced the patch. So, even before firing, the patch was cut. But a blown patch means one which has been incinerated by the powder charge. Holding this patch up to the light after it has been retrieved on the range following shooting will reveal holes.

The cure is usually in the form of: First, get the *strongest* patch material possible. While it may be well to use thicker patch material, sometimes stronger is really what is needed. Second, the ball may be too small for the bore, resulting in a blown patch. Third, the patch material may indeed be too thin. These three points should be observed: well-fitted patch; strong material; and a ball that is not too sloppy in the bore.

Ball Fit and Accuracy

We often tell shooters to "use tight patches." This is fine, but I do not think it's the first step to round ball accuracy. I think we should say, "Use a ball that fits closely to the bore, and *experiment* with patch thicknesses after that." I have shown in a few rifles, for example, that a smaller ball with a very thick patch was not as accurate as a larger, better fitting ball with a *strong*, but thinner patch. This is why I still have a supply of pure Irish linen around, for I have found it in .013" thickness, and it is very strong material.

We want to eliminate powder blow-by. Does a patch do this for us? Every indication by intelligent shooters has shown us that patches are not gaskets. Just the opposite. So, we do not want to count on a cloth patch to affect a perfect seal in the bore. If you want to avoid gas blow-by, then I suggest a ball that fits well to the bore. Obturation or bullet "upset" will help seal the bore better than a patch alone. The patch, of course, could be backed up by hornet nest or another patch over the powder charge to help prevent blowouts. *A torn or blown patch does nothing for accuracy.*

The Over-Size Ball and Accuracy

In one 40-caliber rifle a fellow black powder enthusiast found a superior grade of accuracy only after going to a ball of bore diameter. If this were a totally isolated case, I would not bring it up; however, in the world of target shooting with the round ball, a number of shooters have gone to a round ball that virtually rests in the bore from land to land. In the above rifle, the actual measured bore size was .400". The rifling was .010" deep, so we had a combined dimension from groove bot-

In using a screw to remove a stuck ball, the shooter must be careful that the screw is centered in the bore. This screw was not, and one can see that it could have damaged the rifling.

groove bottom of .020″.

The best combination in this rifle, a highly accurate hand-made barrel by the way, was to use a ball that was miked at .400″ size along with a patch .017″ thick. It had been found that the sharp lands were cutting patches (this discovered by seating a ball and then pulling it with a screw). I immediately had the lands lapped. Because the lands were now slightly rounded, the .400″ ball with the .017″ patch did go downbore; however, a small mallet had to be used to start it. This would indicate a loss in accuracy to us if we had not already tried flat-nosed balls only to discover that they still grouped normally. So, the ball fitted to the bore by mallet-strokes is still accurate.

The cure for this target rifle was a ball that was bore size, heavy (or medium-heavy) patching, and a mallet to start the ball downbore. I would not want to have to load this way in the hunting field, especially for small game where a shooter might have to run a number of loads in a given day afield, but for the bench-shooter, whose ultimate goal is accuracy, the bore-fit ball might be an answer when all else fails.

Rifling and Accuracy

Ever since the first gunsmith found that if he put a bunch of squirrelly-gigs down the inside of the barrel the projectile flew more "true," there have been literally hundreds and hundreds of different styles of rifling. I am convinced that there is one thing experts are best at in this world and that is—disagreement. The funny thing is that I have seen many accurate barrels and yet the makers of these barrels had totally different ideas concerning rifling style and accuracy.

I'm also convinced that there are a number of methods and a number of rifling styles that all produce barrel accuracy. Find a well-made barrel where the craftsman and/or engineer observed precision, and accuracy is going to be inherent in that barrel. One barrel maker I know says that a round ball barrel must have wide grooves and very narrow lands, and that the depth of groove should go about .010″ to .012″. He also crowns his muzzles so that a large ball which fits closely to

the bore can be gotten down *without* a mallet. His barrels shoot great.

Another rifle maker I know has produced barrels of wide groove and narrow land; however, he has used a groove depth of only .008″, and his barrels shoot great. Another barrel maker uses lands and grooves that are equal in width. His barrels shoot great. I know of a target barrel which is superbly accurate, and it is a 53-caliber with a 1:56 twist and the grooves are cut .024″ deep. A .544″ ball is run home with a mallet and 10-ounce ducking is used for a patch, the material being .023″ thick. There you have it.

I believe that there are many ways to make accurate black powder barrels, with some *general* principles applying quite well. These general principles call for a rather shallow groove for barrels meant to shoot the Maxi or the Minie and somewhat deeper grooves for ball-shooters, though the groove depth does not have to be so deep that a wagon train will fall in and never be heard from again. In some cases, we may have gotten carried away with groove depth, though a shooter who wants benchrest accuracy with the ball may well think about very deep grooves, a strong patch, and oversized ball and a mallet to drive the ball home.

Accuracy and Twist

Nothing expressed or implied in Chapter 9 on twist will give the shooter the idea that slow-twist is the only way to go when trying to achieve top accuracy in ball-shooters. After many personal tests on a lot of rifles, I am convinced that slow-twist is right for round balls, mainly so that the shooter can enjoy a wider latitude in his loads. I have mentioned often that my 54-caliber rifle has been witnessed to shoot well with only 40 to 50 grains of FFFg, and also with as much as 120 grains of FFg, and it has a slow twist, only one turn in 79 inches.

But if I were building a rifle for accuracy only, with bench-shooting and target work in mind, my 54 would not have that twist. I'd probably go 1:56 or something like that. As one barrel maker told me, "It takes too much powder to get some of those slow-twist barrels to shoot with match accuracy." For-

We all know that the muzzle of a firearm must be intact for accuracy to remain excellent. Here is a muzzle crown on a 50 caliber rifle. One can see that it is clean and intact. In order for accuracy to remain up to snuff, the crown of the muzzle will have to continue in good condition.

When the crown of the muzzle does become damaged, accuracy is very likely to suffer. Even a small amount of damage, such a shown here, can cause a serious decline in accuracy.

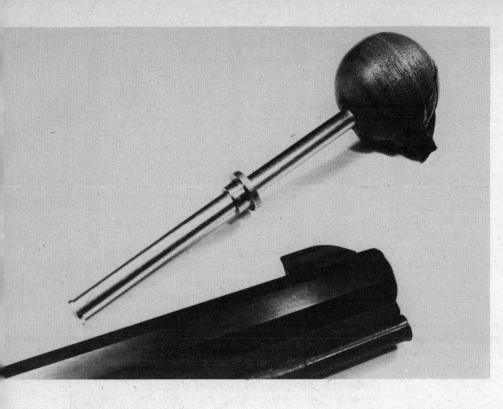

One way to prevent bore damage is to use a loading rod which has a built-in muzzle protector. The Forster Company offers a fine ball-starter which uses a built-in muzzle protector to prevent the scraping of the precious crown of the muzzle.

syth, an intelligent, educated and experienced shooter of 19th century England, showed and proved to all who would look and listen that a round ball from a big 70-caliber or larger rifle would shoot on track to as much as 200 and even 250 yards with only one-quarter turn in the entire length of the bore.

However, as the ball grows larger and larger and attains more mass, it requires less spin or RPS (revolutions per second) to keep it *stable*. So, these very large calibers did indeed, *by proof,* shoot well with only a fourth turn of the ball in the entire length of the bore. But with smaller calibers, we need more RPS. Hence, my own 54 that I mention so often has a 1:79 twist, which is certainly slow. However, in its 34-inch barrel, this would affect about a half-turn of the ball in the length of the bore, not a fourth turn. In fact, if I had to stick my neck out, I would suggest about a half-turn of the ball in the entire length of the bore for rifles of the 50- to 54-caliber class where a shooter wants to use the round ball, and where his goals are hunting and field work.

A famous barrel maker told me that, "I found in a 53- or 54-caliber that a 60-inch overall length is A.1." And he went on to say that, "A 48-inch barrel is more sensitive." He also felt that a full three-fourths turn of the ball in the length of the bore was all right for *target* accuracy. So, in a 50-caliber for target work only, he would call for something like a 1:48 perhaps, knowing that load latitude is cut down. And remember, please, it is scientifically impossible to talk twist without talking caliber. One twist will *not* serve all calibers. One twist will *not* serve all purposes.

In summary, the rifleman interested in bench or target accuracy with the round ball should look to at least a half turn in the bore to perhaps three-fourths of a turn in the bore, while the rifleman interested in the field and in hunting should think of a very slow twist for his ball-shooter. The conical needs more RPS to keep it on track. I have fired very accurate conical-shooting 45-caliber rifles which had twists of 1:22, and I have an accurate 54-caliber rifle meant to fire the 400-grain

Maxi—its rate of twist is 1:34.

Remember, the accuracy (raw accuracy now) of a barrel is not so much in its twist, but in the inherent precision within that bore. I have obtained good accuracy with a round ball from a 45-caliber rifle that had a 1:22 twist, but the accuracy would only come with tiny charges of powder. So accuracy and twist do not go hand-in-hand nearly as much as accuracy and bore precision go hand-in-hand. But we must have our barrel twist suited to our needs.

Compromise Twists

Many rifle companies try to give their products a barrel twist that allows them to be shot with both conicals and round balls. Depending upon our own criteria for accuracy and the need we have for hunting accuracy, those twists can do all right for us. As an example, a 58-caliber with a 1:60 twist managed between 4- and 5-inch groups with bullets at 100 yards, while that same rifle obtained 3-inch groups with round ball, in spite of the shallow groove depth.

While we may not consider groups in the 4- to 5-inch class sufficient to call them "accurate," they are within the demands of hunting accuracy and I'm afraid we can't deny it. Therefore, in this rifle, we are somewhat obliged to say that respectable accuracy was delivered with *both* ball and conical. A 1:60, of course, would be fine enough in a 58-caliber rifle, especially for the lower end charges and the round ball. We might want more than .003" to .005" depth of groove for the patched ball, however, for even better accuracy.

A 1:48 twist in a 50-caliber rifle delivered 3-inch groups at 100 yards with 60 grains of FFg and a round ball, while its best groups with the Maxi were 4 inches at 100 yards using 70 grains of FFg. We have to be careful in our conclusions, because this does *not* say that the 1:48 twist is better for ball than it is for conicals. All it tells us is that this one rifle got slightly better groups with ball than conical, and that could be considered a function of missile more than twist in this isolated case.

TROUBLESHOOTING THE BLACK POWDER LOAD

Often, it is only a "little thing" causing the difference between acceptable accuracy and rewarding ballistics and less than desirable results. This brief troubleshooting guide is geared to help the shooter discover a possible problem with his load and correct it.

Problem 1: There is a whistling sound when firing the Minie ball, and accuracy is poor.

Possible Cure: Try to recover a fired Minie. Chances are, there is a hole blown in the skirt. I have also seen Minies with holes blown totally through from base to nose. To solve the problem you can: 1. reduce powder charge; 2. Switch to Minie with thicker skirt, such as Lyman 577611 or 57730.

Problem 2: Minie is inaccurate.

Possible Cure: Reduce powder charge; switch to different Minie; be certain to fill base of Minie with grease; change from FFFg to FFg powder; be certain to seat Minie without damage to the base.

Problem 3: Maxi is inaccurate.

Possible Cure: Use a Maxi-Ball Starter; alter powder charge first down and then up, keeping good records of the load which delivers best accuracy; switch to another Maxi-ball.

Problem 4: Inaccuracy with cast projectiles.

Possible Cure: First weigh finished projectiles—they should be very close to each other in weight. If they are not, then the lead may be impure and dirty; the temperatures are fluctuating on the heat source; casting habits are poor, or you have a damaged mould. (See *The Black Powder Handgun* for discussion of precision moulding.)

Problem 5: Round ball rifle inaccurate.

Possible Cure: Try larger ball; try stronger patch; try tighter patch/ball fit to the bore; be sure that patch is centered; load a ball and pull it with a screw to determine if lands are cutting patching; if they are, a gunsmith can lap the lands and remove the sharp cutting edge; alter powder charge; alter granulation size; be certain to clean between shots; switch to another lube (might try the Wonder Patch which is impregnated with No. 103 lube); use a backer patch or hornet nest to safeguard the patching on the ball; check spent patches frequently to determine degree of damage if any.

Problem 6: Inaccuracy in the revolver.

Possible Cure: Be certain that no air space exists in the chamber by using a filler material, such as cornmeal, between the ball and the powder charge to take up all air space in the chamber; lower the powder charge; best accuracy was often obtained with a charge of between 50 percent and 75 percent of maximum for the chamber space available (use filler to take up space left after powder charge is reduced). Check adjustable sights for movement; sights must be motionless. Clean revolver, especially the bore, and insure that there is no debris settled in the grooves of the rifling.

Problem 7: Poor ignition.

Possible Cure: Use good percussion caps of reputable quality; change the nipple, especially if it has been used for a long period of time; check for damp powder; in a flintlock, use the methods prescribed in this book under "basic loading." Finally, we must recognize that some black powder arms have poor ignition because of basic design and workmanship; in such a case, the shooter may wish to change firearms. Change powder brand.

Problem 8: Sparks and debris coming back at shooter.

Possible Cure: In a percussion firearm, the shooter may wish to use a metal cup into which the base of the nipple fits. This cup, often of brass, will help to contain debris direction. The shooter may wish to change nipples—the open based nipple often has too much blowback. The hammer nose can be deepened with a Dremel tool to better contain cap debris.

Problem 9: Inaccuracy with powder measure.

Possible Cure: Practice—often, the shooter who practices with the powder measure will learn how to develop a *routine* which will render very reliable load to load weights of powder. Try another type of measure; use a measure that has a swing-in-line funnel to level off the powder supply.

Problem 10: Shotgun patterns inconsistent or blown.

Possible Cure: Reduce the powder charge; switch to a coarser granulation of powder; check all aspects of the wad column to insure that no component is blown out, especially the felt wad; try a one-piece plastic wad, such as the Ballistic Products, Inc., wad; change nipples if they are open-base type; be certain to use a fairly strong seating pressure on the wad column; try to maintain seating pressure within a reasonable range of pounds; change shot size; try a thinner over-shot wad. In the shotshell, try a coarser granulation of powder; use the weakest, not strongest primer you can find, and apply all of the other aspects to the load as mentioned above, shot size, powder charge and so forth.

Problem 11: Black powder cartridge inaccuracy.

Possible Cure: Be certain that there is no air space whatsoever in the case by loading to the full capacity or by using cornmeal to take up the space not occupied by the powder charge. Some shooters also use a card wad on the powder and then fill the additional space with cornmeal. Use mild primers; avoid all magnum type primers. Be certain that bullets are quality run, and use the grease in the grease grooves as prescribed by the mould manufacturer. Even if a small bore, such as the 25-20, try Fg or FFg powder in the case when other granulation sizes have already been tried. Make certain that the correct bullet is used. There are often large margins of variation among original black powder cartridge arms, especially in bore dimensions.

The compromise twist, if indeed we want to name them as such, is viable, depending upon what the shooter wants from his firearm in terms of accuracy. Also, we say again that accuracy is far more a function of a fine barrel than it is of twist, and when we suggest slow twist for ball we are thinking of a greater *range* of accuracy potential, including good accuracy with higher velocity loads.

Accuracy and the Smoothbore

There are several ways to gain decent accuracy from a smoothbore as long as the shooter recognizes that he is not going to be able to challenge the rifled arms to a duel. At least one theory holds that a round ball from a smoothbore would be about as accurate as a round ball from a rifle if we could make round balls with absolute and total perfection. I don't know. Maybe so. I do realize that revolving the ball is important from the standpoint of equalizing the imperfections in the ball around a common axis. But spinning on an axis is also effective in stabilizing a mass on a given "line."

At any rate, I have never seen a smoothbore shoot with the rifled arms at 50 yards, 75 yards, or 100 yards. I believe the British also found this out the hard way during the American Revolution. However, we can get a smoothbore to shoot with a degree of accuracy. Here are the steps:

1. If the rifle is a flintlock such as the musket of the "Brown Bess" type, be certain to use a small metal rod in the touchhole prior to pouring powder down the barrel during the loading process. Then, when the powder is poured and compacted, there will be a clear touchhole for the jet of flame from the priming pan to reach the main powder charge in the breech.

2. Melt a grease such as Crisco or RIG or Young Country No. 103 (a good one for this), and into the melted grease plop a few ½-inch to ¾-inch shotgun wads of the "felt" type. Pull these from the grease and set them aside.

3. In loading the musket, after the small rod has been inserted into the touchhole and the powder poured down, a card wad is run downbore right on top of the powder charge. A "nitro" card wad is useful here. Give that card wad about 40 pounds of seating pressure.

4. On top of the card wad, the greased-soaked felt wad is now run. This is compressed with the loading rod, but it does not have to be forced hard on top of the card wad, just seated completely and firmly.

5. The round ball is now seated firmly right onto the soft felt wad in the bore. No patch is used. Remember, the standard loading rod for the musket is made of steel and a reasonable pressure in seating wads and the ball is easy to accomplish. If the musket is to be carried in the field, I suggest some form of wad on top of the ball to insure that the ball remains downbore on the felt wad. If the shooter is on the range, he will not need this over-ball wad; however, he must be responsible for keeping the ball down on top of the wad and not letting it get away from the wad and roll down the barrel.

Using this method, Don Malson, world champion shooter, improved his groups from a foot size down to 5 inches at standard musket range.

The Maxi-ball loader from Forster is a tool designed to align the Maxi ball in the muzzle and therefore in the breech of the rifle. The unit slips over the muzzle of the firearm and the plunger is pushed downward, inserting the Maxi accurately in the bore.

Starting the Maxi Ball

In a series of somewhat informal tests, we concluded that when a Maxi ball got started down the bore in a crooked condition accuracy suffered. We also found that the best way to start the Maxi was with a Maxi-Ball Starter. One of these is available from Forster Products. The Maxi-Ball Starter centers the projectile in the muzzle. In one of my conical-shooting rifles, I have found that the Maxi-Ball Starter allowed for protection of the important base of the missile, whereas loading by hand sometimes meant nicking the base of the missile.

Accuracy and the Set Trigger

Although this is not a load-oriented comment, it might be wise to mention that in testing a number of set or "sett" triggers, we found that, for our own style of shooting, a letoff pressure of about 6 ounces was right. We actually measured some of our set triggers at as little as 2 ounces, but this was almost too much of a good thing. Others may work well with such small letoff weights. RCBS offers a trigger pull gauge for a nominal fee, and users of the set trigger may wish to invest in one, in order to determine how light a trigger pull should be, and then standardize the battery of rifles by using the gauge.

This important chapter cannot go into every detail of accuracy in black powder loading, for many of those details are personal to either the shooter, his firearm or both. As the shooter safely experiments with his own muzzleloaders and black powder cartridge guns, he will determine for himself which tricks and tips work best. This chapter serves to give the shooter a starting point from which to develop the best accuracy from his own shooting irons.

chapter 8

Loading for Power

THE CONCEPT of "optimum load" fairly well takes care of our "power loads," since it is my belief that the shooter should not go beyond a certain maximum powder level in the first place. However, as with all things in the fascinating, but often bumpy journey through black powder valley, "it ain't that simple." The shooter, I feel, should have an understanding of what he is getting in terms of useful ballistic force, and that is the reason for this rather important chapter.

Also, and I hate to continually dwell on safety, we *must* include some facts about recommended loads out of the past because some of these "power loads" are actually unworkable in modern day usage. We will explain why. The shooter often questions today's loading advice in light of the fact that the old-timers seemed to burn so much more powder in some rifles and on some occasions. I have already answered what must amount to over 100 letters from readers who have dug into old manuscripts and found huge black powder loads in them. These fellows want to know why they can't load their rifles the same way.

First, all was not rosy in making power loads in days gone by. In the fine document by Osborne Russell, called *Journal of a Trapper* (1834-1843), the author documents a few gun accidents in terms of a firearm coming apart at the seams. Also, he speaks of a "bursted tube" on a rifle. (Tube, by the way, was the term for nipple.) Russell said, " . . . we found the whole country [Yellowstone today] swarming with Elk we killed a fat Buck for supper and encamped for the night the next day Allen shot a Grizzly Bear and bursted the percussion tube of his rifle which obliged us to return to our comrades on the 13th and make another tube." (p. 66)

Such occurrences were common, and I note, too, that when a man came up missing, they assumed that he may have had a fall, been scalped by the Indians, or that his rifle may have blown up. If rifles did not blow up with at least some regularity, then why would the party assume a rifle had blown up? At one point in the Russell saga, the author and his friends are contemplating the disappearance of a comrade. Russell says, "It was then agreed that either his gun had bursted and killed him or his horse had fallen with him over some tremendous precipice. He was a man about 55 years of age and of 30 years

experience as a hunter." (p. 28)

I'm saying all of this to tell the reader that loading for power, which is what these mountain men were no doubt doing, is to be considered a science. I'm led to believe that the old-timers in some isolated cases simply poured a great quantity of black powder down the bore when power was sought for. However, they probably were not getting the actual punch they wanted. We know now, thanks to the chronograph, that a lot of that powder went for naught, except to cause more kick and blast and very little useful velocity.

We also know that the powder used in the old days was not the same as used today. I think we have the finest black powder ever manufactured at any given time in the country, and it seems to show in terms of actual velocity per charge. With this, I'll conclude step one of our loading for power process—forget old-time data. Do not rely on it. Do not use it. When reading about the Englishman who poured a half bucket of black powder down his big bore to bag a bull elephant, remember that his rifle was of truly large caliber, that this caliber helped in dissipating the energies created by the burning powder, and that his powder was not the same propellant that we use today.

Power in Bore Size

Elsewhere in the book we show how increases in caliber mean a great deal to black powder shooters who want truly powerful firearms for hunting. At the same time, we have to admit that America was won with small-caliber longrifles, and that the early Eastern Seaboard adventurers, such as Dan'l Boone, probably bagged their venison with something under 40-caliber. I mention this fact because I do not want to confuse optimum hunting loads with forsaking accuracy factors. A good shot with a 40-caliber rifle will put the meat on the table because the ball will be placed in the head or neck, not the rump—a 40-caliber slug in the head is worth two 50s in the tail. *Nothing we say here about optimum power loads is to replace the value of ball/bullet placement on the game.*

However, there is no denying that we cannot attain top rated velocity with black powder, nor would we want to. The thrills in black powder shooting stem from many facets; how-

A progression of black powder pure lead round balls shows the great differences in dimension as the spheres increase in diameter. On the left is a 36-caliber ball (.350″) which weighs 65 grains, followed by the 40-caliber ball (.395″) at 92 grains. Next is the 45-caliber (.455″) ball at 133 grains, followed by the 50-caliber ball (.490″) at 177 grains. The 54-caliber ball (.535″) is next at 230 grains with the 58-caliber ball (.570″) last in line at 280 grains.

ever, one is the challenge, and if we lost that aspect of the sport, a lot of the good feeling we have about top scores and cleanly harvested meat would also be lost. So, without a lot of velocity, we turn to mass for our "power." The old-timers knew this. When they said *big bore,* they meant it.

Sir Samuel Baker was an Englishman of the 19th century who hunted much in Ceylon, and he wrote an interesting book on the subject, entitled *The Rifle and Hound in Ceylon,* long out of print but often available in reprint. Baker used "huge-bore" rifles and often bagged his elephants with the round ball, which he preferred over the conical. But he used the conical, too. How about this one: "A four-ounce [conical] ball, raking an animal from stem to stern, must settle him at once" (p. 137 of Arno Press edition). I should say so. The projectile of four ounces amounts to 1,750 grains. One can see that a 180-grain 30-06 bullet would be dwarfed by such a slug.

Certainly, power does hold hands with the big bore. They are companions. And penetration, along with wound channel and of course diameter of that wound channel, is increased as ball or bullet mass is increased. As long as we never leave shot placement out of the picture, we can rest assured that larger is stronger in the game fields.

Using the Data

First, how close is the data from one firearm to another? If a shooter has the tables before him, showing actual measured velocities, can he count on these in terms of "power" and in terms of trajectory? I think the answer is, strongly, *yes.* For example, I was examining the velocities printed by Thompson/Center and Lyman for 36-caliber rifles. We have:

1. Thompson/Center, 36-caliber, 28″ barrel, .015″ patch, T/C 13 lube, .350″ 65-grain round ball, No. 11 cap.

RESULTS:

Charge	Powder	Muzzle Velocity
40 FFFg	duPont	1,894 fps
50 FFFg	duPont	2,034 fps
60 FFFg	duPont	2,150 fps

2. Lyman Data from *Black Powder Handbook* 36-caliber, 28″ barrel, .015″ patch, Crisco lube, .350″ 65-grain round ball, No. 11 cap.

RESULTS:

Charge	Powder	Muzzle Velocity
40 FFFg	GOI	1,706 fps
50 FFFg	GOI	1,956 fps
60 FFFg	GOI	2,090 fps

How come these two highly reliable companies differ in their printed data? It's a matter of variables, being: powder (note two different brands); powder lot (actual "runs" of powder); actual bore dimensions; rate of twist (varying bore friction); configuration of rifling; altitude above sea level; atmospheric temperature; powder temperature; precise patch thickness; precise lube effect; actual dimension of ball in thousandths of an inch; percussion cap (to a small degree); the chronograph used for testing; how the chronograph screens were baffled, and so forth.

Yet, I can take the above loads, including the 40-grain charges, which differ by 188 fps, and create exactly what I want in the field, both in terms of expected "power," and in terms of trajectory. Fortunately, the ballistics from the chronograph are always close enough to be highly useful to us, indispensable for the shooter who truly wants to make the best loads. Kick and noise do *not* spell out power. In a moment, we will see that other researchers (as well as the one beating the typewriter here) have actually recorded *lower* velocities in cases of extremely high powder charges—more smoke, more kick, more noise, and LESS POWER. That is why we have labored to give the shooter a suggested optimum hunting or "power load" in this book.

Let's take the two velocity figures above for the 40-grain charge and see what we could actually do with them in terms of using the information for our own loading purposes. First, I see that the 1,894 fps load is worth 518 foot-pounds of muzzle energy. The 1,706 fps is worth 420 foot-pounds of muzzle energy. I can see right away that I do not have a deer load, even though I do not believe in kinetic energy ratings as the only means of assessing black powder power. But these loads won't qualify as big game in punch.

I can also see that they will bag small game with no problem because we know a 22 Long Rifle will do it, and with the 40-grain bullet at even 1300 fps we only have 150 foot-pounds of energy. I have already learned much, even if the figures are not precisely the same. I further know that if I sight the rifle in to strike right on at 50 yards, I will be about 1½ inches low at 75 yards, which tells me I have a very good small game trajectory for my purposes with either load because I will seldom shoot small game beyond 75 yards.

In this book, we did not use standard test barrels because we wanted to record any differences that a barrel, due to twist, actual bore diameter, or a number of other things, might offer us. So, the shooter should, in building his optimum hunting load for power, consult the tables and find his own rifle. He will then know two things: he will have a good idea of the "power" of his particular load, and he can consult our simplified sighting-in chart and head for the range with his own smokepole to sight it in for hunting purposes, taking complete advantage of the trajectory potential of the load.

Velocity and Ball Penetration

There are a number of shooters in the country today whom I call "Black Powder Preachers." They stand at the range, or they bang away on the Remington Portable, telling all black powder fans who will listen exactly how to load their rifles and what the results of such loads will be. These folks don't use such mundane instruments as chronographs to verify their preaching. They simply know what works best and how it works from intuition. Sometimes, they have bagged a deer in the brush at 50 yards, and they therefore know that 50 grains of black powder behind a 50-caliber ball will kill a deer, and sometimes they haven't bagged anything at all. But they are willing to advise anyway.

Quite a number of these "black powder gurus," as a friend of mine calls them, have stated that you do not need an opti-

mum safe charge for hunting because as the ball increases in velocity, it no longer penetrates. I am not suggesting that they are entirely wrong. However, the rule of thumb they set forth must be explained to the shooter, and he must not buy this rule wholesale. It is more wrong than right.

Actual experience is a good teacher, though sometimes we only think we saw what we saw when we really saw something else. However, I'll point out that I have shot clear through elk, bison and big mule deer, plus smaller antelope, with round balls of the 50- to 54-caliber class steaming along at what we consider higher velocity in black powder loads. The idea that a round ball achieves *less* penetration at higher speeds (as propounded by a number of black powder gurus), seems to be false based upon my own field experience.

More energy usually means more penetration, *provided that the projectile remains intact* and that it retains some semblance of its original form. Change of shape in a projectile transfers energy from the projectile to the medium it is passing through, and thereby energy is lost in the projectile itself and without energy the ball cannot travel on. So, a ball smashed flat in an instant would not indeed penetrate as well as one which remained somewhat true to its original shape, even though a ball is hardly ideal in shape to begin with in terms of penetration.

I have, however, taken a round ball flatter than a pancake from the off-side of a bison bull, and yet that ball traveled through the entire chest cavity from point-blank range out of a 54-caliber rifle firing a .530″ round ball at close to 2000 fps muzzle velocity. I'm sure the striking speed had to be something like 1900 or in that range. First, we need to remind ourselves that a pure lead projectile does not fragment. This ball weighed exactly 224.9 grains after it was recovered. It had weighed 225.0 grains prior to being shot out of the rifle. (I weigh all of the balls I shoot prior to hunting so I can tell exactly how much the balls weighs if I recover them later from game.)

Pure lead is very cohesive. The molecular cohesion means

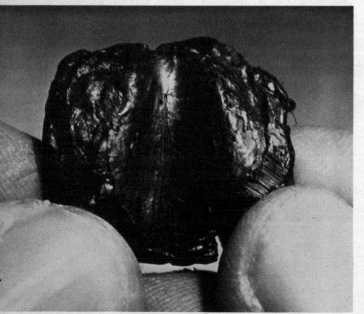

This highly flattened hunk of lead is a .530″ round ball taken from the offside of a bison bull hit in the chest cavity from point blank range. The hunk of pure lead travelled the entire breadth of the chest, knocking a rib piece out. Loss of lead was almost nil, which is typical of a pure lead pill. "Power" in black powder is of course tied in with velocity, however, mass plays a big role, too, and so does sheer caliber size. Remember, the bison is the largest four-footer on the continent as compared with game animals. And a bison bull, full grown, can weigh more than a moose or a "Kodiak" bear.

that it sticks together like Abbott and Costello. A fragmented round ball, if it had been moulded from pure lead (as pure as we can obtain), is more rare than prices going down or winter in the Arctic turning mild. So, at high speed, we do have a projectile that will flatten out, but that ball of pure lead *will* stick together.

Furthermore, the idea of loading way down to give us a nice low velocity ball so that it will "penetrate better," according to the gurus, is somewhat meaningless when we consider that the ball loses velocity so rapidly anyway! If a round ball of .490″ starts out at a flat 2000 fps from the muzzle, it will be

The scapula (shoulder blade) of a bull elk is shown here. The hole was made by a .530″ round ball. The ball exited at the root of the tail, rather unusual, since we usually find the round ball stopped in the off-side of the game animal, usually against the hide.

down to something like 1500 fps at only 50 yards from the muzzle.

I've belabored this point because I would like to see shooters who are striving for "power" load a *safe,* but optimum chain. In fact, I also tried a few informal penetration tests on various media to see if I could arrive at an estimation of what happens when the ball strikes at high speed. Remember, I had witnessed cases of round ball from a 54-caliber rifle passing though a bull elk and penetrating the entire chest cavity of a bull bison—the elk taken at 70 paces, the bison at a comparative few feet from the muzzle after rising back to his feet from a brain shot. (Six men saw it happen, and the brain was pierced all the way through.) So, let's take a glance at one of these informal test runs.

Four test media were used in these informal runs. I wanted indications of what would happen when a round ball struck hard objects as well as softer objects. The first test medium were catalogs of the "wishbook" variety, such as offered by Sears, Wards and other companies. These are very hard on projectiles and are one of the few items I have ever used which will cause some fragmentation in a pure lead missile. The second test medium was a damp clay bank. This natural material was terribly compacted and tough, but it did not contain rocks or other debris upon inspection. The third test material was a series of ½-inch thick marine grade plywood planks. The fourth medium was modeling clay, such as may be purchased from an art shop.

Caliber 50, .495″ Round-Ball Test

At 1,400 fps from the muzzle, the .495″ pure lead round ball weighing 182 grains, made it through two "wish book" catalogs from a distance of 10 feet. The same ball at a velocity of 2000 fps made it through the same two books and into the first few pages of the third book, showing no improvement upon penetration and indicating not only by penetration, but also by the fact that lead was lost, that fragmentation was taking place.

The 182-grain round ball weighed 146.7 grains on the average recovered from this first test, and this was at a starting velocity of 1400 fps. The 182-grain .495″ ball weighed a flat 150.0 grains, or about the same, actually, fired into the hard paper books at a starting velocity of 2000 fps. Incidentally, a 7mm Remington Magnum, firing a toughly constructed 160-grain bullet at a velocity of a bit over 3100 fps, also pehetrated only two wish books and a bit into the third book when fired from 10 feet.

In the clay bank, the .495″ round ball penetrated a flat two-inch average for 5 shots, with the variation between each pen-

This is a 45-caliber Maxi ball in a "before-and-after" pose. Once again, high lead retention was evident. Pure lead projectiles lose very little weight in soft-skinned game animals or, in this case, in the test medium.

The plain spherical lead ball will drop game from mice to moose. The mule deer on the left was taken at 50 yards with a .530″ round ball and cleanly harvested with one shot. John Fadala poses with the two mule deer bucks.

etration absolutely minor. This was with the 1400 fps starting velocity. At 2000 fps starting velocity the same ball made it into an average of 2¼ inches of the tough clay bank for five shots. In this case, both balls weighed right at 181 grains upon recovery, so fragmentation was not evident. So, there again was little difference, but the higher velocity ball *did not penetrate less* than the lower velocity ball, as the black powder gurus had told us it would. Nor did it gain much penetration in the hard clay bank, only ¼-inch on the average.

On the boards the .495″ ball, at 1400 fps, traveled through five planks and actually stuck in the sixth plank with just enough penetration to hold it there. The average weight of the recovered ball in this case was 176.8 grains. At 2000 fps, the same ball penetrated nine boards. The faster ball now, in this medium, was gaining in penetration, and the recovered ball now weighed an average of 173.0 grains.

In the modeling clay, the .495″ ball at 1400 fps made it through 15½ inches of material on the average. But the same ball at 2000 fps made it through 22½ inches of clay. In both cases, the balls lost nil mass, weighing about the same as their starting weight before firing. While the nominal weight of the .495″ ball is 182.4 grains, I want to point out that the average heft of the Speer .495″ swaged round balls was 182.9 grains, for those who insist upon keeping things accurate as well as precise.

I will not go into the figures earned by a .530″ ball which averaged at 224.5 grains in actual weight; however, I would like to point out that this ball, at a starting velocity of 1,250 fps fired from 10 feet, made it through 27 inches of modeling clay, but at 1,850 fps, the same .530″ ball flew all the way through the 30-inch clay block, so we got no usable measurement.

In conclusion, field experience and informal shooting tests indicated that round ball penetration did not fail because velocity was boosted with reasonably safe charges of powder. In fact, in accord with laws of physics, on media which did not smash the ball flat or fragment it, penetration was enhanced by added velocity. Also, I want to point out that with the coni-

cal the results of one informal test came out the same. Higher velocity did not retard penetration in the test media.

Another Reason for Safe Optimum Hunting Loads

I tend to agree wholeheartedly with the rule of thumb calculations of black powder writer Max Vickery when it comes to loading for "power" in hunting. Mr. Vickery is not for overloads, and neither am I. But he wants loads of flat trajectory, by black powder standards, and some striking power. He says, in *Muzzle Blasts Magazine* for May, 1976, p. 21, "I think the states that require the muzzle-loading rifle for deer to be a .45 or above did the right thing. At target, all you have to do is get a hole in the paper; in hunting, you have an animal to anchor or you have a cripple." In the same article, he further stated, "What I'm driving at is: Somewhere between extreme velocity and ultimate accuracy is probably the correct hunting load for your rifle." Mr. Vickery goes on to ask the shooter to look for a starting velocity in the 2000 fps domain, roughly, if the rifle will shoot that round ball load with accuracy. I agree.

When You Use Too Much Powder

Pumping the black powder down the hole as if it were blasting powder may well be a waste of fuel. My own tests have shown this to be a fact, and I have actually obtained *decreased* muzzle velocity with some hot loads. I am, of course, speaking of very, very heavy charges of powder.

Let us not confuse theory with actual practice. In theory a round ball, during firing, can consume about its own weight in fuel, with at least minor increases in velocity. This was proved in a *test* barrel, under *test* conditions. *Don't* try this yourself. Remember that the black powder charge itself may be as much as 50- to 57-percent unburned. We speak of this in our chapter on black powder. So, the charge has to push itself out of the bore, and it also has to push the missile out of the bore. That is a lot of work to be done.

Mr. Ed Yard, respected tester, found that after a certain amount of black powder was fired in a 50 caliber test rifle, the

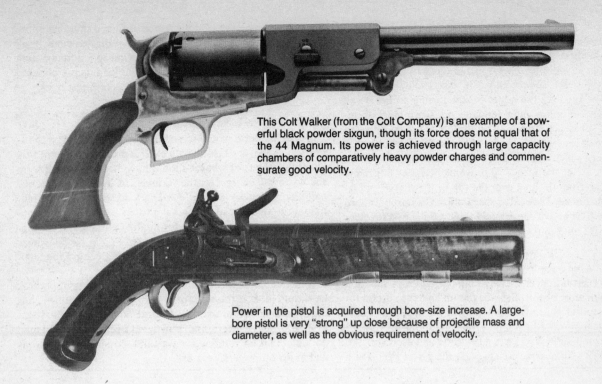

This Colt Walker (from the Colt Company) is an example of a powerful black powder sixgun, though its force does not equal that of the 44 Magnum. Its power is achieved through large capacity chambers of comparatively heavy powder charges and commensurate good velocity.

Power in the pistol is acquired through bore-size increase. A large-bore pistol is very "strong" up close because of projectile mass and diameter, as well as the obvious requirement of velocity.

next addition of black powder actually brought the velocity *down*. He turned to a 45-caliber test rifle and got the same results. Under test conditions, Dr. Gary White found the same phenomenon. After he reached a certain level of fuel, more powder brought the velocity *down*. These, as we have stated, are in very heavy doses of powder.

In our own tests for this book, we did not reach these levels, because we did not use enough powder to see an actual *drop* in velocity. However, we did see many cases of a good, workable velocity being reached with a charge that is well under the recommendations made by some shooters. So, while in most cases we will indeed attain higher velocity by going up to the full, maximum, safe load as recommended by the gunmaker, our chronograph will often prove to us that a load of a bit less powder will get just about as much effectiveness, and in such cases, we'll recommend the lighter charge.

Using Too Little Powder

In a few rare cases, too little powder can be questioned. I have no proof, and I know of no one else who has proof which will stand up to the scrutiny of well-constructed tests, but we do have a rather substantial body of data to look at which suggests that some firearms have blown when the breech was, in effect (or actuality), only partially loaded with powder. We have seen this in modern arms, such as the 270 Winchester with half-charges of slow-burning smokeless powder. The recommendation of those who shoot a lot of black powder cartridges is to keep the case fairly full of powder, too.

When we only short-start a ball or bullet in the muzzle-loader, we have, in effect, created a chamber which is not full of powder. I can only speculate upon what actually happens in such instances. Frankly, the mystery lies in the fact that we have not been able to duplicate, time after time, the actual event of blowing a gun barrel to pieces using partially loaded chamber areas. We do, however, have isolated cases of this happening. I was told only two days before writing this chapter that a documented case of a gun becoming injured with a short-started ball was again documented.

One possible answer may rest in the idea of *detonation*. In the words of dedicated black powder shooter Reverend Joel Chiri, who wrote me a letter on the subject, we will briefly explore this situation. The reverend said, "As a reloader I ultimately heard of an unusual occurrence called *detonation*. Detonation occurs when large pistol cases are charged with small amounts of fast-burning [smokeless] powder. The result usually destroys the gun. I have seen quality guns destroyed in this manner. The strange thing is that it does not always happen. In fact, it rarely happens."

Reverend Chiri goes on to explain that the theory behind detonation suggests that the powder, lying in a "trough" along the bottom of the barrel or the cartridge case, does not burn as such, but instead goes off all at once, giving very high pressures. And, some shooters feel that if the powder is kept to the back of the case or chamber, by the use of filler materials, detonation will not occur.

Power in the Shotgun

I have listed volume-for-volume loads because these have been given over the years as safe and powerful. I have tested a few dozen shotguns with volume-for-volume loads and have never had a problem with them. At the same time, I have never found a lesser charge of powder to produce a worse pattern. I always consider using *less* powder in my own shotgun loads whenever I can.

While a volume-for-volume load—equal volumes of shot and powder— has proved to be safe time after time, mainly due, I am sure, to the tremendous size of the effective chamber area of the shotgun, my own thought is that such a charge is about maximum, at least in my philosophy. In my own 12-gauge hunting load for upland game, I seldom use the volume/volume charge. Often I will use 1¼ ounces of shot backed by a charge of FFg that's 20 percent less than the volume of shot. The birds drop as cleanly as they ever did with any shotgun I ever used in the past.

Power in the Revolver

The chambers of the revolver limit the amount of powder which can be used. Therefore, the shooter has a built-in maximum he must adhere to. As for fuel, I think FFFg is usually preferred; however, some companies recommend FFFFg pan powder. The revolver fan might consider using a filler on all loads which are below chamber capacity. Corn meal or another inert substance is generally considered all right, the idea being to keep the powder charge to the back of the chamber near the vent which will allow the jet from the percussion cap to ignite it. Also, the idea is to prevent the jet of hot flame from the cap from flashing over the top of the charge and igniting it all at once. Such is the speculation. The proof is hard to come by. But I have consistently achieved my best revolver accuracy with filler in the chambers.

Power in the Pistol

The larger bore single shot pistols do well with FFg, and I can see no reason to ever use anything of smaller granulation than FFFg in most pistols. Safe maximum loads are useful for hunting purposes for those few who will pursue larger game with the black powder handgun. Primarily, the black powder pistol is a companion piece, and a beautiful and useful one, to the rifle. With light accurate charges, the pistol becomes a small game meat potter in the hands of a good shot. I suppose if the black powder hunter lived where some ferocious beast might make lunch of him, he might want to load maximum charges. I can't think of much reason to load up the pistol to anything beyond top-rated accuracy levels for most of us.

The Double Charge

I wish this term would have followed the dinosaur into extinction; however, it is still with us. It is precisely the opposite, in actual effect, of what it should have been. The real term should be *half charge*, for the "double" charge is just that, *two half charges or the nominal hunting load.* However, the old-time term was used to mean that a rifleman was going to double the *target* load in his rifle for hunting purposes. If he happened to enjoy a load a of 50 grains of FFg in his 50-caliber rifle, he might then load 100 grains of FFg behind the .490″ ball for hunting.

If the reader does see references to double charging, I think he should look at the term in light of a hunting load which is only two times larger than a *light* target load in that rifle. Ideas of shooting 80 or 90 grains of powder in a certain rifle and then doubling that for hunting are wasteful, potentially dangerous and in my opinion not correct.

Simplified Sighting Chart for Optimum Loads

The chart below will show the reader how to start his sighting-in procedures. In no way does it give the exact line of flight for a bullet or ball, nor does any other chart in existence. The best we can do is get a shooter started in the right direction, and then he will have to take it from there, finding out precisely where his own rifle or handgun strikes the target at the various ranges at which the shooter fires.

SIMPLIFIED SIGHT CHART FOR OPTIMUM RIFLE LOADS

45- to 58-caliber (ball [2000] or conical [1500])*

13 Yards	50 Yards	100 Yards	125 Yards
0	+1″	−1″	−6″

38 to 40-caliber (1500 fps range)

25 Yards	50 Yards	75 Yards
+½″	0″	−2″

38 to 40-caliber (2000 fps range)

25 Yards	50 Yards	75 Yards
+½″	0″	−1″

32 to 36-caliber (1500 fps range)

25 Yards	50 Yards	75 Yards
+1″	0″	−2″

*This is based upon the ball beginning at about 1800 (lowest) to about 2000 (highest) fps range. The conical is calibrated at about 1500 fps in this case, but it will print close to the same pattern of trajectory, perhaps a bit *lower* at 75 to 125 yards, due to its ability to retain velocity better than a ball. So, a ball at about 1800-2000 fps and a conical at about 1500 fps print close to the same pattern, with the ball slightly flatter overall.

We have calculated the following trajectory patterns from the test rifles coming over the transom. One will see immediately that calibers 45 through 58 are given no special sighting-in consideration. This is because in practical, real-life terms, there are only minor differences in these calibers from zero to 125 yards. There are differences, of course, and the larger balls carry up better than the smaller ones; however, the shooter, in the process of precisely sighting his own rifle, will find that our figures not only "put him on the paper," but also come fairly close to actual patterns of trajectory.

The Process

1. Sight in 45- through 58-caliber rifles by beginning at 13 yards from the muzzle. This gives the shooter a very good chance of hitting paper the first shot out of the barrel. If the shooter tries sighting at 75 to 100 yards for starters, then he may find it difficult to hit paper right away, or he may find that adjustments are quite difficult to make with accuracy at such ranges where minor adjustments account for big changes in point of impact.

2. After the gun is sighted for 13 yards, the shooter can move the target out to 50 yards. He should concentrate *only* on windage problems at 50 yards, leaving any change in "up/down" or elevation changes on the target to be conducted at 75 yards.

3. Now, with the target at 75 yards, the shooter can see how his grouping is on the bull's-eye. If he wants to be right on at 75 yards, which is not a bad idea, he can adjust the sights so that the group prints center of the bull. Now, he can shoot from zero to 75 yards knowing that his ball or bullet will print on at about 13 yards or so, about an inch high at 50 yards, about an inch or so low at 100 yards and about ½-foot low at 125 yards. The man with a rifle in 45- through 58-caliber firing the

Building the Optimum Load

This important topic is touched on more than once, but we will cover it again:

1. *Never exceed the maximum charge as recommended by the gunmaker.*
2. Begin all testing with about half of the top recommended charge.
3. Use a ball which fits the bore well or a proper-sized conical.
4. Make certain the patching material is strong, not always thick, necessarily, but strong.
5. Inspect patches—if they are torn or blown use a piece of hornet nest (or second patch) on top of the powder charge to prevent patch burnout.
6. Increase the powder charge—to safe levels—5 to 10 grains at a time, by volume, while shooting several 5-shot groups from a solid benchrest. When accuracy falls off to the point where precise ball placement becomes doubtful, go back to the last charge that produced at least an optimum in hunting accuracy, hopefully something in the area of at least 2 inches at 50 yards. Do not, however, exceed the factory's maximum recommended load for your rifle.
7. Sight the rifle in for this load. It is your optimum hunting load.
8. Looking at the data you have carefully kept, beginning with the groups made with the half-charge of powder on up, select that load chain, powder, lube, ball and patch, or conical and lube, which gave the greatest accuracy of all, time after time.

This is your everyday load, your target load, your plinking load, your small game load, and sometimes even your big game load when conditions allow for close-range shooting.

Loading for power, then, is to create a charge along with other components of the load chain which delivers sufficient accuracy to get the job done, while still allowing for optimum *velocity* and a flatness of *trajectory*. This load will give the hunter a chance to take his game over reasonable, prudent black powder ranges. As the hunting black powder shooter studies our "Simplified Sighting-In Chart," he can see that our optimum charges with optimum velocities will allow for a reasonable flatness of trajectory. He can sight in at a given range and he can hit a target at 100 or even 125 yards without undue "Kentucky windage" and guesswork. This means putting the projectile in the vitals, rather than in the non-vitals. And that, is the most important aspect of cleanly harvesting game.

round ball or the conical can bag game from zero to 100 yards with no sight hold-over. On deer-sized game he can still hold dead center on the chest out to a full 125 yards and expect a strike in the vitals.

No person can judge range in the field to perfection, and as I continually work within the confines of black powder shooting (mostly not exceeding 100 to maybe 125 yards), I seem to get worse and worse in judging longer ranges. I, not long ago, mistook a mere 190 yards for 300 yards. It had been so long since I had worked beyond 125 yards, that nearly 200 yards seemed very far away indeed. I used to be able to arrive at a fairly close approximation of 200 yards in the field.

However, with the sighting as stated above, a shooter can do quite well if he will study field distances and learn to judge the range to the best of his ability. I try to keep my hunting shots under 125 yards, and I hope for much closer shots and work for much closer shots when I can get them, which is most of the time.

The Sub-Bores

With the 32- and 36-caliber rifles, I feel that a muzzle velocity of about 1500 fps is plenty for small game and informal plinking. Therefore, I sight in to hit 1-inch *high* at 25 yards. This puts me about on at 50 yards, or perhaps a very small degree to the high side. At 75 yards, the ball dips only 2 inches low. In other words, I can hit a cottontail-sized target from zero to 75 yards without worrying about how much to hold off-target.

One caution: When the shooter is at point blank range, and I mean a few yards only, he must remember that his sights are *over* the target. Recall that with our 32/36-caliber sighting, we are a bit high at 25 yards, so we hold a little *low* to make a perfect strike center. But . . . at only a few yards, which is where I take most of my

mountain grouse, the shooter must aim at the very top of the bird's head or a bit over the head in order to affect a hit on the head itself, thereby preserving meat.

The 38- and 40-Caliber Rifles

These two fine calibers (and the 40-caliber is one of my favorite numbers), sort of fall in between the 45/58 and the 32/36 sight suggestions. If either is to be used for larger game, such as javelina, and the hunter gets the velocity up to about 2000 fps or perhaps 1900 fps, then a sight-in right at 50 yards is not bad. The ball will be ½-inch high at 25 yards and maybe 1-inch low at 75 yards.

If the 38/40 range is used for small game and the like, then a 1500 fps range is expected, and the shooter can print ½-inch high at 25 yards again, but he will probably drop a full 2 inches at 75 yards.

Remember, all of the 45/58 figures are based upon a muzzle velocity in the 1800-2000 fps domain, true optimum hunting charges. Of course, this includes the 54s which start out at 1850 fps, and the 58s which begin at 1800 fps. We are trying to get on target, fellow shooters, and the fine-sighting is left up to the individual.

Handguns

I sight in for 25 yards with my handguns because I find no reason for longer range work. The 44-caliber handgun sighted to strike 1-inch *high* at 25 yards will give a little better usefulness from the potential of the trajectory pattern. Sighted 1-inch high at 25 yards, the 44 will be nearly on, and only a little low, at 50 yards. The larger pistols in the 50/54 range will be about the same, but sighted 1-inch high at 25 yards, these will hit more "dead center" at 50 yards. The latter class of pistol caliber will only be about 4 inches low at 75 yards, incidentally.

chapter 9

Rate of Twist and the Muzzleloader

AN IMPORTANT aspect of muzzle-loading is the concept of twist, that is, the actual spiral that the rifling makes in the bore. The subject of twist has been badly convoluted over the years, with some diehard writers still swearing that the only possible twist is 1:48 or one turn in 48 inches. Why do they believe this untruth? Part of the reason stems from the current popularity of that particular twist rate. Part of the reason stems from the fact that Sam 'n Jake Hawken, the famous Hawken Brothers of St. Louis, whose name became synonymous with "plains rifle," apparently rifled everything from their cat to their canary with a 1:48 twist. They probably had their reasons for doing so, and certainly their firearms "worked" fine. However...

THERE IS NO SUCH THING AS ONE PERFECT TWIST! That would be impossible and contrary to the rules of science. In the first place, you cannot talk twist without talking caliber. In the second place, it matters very much which style of projectile is to be used in the rifle or handgun. Therefore, the shooters (modern or old-time) who have sung the praise of a specific rifling twist with no regard for caliber or missile are way off base and do not have a viable argument. I have picked on the 1:48 twist as an example, and I want to make certain that the reader recognizes the fact that there is nothing wrong with a 1:48 twist, lest we have a grave misunderstanding here. I'm just pointing out that *no one twist* can be right for all circumstances, and that is all that I'm saying. I have fired many rifles with 1:48 twist which were simply excellent, and in terms of hunting accuracy, I have achieved excellent accuracy from many over-the-counter 1:48 twist rifles. In other words, if you own a 1:48 be happy. It is probably fine.

However, the shooter who is interested in knowing the ins and outs of his muzzleloader *must* have a grasp of twist because it is one of the basic factors which dictate how much powder he can use. It is also wise to have a working knowledge of twist simply because it is an interesting subject associated with all shooting.

In this chapter, we'll talk about twist and why we need to understand its effect upon the loads we pour down our smoke-belchers. I long wrestled with the problems of twist and still find myself duking it out with the subject. I hardly know all there is to know about it. But what I've learned has come by way of making mistakes, making a fool of myself at times and also from listening intently to my mentors on the subject.

For starters, let's take the comparison of a nut moving on a threaded bolt as a teaching aid to understanding twist. We have a ¼-inch diameter bolt and a ½-inch diameter bolt. We can think of them as two different calibers, if we like. Let's make the ¼-inch bolt a 50-caliber and the ½-inch bolt a 60-caliber. Both are threaded *exactly the same*. Both have 20 threads to the inch. Or in rifle talk we can say that both bolts have 20 turns to the inch—the nut will turn 20 times in 1-inch of bolt shaft, or one revolution per each ½₀th of an inch. It's all the same thing.

If *either* nut, the ¼-inch or ½-inch, is moved down its respective bolt 1-inch, that nut will make 20 turns or revolutions. Think of the nut as a bullet or ball. So, of course, in spite of the size or "caliber" of our nut/bolt setup (the different diameters of the bolts), the number of turns is *dictated* and *commanded* by the "rate of twist" of that bolt. Let's also think of the threads on the bolt as the rifling in the bore of a firearm. So, the threads or "rifling" dictate the twist. However, the nut can move down the length of the bolt in one second or one minute or one millisecond, or any other prescribed *time* unit depending upon the velocity given the nut, just as the bullet or ball moves down the bore at a certain speed depending upon the velocity imparted to it by the powder charge.

So, the revolution of the nut or the projectile—in terms of *time*—can vary. This is the key, and it is very important to understanding the variations in powder charge dictated by different rifling twist. RPS or RPM (revolutions per second or revolutions per minute) in the firearm will also be controlled by two factors: the rate of twist and the velocity of the missile. So, if a 50-caliber ball is fired in a 1:48 twist and a 60-caliber ball is fired in a 1:48 twist, both will enjoy the same number of turns. How *fast* these balls revolve will be controlled by the speed of the balls as they exit from the muzzle.

If both the 50- and 60-caliber balls are given the *same* velocity, in the same rate of twist bore, they will spin at the same speed irrespective of barrel length. But the energy required to

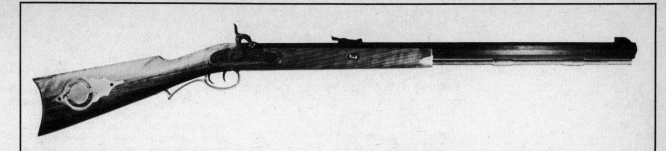

There are many non-replica "Hawken" rifles which do just fine with the 1:48 twist. Actually, this twist is thought by many to be somewhat "fast" because there are other rifles of the same caliber with twists so much slower. In fact, we must admit that the 1:48 is still in the "slow" domain. After all, a "Hawken" of 1:48 twist in 45-caliber would be compared with a 1:20 45-caliber Ruger 45-70, so we can see how much slower the Hawken is. On the other hand, it has been well established that the ball is stabilized with very, very little RPS, hence the 1:48 twist *for ball shoot-ing and in the larger calibers* can be considered a bit on the fast side. The owner of a 50-caliber rifle with a 1:48 twist should, for example, strongly undertake a test program to see which powder charge develops the most accurate load in his rifle. He may be very pleasantly surprised when he finds a specific charge which is more than adequate in the accuracy department. Since RPS is related to *velocity* (as well as rate of twist), many target rifles, even in ball-shooting, do *not* need a super-slow twist—a faster twist for balls is fine for target loads.

bring the 60-caliber ball to its RPS is going to be greater than the energy required to bring the 50-caliber ball to the same RPS, being proportional to the greater mass and diameter of the 60-caliber ball. So, while both spin at the same rate of turns or number of revolutions per second or per minute, the 60-caliber ball has $\frac{.6^3}{.5^3} \times \frac{.6}{.5} = 2.07$ times *more* kinetic energy of rotation than the 50-caliber ball. It also has $\frac{.6^3}{.5^3} = 1.73$ times more translational energy at the same muzzle velocity. Hunters who want power from the round ball go up in caliber to get it, and the latter figure supports the fact that more "raw power" is obtained with a larger ball, and not in direct proportion to the increase in ball size either.

Obviously, the charge of black powder used to push the 60-caliber ball will have to be greater than the charge of powder used to drive the 50 in order for both balls to reach the same velocity, hence the same RPS. We cannot simply add 1.73 plus 2.07 to determine how much more energy is needed to push the bigger ball, because the energy of twist is a very small figure to begin with, and the *area* of the 60-caliber ball allows for more effective exposure to the expanding gases pushing on it. If we take $\frac{.60^2}{.50^2} = 1.44$ we see that the 60-caliber ball has 44 percent more area exposed to the expanding gases of the powder charge.

So what? The importance will soon show up and it might be well worth the reader's sticking with us a minute longer. What it boils down to is the fact that we require different rotational speeds for different projectile sizes as well as differently shaped projectiles (ball *vs* bullet). Therefore, the statement which is often made in print today that "one twist is correct" is totally without foundation, and the modern black powder shooter should know it. The topic is part of his overall "gun savvy."

I have a 54-caliber hunting rifle which has a twist of 1:79, or one turn in 79 inches. What does this tell us immediately? It says that the rifle was made to shoot the round ball and not a conical. How do we know that? We know because hundreds of tests have confirmed the fact that a ball requires very little RPS to stay "on track." Therefore, it takes a very little bit of

twist to stabilize a round ball. We also recognize that the rifle is made for hunting loads because we wish to use *safe* but strong black powder charges to propel the ball at good velocity, and we do not want the ball "stripping," or "tripping on the rifling," as some of the old-timers used to say. In other words, we do not want a tight twist which might allow the ball to jump off the lands. Now, because this rifle is in 54-caliber, we use a very little bit of twist, less than a half-turn on the ball in flight. As the mass of a ball increases, less and less twist is necessary. As the mass of the ball decreases, more twist is required to get a higher RPS rating, since balls of less mass need more spin to stabilize them.

A dedicated gunner from the past did a great deal of testing along the lines of round ball shooting. Being a mechanical engineer, as well as an officer in the English Army, our man was able to construct many studies. We refer to his book here, *The Sporting Rifle and Its Projectiles,* by Lt. James Forsyth, MA,

These big 58-caliber, 530-grain cast Lyman projectiles have a special thick skirt designed to take the expansion of strong black powder charges. While the "length-per-caliber" ratio is not overly impressive in a 58-caliber, 530-grain bullet, there is still sufficient "sectional density" to require the stabilization offered by a more rapid twist.

Here are two 58-caliber projectiles, the .570″ ball on the left and a 600-grain Minie from the Lyman 570-grain mould. Apparently, the latter mould was designated "570" with an alloy as, in pure lead, the 570-grain mould does throw a 600-grain bullet. Rate of twist in rifles using these projectiles would have to be different for a perfect spin for either missile; however, compromise rates of twist will work with both projectiles. As an example, a 1:60 twist kept both of these missiles on track with hunting accuracy, though neither was seen to produce truly tight groups.

1863. One of his findings has already been discussed above, twist and ball mass. On page 99 of the book (which is now available in reprint from Buckskin Press, POB 789, Big Timber, MT 59011), Forsyth says, "A larger gauge will require *less* spiral than a smaller." We understand why—mass—the mass of the larger projectile. Again, we show that no one twist can be right for all bore sizes. Forsyth goes on to say, same book, p. 57, "I have found that a 14 gauge barrel rifled at the rate of 1 turn in 8 ft. 8 in., if correctly made, will throw a plain spherical ball with sufficient accuracy for all practical purposes up to 200 or 250 yards, and if a range of 150 yards only is required, the same accuracy will be obtained by a turn in 12 feet." That "turn in 12 feet" means a twist of 1:144, which makes my 1:79 above seem fast.

But remember we need less RPS for the larger ball, and Forsyth's 14-gauge is about 70-caliber. When Forsyth suggests a twist for the 25-gauge, which is about 58-caliber, he calls for a twist of 1:78, not exactly that of course, as 1:70 to 1:80 would not mean all that much. It just happened that his rifle turned out with 1:78 twist from the barrel maker, as my custom barrel turned out to be 1:79. We should note here that there is no compiled table I know of which shows precisely how much RPS is required of each round ball caliber size to stabilize it. Finally, Forsyth makes a statement which we want to present here:

Now, if the principles of rifling above laid down be attentively considered, it will be easily understood, that the rifling, if suited to any one of these, [speaking of various calibers as well as differences in ball or bullet] must be perfectly unfitted for the use of either of the others. (p.45)

In other words, if we have a bore twisted to be just right for a *bullet,* chances are it will not be perfect for a *round ball.* If we have a bore with a twist just right for a 36-caliber ball, that twist will not be perfect for a 54-caliber ball. What is very important to us is the fact that we are continually speaking in terms of RPS here! We have to remember that. Twist in itself does not mean that much. The number of turns in the air the ball makes are not as important to us as the rate of speed of those turns, or RPS. RPS dictates stabilization.

We agree, I think, that the velocity determines the RPS along with the rate of twist. In other words, velocity plus rate of twist equals RPS. So if we change the velocity, we change the RPS. This is very important for accuracy reasons. We can actually alter accuracy by changing the velocity in some black powder muzzleloaders. This, among others, is one reason we suggest the shooter going to the bench and trying various powder charges to see which works best in the specific firearm in question. That is one part of the payoff in understanding something about twist factors.

If we have a rifle, for example, which is not firing accurately with a specific charge, we can change the charge, never exceeding the maximum suggested loads of course, and usually going downward for our first attempts, and we might immediately improve accuracy. In our own tests we found that rifles with a rather tight spiral shot the ball well in reduced powder charge loads. We also found that in some rifles the conicals did better with modest instead of very light charges of powder.

Then, of course, there is the problem of what "kind" of accuracy we are after. I'd prefer a slightly larger group at 100 yards with plenty of steam left on the projectile, rather than a little bit more accuracy, but a blooper load which might give us trajectory problems and perhaps a wounded game animal. It is a compromise, and the "twist-smart" shooter can take advantage of his knowledge and produce a load chain which strains the most accuracy from his firearm for the purpose at hand, hunting or target work.

People thought, still think, and continue to put in print that "light loads always give the best accuracy." Well, while this is true in many cases, it is not really the "light" load which is accurate, so much as the "right" load. Light loads are not always correct for accuracy. A custom barrel maker I know has some special round ball shooting guns which he built to drive the round ball at over 2100 to 2300 fps muzzle velocity and still group into an inch and under at 50 yards for a 10-shot (not 5-shot) string. When the old-timer spoke of a ball "tripping over the rifling" he meant a ball jumping out of the hold which the lands had on it and riding on top of the lands instead of being contained by them. This was often a case of too much twist. The way to correct the problem was to lower the powder charge, thereby lowering the velocity. This would also lower the RPS. But at least the ball would remain in the groove and be guided by the land of the rifling, (a ball needs very little RPS anyway) so the lesser charge was the answer to better accuracy in rifles with too much twist.

I have often wondered if the deep groove concept did not arise from the wrong twist being used in some of the early round ball guns. The scenario goes like this: the shooter tries to load his fast twist shallow grooved bore for flat trajectory. When he does this, the ball jumps out of the control of the rifling. He complains. So, the gunmaker fixes things by making the groove deeper, creating a land about as tall as a basketball player. Now, by golly, the ball is better gripped. While the idea is OK, it's kind of like cutting a drinking glass in two in order to get half a glass of water.

I have no quarrel with deep grooves! Many deep groove arms we shot were superbly accurate. Also, some shooters prefer deeper grooves because these rifles will shoot longer before needing cleaning than will the shallow groove bores due to the groove being filled up less quickly with fouling. On the other hand, a more shallow groove is easier to clean and keep clean. So that is a trade-off. We did test shallower (not overly shallow) groove depths and found ball-shooting accuracy with .007" and similar depths. In fact, when I had my custom 54-caliber built, the barrel was supplied with a groove depth of .008" and it often shoots 1-inch groups at 50 yards. Forsyth had special barrels made for him with shallow grooves—they shot round balls just fine.

Black powder facts seem to be about as stable as a feather in the wind. However, to recap, let's agree that round balls do best with very slow twist, while the conicals need more twist. Let's also agree that while deep groove ball shooters are truly superb, the shallow groove can also be very accurate in ball-shooting. We can also agree, I hope, that changing powder charges to alter RPS can have a strong effect on accuracy. In short, the black powder shooter is going to know the twist of his firearm and he's going to load accordingly.

Twist and Barrel Length

This is another subject within the topic of twist. Assuming that the ball or bullet is contained by the rifling, once the rate of twist is established, such as 1:48 or 1:60, then the rate of twist is independent of barrel length, no matter if the barrel is 1-inch long or 100 inches long. The length of the barrel does not dictate the RPS. The key word in twist is "rate." "One in forty-eight" does not imply a turn in 48 inches of barrel. It implies a turn in 48 inches, period.

As an example, let's say we have a barrel with a 1:60 twist. The barrel is 30-inches long. Therefore, the ball will experience one-half revolution in its journey through the bore. It cannot revolve any other number of times in terms of raw *turns* in the bore because the rifling won't let it. Now let us cut the barrel in half, down to 15 inches. We have not changed a thing as far as *rate* of twist is concerned. In the 15-inch barrel, the ball will not emerge from the bore with a different *rate* of twist. In fact, 15 inches out in front of the 15-inch barrel, the ball will *still* maintain the same half revolution mentioned above. The actual number of turns, however, is of small value to us, which is important to remember. We are not interested in the *number* of turns. We are interested in the *velocity* of spin. RPS is determined by *muzzle velocity* and *rate of twist*.

Well, if the *rate* of twist remains the same, irrespective of barrel length, how come the majority of gunmakers turn out pistol barrels with a faster twist than rifle barrels *in the same caliber*? RPS is the reason, not turns per inch of barrel. Because the pistol barrel is going to get less velocity than the rifle barrel, we can use the greater rate of twist to get the RPS back up. Projectile spin is going to be muzzle velocity times turns per inch. Here's an example:

$$\frac{feet}{seconds} \times \frac{12\ inches}{one\ foot} \times \frac{turns}{inches} = \text{Turns per second (RPS)}$$

$$\frac{1500\ feet}{seconds} \times \frac{12}{1} \times \frac{1}{60} = \text{300 RPS or 1800 RPM}$$

Looking at this from a practical point of view, let's see what a professional barrelmaking outfit does about rate of twist and barrel length. We'll take Green Mountain as our example, as

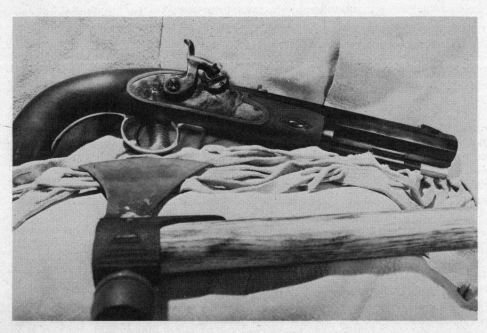

When Lyman produced their Plains Pistol in large bore, they produced it with a faster rate of twist than the same caliber would receive in a rifle, because velocity will be less with a pistol, and therefore the RPS will be less. RPS, not number of actual turns, gives the projectile stabilization.

While these are all elongated missiles and could all be called "bullets" the fact remains that they will call for different rates of twist in a rifle. Since the 7mm bullet on the left is of higher sectional density than those on the right, we would expect the firearm to use a bit more spiral for this bullet. In fact, if we look at the modern 7x57 you will find that its barrel has a rate of twist in the area of 1:9 to stabilize its longer 7mm bullets at moderate velocity. The 7mm Mag will often wear a 1:9 twist also. In the middle is a 625-grain Minie in 58-caliber. Rate of twist should be modestly "tight" for this projectile and our custom arm with 1:34 twist (in 54-caliber) did prove accurate with the conical. The .458", 500-grain bullet on the right is generally used in rifles with about a 1:14 twist, being a projectile with good mass.

they are known for accurate barrels. They offer a 50-caliber rifle barrel for ball-shooting with a rate of twist of 1:70. But when they offer a 36-caliber round-ball barrel for the rifle, the twist goes to 1:48 due to less ball mass. And their pistol barrels are faster twist. A 1:22 is standard.

This is not to say that a pistol barrel in round ball shooting must always have fast twist to get any accuracy at all. You see, we still have not put a *specific* RPS figure on each ball size to show *exactly* how much RPS is required to stabilize that ball and for how far in terms of range. The latter is not as much a problem as one might think, and it is no wonder that Forsyth got good accuracy with slow twist even out to 250 yards, because the matter of RPS loss is not as crucial as the matter of raw velocity loss. The two factors are not treated the same by the laws of physics. Spin slowdown is not as profound as forward motion slowdown of the projectile. Naturally, we are still dealing with mass, and the heavy ball does not slow down as rapidly as the lighter ball. We found this to be true, of course, in actual practice with the loads we fired over the chronograph at 100 yards. The heavier balls retained velocity better than the lighter balls, of course.

Another practical test, if not a conclusive one in all aspects, was the shooting of round balls into media and collecting them again to determine in which direction the balls struck the target. We backed off 200 yards from a homogenous clay bank free of rocks and fired 10 rounds from a custom 54-caliber rifle with 1:79 twist using two loads—70 grains of FFg and 120 grains of FFg. In all cases, the sprue of the ball was facing inward in the clay—they were loaded with the sprue towards the muzzle—indicating that the balls arrived on target facing the same way they left the muzzle of the gun. Not one was pointing in a different direction; however, I must admit that this short test is inconclusive.

Forsyth concluded that a ball receiving a rate of twist to give it about a quarter turn in the bore was good enough to stabilize it. This was for very large round balls and it was made from practical trial-and-error tests. Since Forsyth was speaking of 70-, 80- and larger-caliber bores, we cannot conclude that smaller balls will do just as well with only a quarter-turn *rate* of twist. However, in our own meager tests, we found that

50- to 60-caliber arms which offered a rate of about one-third to one-half turn seemed to stabilize the ball at least to the 100-yard range, and remember that RPS slowdown is not as critical as forward motion slowdown, so those balls were quite probably stabilized well past our 100-yard target butts.

We also found that many target arms did just fine with much more rapid twist, and we can only "tell what we saw." However, in the tests it did seem that the slow-twist rifles had a much greater *range* of accuracy. Our often-mentioned 1:79, 54-caliber rifle was accurate with as little as 40 grains of FFFg and as much as 120 grains of FFg. A custom 50-caliber rifle with a 1:40 twist was accurate with 60 FFg, but over that we felt that our test concluded accuracy was falling off. Naturally, there are *many* factors to consider, and the deeper grooves might indeed mean that some barrels with a faster twist might enjoy a larger range of accuracy in terms of powder charge. In one 40-caliber rifle, only fair accuracy was obtained with a .395" ball, but a .400" ball (bore size in other words) backed by hornet nest and a strong Irish linen patch produced fine accuracy. This rifle had about a 1:40 twist.

There's a lot to the game of twist. This little discussion does not cover all the bases, nor do I have sufficient knowledge to feel comfortable in saying much more on the topic. But the general rules of thumb we have established do seem sound, such as slow twist for ball, faster twist for bullet, with groove depth playing not quite the role we thought it to play at first. Naturally, just to make a point, even our .008" groove depth is quite deep as compared with slug-shooting guns which use very shallow depth of groove. As an example of the latter, a rifle which won a black powder bench competitive match (shooting slugs) had a groove depth of only .0057". In many of the modern arms meant to shoot the conical, we find groove depths of .003" or .005" (roughly) and accuracy is good.

As long as the shooter has an idea that twist is important to his loading knowledge, then this chapter has done its work. Our goal is to help the shooter build that optimum load for his rifle, a load which is made for a specific task—game harvesting or target work. The shooter who knows that he must think in terms of barrel twist when he builds that custom load will have one more valuable bit of know-how going for him.

chapter 10

Shotgun Loads and Patterns

THE BLACK POWDER SHOTGUN was the firearm of the common man during the settling of this country. To be sure, America and Canada have always been nations of riflemen, and the rifle, smokepole or modern, is still "number one" in both countries. The shotgun did not win any battles in those golden days of taming the wild lands; however, it was in the hands of the homesteaders, and it supplied plenty of food for the pot, while still offering the advantages of close-range protection for life and limb. Today, the black powder shotgun is back, not in the force applied by the muzzle-loading rifle, but certainly not in the shade either.

The versatility of the shotgun has always been a strong feature. Often, we like to talk about that hypothetical "all-around" firearm, and whether in black powder style or contemporary, the shotgun is likely to win the field in this argument. Our loading data shows some round-ball ballistics for the smokepole scattergun, and anyone who thinks a deer or similar game will stand up to that much force is dreaming. With the Denver Bullet Company .690″ 494-grain round ball tested in the 12-gauge guns, and a safe, reasonable charge of black powder, a well-placed shot on any North American game is going to be quite effective.

At the same time, the shotgun remains the only tool to throw multiple projectiles with good results. I have tried the double-ball loads, under test conditions, in rifles, and accuracy was very poor. So, when we want a lot of missiles in the air with a useful pattern, it is the shotgun we turn to. The black powder shotgun, in spite of the fact that it is not the most popular of the muzzle-loading firearms available today, is an obedient servant of the shooter. It performs very well, and its ballistics are quite close to those of the modern scattergun. But is it really any good in the pattern department? After all, the true effectiveness of a shotgun lies in its patterns more than any other single factor. Given as little as 850 fps muzzle velocity I have cleanly taken small birds such as quail at close range, due to good patterns. But with 1400 fps and a poor pattern, the same birds may have slipped through the "holes." You've got to hit 'em before you can put 'em in the fry pan.

I love the black powder shotgun, but I am not going to trump up any wild stories about its patterns. That would not be honest. After having shot quite a number of loads with many variations in the wad column and shot charge and powder charge, I have reached some, hopefully, valid conclusions about black powder shotgun patterns in general. These, I'll share with the reader presently. We need to approach the discussion step by step, because there is more to a good load with the black powder shotgun than at first meets the eye.

Useful Patterns

My first field experience with the black powder shotgun came on a cloudy day in the sagebrush flats, where the object was to harvest three big birds called sage hens. A large male sage hen can weigh more than 3 pounds, but the birds are soft-feathered and my No. 5 shot would penetrate well and take this upland game cleanly. By the time the day drew to a close, I had my limit of three sage hens. I had taken them with a 12-gauge black powder shotgun. However, I had fired 12 times to do it, and I took no long shots either.

The problem, as I later learned through testing, was pattern. For that kind of work, especially at that stage of the season, with the birds jumping at 30 yards and more and being fired at, probably, at 35 to 40 yards, I needed a fairly tight pattern. I wasn't getting it. I wounded no game that day, which made me think at first that my pattern was perhaps too tight. But that was not the case. I was lucky not to "dust" any of those birds because my pattern at 40 yards was no better than 45 percent strong.

We must stop the story here to determine what the 45 percent really means to us. Below, the general meaning of full choke, modified choke, improved cylinder, and so forth, is discussed. Let's see what these values are:

Extra Full Choke	= 80 percent or better
Full Choke	= 70 to 79 percent
Improved Modified Choke	= 65 to 69 percent
Modified Choke	= 55 to 64 percent
Improved Cylinder I	= 50 to 54 percent
Improved Cylinder II*	= 45 to 49 percent
Cylinder	= under 45 percent

*This is the usual Improved Cylinder; Improved Cylinder I is "strong" or "quarter choke."

Enjoying the black powder shotgun means learning how to load for it, and we must prepare each load for the specific intended use. Here, sons of the author, John on the left, Bill on the right, practice with the smokepole on informal aerial targets using old-fashioned cardboard wad loads for open patterns.

As the reader can see, by my own judgement of choke meaning above, my pattern was barely at the edge of the Improved Cylinder rating, and also on the upper edge of the straight cylinder rating. Since this black powder shotgun had no choke, as most black powder shotguns do *not*, then I'm not sure why I was surprised to learn later that I was trying for 40-yard birds with a 25-yard pattern.

On the other hand, with that same gun and the same loads, with the exception that the 1¼-ounce shot charge of No. 5s was replaced with a 1⅛-ounce shot charge of No. 8s, I absolutely cleaned house on quail. Know what the rough average range was on those quail? I tried to keep a record. I'd guesstimate about 15 yards. The point of telling these two experiences is simply this—my shotgun and its pattern were not correct for the sage hen hunt, but they were just right for the quail hunt.

A friend of mine was with me when I ran one of the many patterning tests for this book, and I failed to see the trend in his exclamations about the patterns until we had been shooting for about 2 hours. "Ah, that's a good one," he said after we averaged the percentage for a particular load. "It's not like that last one, thank goodness." I began to see that my buddy felt that anything under at least modified choke wasn't worth a hoot. I wonder how many shotgunners really do feel that way?

So, before looking at specifics, let's recognize the fact that "good" for one shotgunning situation may not be "good" patterning for another shotgun situation. If full choke were the only choke worth anything, the makers of shotguns would

have long ago abandoned the other choke ratings. I say this, because the reader is going to find out quite soon that the straight-tube black powder shotgun is highly unlikely to deliver much better than 45 percent to maybe 50 percent patterns.

Finally, and then I'll press on, I want to point out that by using two methods I have been very successful in my own upland gunning and waterfowling with the old-time muzzle-loading smokepole shotgun. First, I changed my hunting tactics. Last season, I bagged my sage hens, which are not that hard to hit, with about three total misses for the season, rather than that initial poor showing of three birds in the bag for 12 shots. How did I do It? I hunted differently.

When I was out the first time, I busted through the cover not caring how I broke a covey. Let them fly as they will, I thought. I counted on the pattern to bring the birds down. After patterning my shotgun and knowing what I had going for me, I changed tactics. I was on high ground from time to time all day long looking for birds, and I moved more slowly through cover, hoping to get a rise up close, not at 30 yards. And the change in hunting style brought closer shots and bagged birds.

This same change in style attended all of my black powder shotgunning and my success ratio improved along with the switch in hunting patterns. After all, I decided that I had swapped tactics when I turned to the muzzle-loading rifle. I no longer hoped for across-the-canyon long shots, but rather hunted so that I had a good chance of getting closer shots, and the system worked. We still had plenty of good meat harvested to the table.

The second change came later in my study of the black powder shotgun pattern. I discovered the components offered by Ballistic Products, Inc., components designed for long-range patterns. And they worked in improving the percentage of shot in my 30-inch circle at 40 yards. They did not turn my old-time straight-tube scattergun into a full-choke modern wonder. But they certainly did offer patterns that were much closer to those experienced with the modern choke-bored shotgun.

Wad Columns

We therefore say to the reader that full choke is not always best, even though we tend to think in these terms based upon a concept of more shot in a tight circle being better for all things under all conditions. So, as we proceed here, the reader should keep in mind that his patterns should match the shooting conditions. If he's jumping quail at 10 yards and popping at them from 15 to 20 yards from the gun's muzzle, full choke is not so dandy. If, on the other hand, the geese are 55 yards out, the 45 percent choke is not the right one to do the job.

The Basic Wad Column

The grand old man of black powder shotgunning is Mr. V.M. Starr of Edin, South Dakota. He's been known for many years, decades actually, as "The Muzzle Gunsmith." He has also been badly misunderstood by some shooters. Recently, I read the work of a fellow writer who was complaining about the basic wad column that Starr taught. The fellow was getting poor patterns with the wad, and he had to turn to a modern one-piece plastic wad to make things all better.

You see, Mr. Starr's basic wad column, which I will explain in a moment, said nothing of turning a straight-tubed shotgun into a full choke shotgun. Mr. Starr, in fact, gained his fame through *building chokes*. He was a choke-maker. His shot-guns in black powder style were not straight tubes. Therefore, his basic load, which I shot over the screens for chronograph-ing and at pattern boards for patterning, worked quite well.

The basic wad column consists of: two ³⁄₃₂-inch heavy card-board wads on the powder charge; and one wad over the shot charge.

Mr. Starr tells it this way, on page 8 of his little booklet, "The Muzzle Loading Shotgun."

> I only use one kind of wads and those I cut from cardboard like display signs that are extra thick, about ³⁄₃₂" is about right and use two of these on the powder and one on the shot. I have had several pretty wise gun men tell me that that is not enough wads before they saw the results but never have had one say a word further on the subject after they had seen one of my guns perform so loaded. You can put in more wads on the powder if you wish or if you enjoy cutting them but my experience tells me that you are just wasting your time and cardboard and in spite of the fact that shot gun shells have felt wads in them and always have had as far as I know I don't think that they are at all necessary in a muzzle loader. Anyhow, if my guns shot any better I would not know what to do with the extra efficiency.

I think it is worth noting that Mr. Starr was once in a contest against a large body of modern shotshell shooters and he won. Of course, this proves nothing since basic skill was probably responsible for Starr's victory. However, in a two-team con-test of about 100 participants in 1948 Starr managed to score 410 hits against the runner up scoring 182 hits. I also should point out that some of Mr. Starr's muzzleloaders have been checked to have a full choke pattern of over 80 percent at 40 yards.

In a moment, we will see what happens in the modern no-choke muzzleloader with Starr's basic load. But for now, let's go on to the next wad column which we checked out in our test runs. I think we will call this one the "felt wad basic columns."

The Felt Wad Basic Columns

Here, we simply put a nitro card wad over the powder charge, followed by a felt wad, followed by shot and then an over-shot wad. In effect, we have the wad column used in shotgun shells for a great many years, prior to the advent of the modern one-piece plastic wad columns. The nitro card seemed vital to good patterns in my tests, because without it the felt wad was found to be burned all the way through in many cases, and this would disrupt the very base that the shot charge is resting upon.

The One-Piece Plastic Wad

Yes, the old-time smokepole shotgun will use the one-piece plastic wad effectively. We will talk about patterns with this unit soon, and for now we will remind the shooter to watch for plastic "wash" in the bore after firing a few too many rounds of shot with this wad column. I have found the coating in the bore to be no problem whatsoever. But I do like to clean the bore of any residue and that includes plastic fouling. This coating was quite easily removed by a swipe or two with a tight-fitting bristle brush and rubbing alcohol.

Ballistic Products Long-Range Wads

Finally, the fourth type of wad column to undergo testing was the Ballistic Products, Inc. wad in both 10-gauge and 12-gauge. In the 12-gauge, I used the Magnum Shotcup with the BPGS wad underneath it. This latter unit combines with the first to create a good gas seal in the bore, and it also drives the Shotcup unit in front of it. Remember, let us not confuse cloth ball-patches with plastic or even nitro shotgun wads. Cloth does not make for a super gasket, but other items do.

Results of Patterning

Procedures:

1. All shooting was accomplished with the muzzle of the shotgun a measured 40 yards away from the patterning sheet.

2. The patterning paper was a bit over 40 inches square.

3. No aiming point was used on the patterning paper. A shot was fired at the paper, trying to center the shot as much as possible.

4. A cardboard cutout circle (30 inches in diameter) was

The Remington SP10 one-piece 10-gauge wad was used in two 10-gauge muzzle-loading shotguns with success. Patterns with these two shotguns were dense at close range. Since the 10-gauge guns in black powder style are quite light in weight, they would serve well for some upland gunning, especially for the larger birds such as pheas-ants and sage grouse.

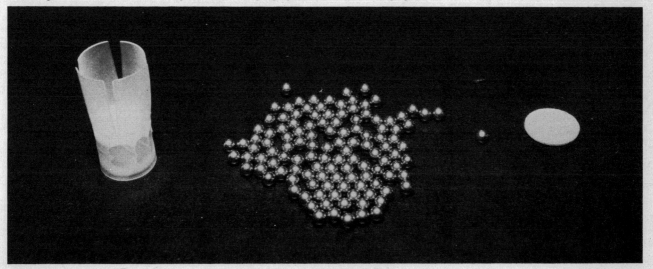

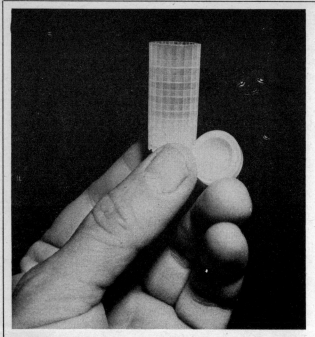 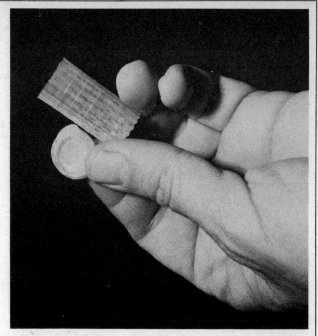

(Left) More sophisticated black powder shotgun loads include one-piece plastic wads. The wad shown here is the Ballistic Products, Inc. 1½-ounce 12-gauge Magnum Shotcup, a ribbed wad which is loaded with the BPGS 12-gauge *gas seal*. The gas seal goes downbore first, of course, to rest on the powder charge. Pat-

terns can be varied by splitting the one-piece BPGS shot wad as per instructions which come with the package of wads. (Right) Here are the Ballistic Products one-piece plastic wad and gas seal picked up after use. Note that they are totally intact, with the exception of some slight flare around the lip of the gas seal.

placed over the shotgun pattern on the paper to encompass the major bulk of that pattern.

5. With the pattern well covered with the 30-inch cardboard cutout, a pen was used to inscribe a circle around the shot pattern. Now the pattern was removed.

6. The result was the most dense portion of the shotgun pattern on the paper being encompassed by a pen line circle.

7. The number of shot within that 30-inch circle was counted.

8. A percentage was arrived at by division, that is, dividing the number of shot counted within the 30-inch circle on the pattern paper with the average number of pellets to be found in the load that was used.

To explain the last step further, we might suppose that we have a 1¼-ounce shot charge using No. 7½ shot size. If this were the case, that shot charge would have *about* 438 pellets in it. Let's say we have counted 220 pellets within the 30-inch circle prescribed on the patterning paper. If we divide 220 by 438 we end up with .50, or 50 percent pattern. If we look at our established norm for 50 percent pattern, we can call that pattern just barely an Improved Cylinder. It almost goes to Improved Cylinder II levels.

Two 12-gauge shotguns were tested for pattern, both with no-choke bores, one a single-shot, the other a side-by-side double gun, both in percussion. Let me explain that there is a difference, albeit a minor difference, among some of the modern black powder shotgun bore sizes. Some companies are offering the gauge size so that it actually corresponds to the interior dimensions of a shotgun shell or hull. For example, a 12-gauge shotgun bore would be about 13-gauge actually, so that

it will accept, tightly, the normal modern 12-gauge components which are made for a 12-gauge shotgun hull.

On the other hand, there are shotgun bores which more closely correspond to the actual dimensions established as 12-gauge, or whatever the gauge may be. In these firearms, the one-piece plastic wad may be a bit on the loose side, but in chronographing various shotguns of the two bore sizes, I found no appreciable differences using the BPGS wad mentioned above. Apparently, that wad expanded sufficiently to fill the bore so that there was not enough gas loss in the larger bores to cause a loss in velocity that amounted to anything.

Number 7½ shot was used in our tests. Here are some actual patterns. First, we can look at these and then we can consider what they mean to us.

1. 12-gauge
   Wad:
   2 nitro cards on powder (.125″ cards)
   Shot:
   1 over-shot wad
   1¼ ounces of No. 7½ shot/100 grains FFg GOI
   Pattern Percentage: 42 percent

2. 12-gauge
   Wad:
   1 nitro card wad
   1 ¼″ wool felt wad
   1 over-shot wad
   Shot:
   1 over-shot wad
   1¼ ounces of No. 7½ shot/100 grains FFg GOI
   Pattern Percentage: 45 percent

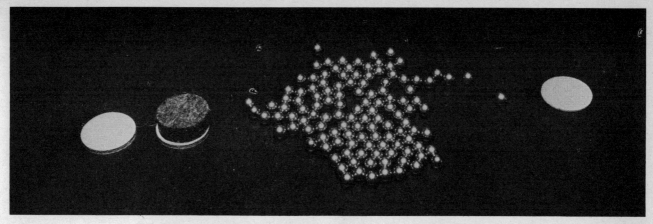

A simple over-powder felt wad is commonly used in the black powder shotgun. However, the shooter is urged to put one or two over-powder wads downbore *before* loading the felt wad. The felt wad can be burned through by the hot gases of the powder charge, thereby spoiling the pattern. Note over-shot wad, far right.

In one bore, we found that the side of the Ballistic Products, Inc. one-piece Magnum Shotcup was torn away after firing. This problem was cured when a roughness in the bore of this particular old shotgun was corrected. While the black powder loader is very wise to check his rifle's patches, he is also wise to take a look at fired components from the shotgun. They might tell a story.

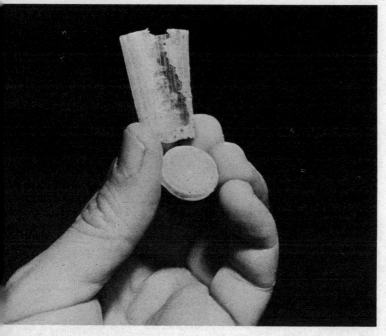

3. 12-gauge
Wad:
1 Pacific Verelite Blue Wad
Shot:
1 over-shot wad
1¼ ounces of No. 7½ shot/100 grains FFg GOI
Pattern Percentage: 47 percent

4. 12-gauge
Wad:
1 Ballistic Products, Inc. PBGS wad*

_____
*Gas seal.

Shot:
1 Magnum Shotcup
1¼ ounces of No. 7½ shot/100 FFg GOI
Pattern Percentage: 60 percent

We must, in the interest of accuracy, explain that in the last situation, results were not always consistent. More study is necessary to determine exactly how to load the very interesting and useful Ballistic Products one-piece plastic wad with gas seal. In some cases, the patterning paper had a hole in it, and inspection proved that the hole was caused by the plastic unit itself, which made it all the way from the muzzle of the shotgun to the 40-yard pattern board. The gas seal (BPGS) wad was also behind the paper indicating that this unit was probably intact on the back of the one-piece Magnum Shotcup. Furthermore, the plastic wad in two cases out of 25 trial runs actually penetrated not only the patterning paper itself, but also the soft backer board which was used to hold the patterning paper.

In one individual trial run, a 12-gauge was fired at only 25 yards and the pattern was 100 percent. All of the load struck into a 30-inch circle at that distance, and there was a hole in the paper pattern where the plastic unit(s) had torn through. All the same, it's my opinion that further work with these modern components could produce a reliable pattern at waterfowl distances. But this is speculation at this point.

In spite of some problems with the uniformity of results with the latter wad columns, it was the only type of wad which indicated that tighter than 50 percent patterns might be possible from a straight-tube, no-choke black powder shotgun barrel. Now, what about the second shotgun to be tested? The results were almost identical to the first data, and these will not be recorded here.

We will draw some conclusions in a moment, but first, let's take a look at the 10-gauge data, which, in effect, were about the same pattern-wise as the 12-gauge, the exception being, of course, that we were tossing 1½ ounces of shot in the 10-gauge and that there were more actual strikes on the 30-inch circle at 40 yards. In fact, our chilled shot, Lawrence Brand, computed to about 525 pellets in the 1½-ounce load of shot.

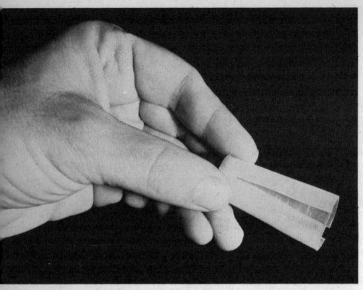

This is the Ballistic Products 10-Gauge Magnum Ballistic Pattern Driver—a one piece wad which does *not* come with the slit sides. The shooter is encouraged to follow directions when he slits the sides of these units. The author got some better patterns in terms of density by leaving the sides unslit. However, each shotgun may vary and the individual shooter must pattern his own shotgun to be sure of his gun's specific pattern.

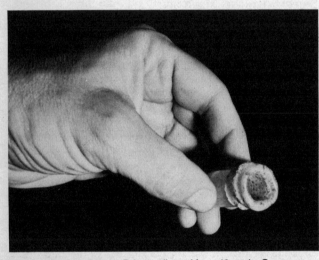

This is a Ballistic Pattern Driver collected from 40 yards. One can see that the unslit sides of the shotcup did not allow for the escape of all the shot and the unit was still carrying shot out to 40 yards. However, this was not the case with all unslit units.

1. 10-gauge
   Wad:
   2 nitro cards
   Shot:
   1 over-shot wad
   1½ ounces of No. 7½ shot/120 grains FFg GOI
   Pattern Percentage: 44 percent

2. 10-gauge
   Wad:
   1 nitro card
   1 cushion fiber wad

Shot:
1 over-shot wad
1½ ounces of No. 7½ shot/120 grains FFg GOI
Pattern Percentage: 48 percent

3. 10-gauge
   Wad:
   1 one-piece plastic wad
   Shot:
   1 over-shot wad
   1½ ounces of No. 7½ shot/120 grains FFg GOI
Pattern Percentage: 48 percent*

4. 10-gauge
   Wad:
   1 Ballistic Products, Inc., Ballistic Pattern Driver
   Shot:
   1 over-shot wad
   1½ ounces of No. 7½ shot/120 grains FFg GOI
Pattern Percentage: 62 percent

Once again, we had varying results with the one-piece plastic wad in the last test. However, this was also the only wad which delivered over 50 percent patterns in the big 10-gauge gun. The resulting patterns were 62 percent on the average.

Test Problems and Conclusions

There is no way that a grand total of three test shotguns can tell the world of black powder shooters what to expect from each and every shotgun out there. Also, tests of this nature must be run over and over again, using slight variations in the wad column, though never getting carried away and going to extreme measures, because the creation of a wad column that *will not* proceed up the bore and out the muzzle can become, in effect, a bore obstruction which can result in a ruptured barrel.

On the other hand, we can say something in general terms about the black powder shotgun as it is given to us these days. I will state that, in my opinion, there is no way to make the no-choke shotgun act the same as a shotgun with a choke. At the same time, I was impressed by the potential of the Ballistic Products wad system—the only patterns to exceed 50 percent were made with those wads. In one inconclusive side test, an average of five shots on the pattern board using a single nitro card wad downbore first, followed by the BPGS gas seal and the Magnum Shotcup seemed to promote patterns of slightly better distribution with few holes from that one test shotgun.

The scope of this work did not include further testing of the black powder shotgun in terms of patterns. Our major aim was to provide for a ballistic story on the black powder shotgun, as well as an *indication* of pattern possibilities. As this is written I would have to call the black powder no-choke, straight tube shotgun a very fine tool for close work, but not necessarily the right choice for those very long shots.

The use of standard plastic wads did improve patterns somewhat, but in my older tests, I think I was somewhat hasty in jumping on the 10 percent better pattern theory. The one-piece plastic wad did seem to tighten patterns a bit over the

---

*I could gather no statistically significant difference here over the cushion fiber wad pattern, but the pattern was better distributed.

more simple card wad loads, but not appreciably so, with the exception of the Ballistic Products wads, which need to be worked with more fully in order to control the results obtained with them in the black powder shotgun.

By slitting the 10-gauge Pattern Driver with two long slits, as described in the instructions with this wad, the 10-gauge pattern was not as good as when the wad was used straight out of the box. I am sure that the instructions for the use of this wad are correct with modern shells, and perhaps in another 10-gauge black powder shotgun, the slits would have been successful. But in the one 10-gauge test gun, better patterns were made with unslit pattern drivers.

FFFg vs. FFg/Fg Black Powders

I was also anxious to rerun a few tests I had conducted a long time ago, mainly pertaining to patterns in terms of FFFg black powder vs. Fg or FFg black powder. Previously, and with no doubt whatever, I had learned, so I thought, that the use of FFFg would just about blow a good pattern most of the time. Now I have to revise my opinion somewhat; however, before going into this new data, I still want the reader to know that I heartily recommend Fg and FFg in the black powder shotgun. *There is no reason to use FFFg in the black powder shotgun.*

However, in trying to determine pattern differences between the granulations of black powder, I was taken back when the patterns with FFFg and FFg showed no variations that I could call truly different. What had happened before when patterns definitely did open up and become spotty and "blown" with FFFg? I ran across some of my old data and looked at the wad columns.

It is now my opinion that the hotter FFFg produced the lousy patterns because it was more effectively cutting into my wad column, thereby ruining the seat and base for the shot. In other words, it was not the somewhat higher velocity attributed to FFFg powder which was causing a loss in pattern density, most likely, but rather the fact that the wad column was more "chewed up" by FFFg than by FFg or Fg.

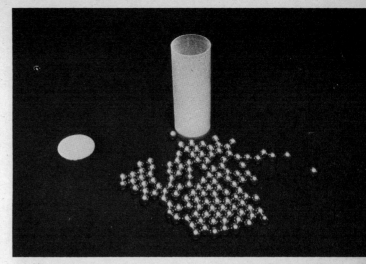

The big 10 gauge Ballistic Pattern Driver was used in unslit form in a couple of the 10-gauge shotguns with very good performance. Here, a charge of No. 2 shot is shown with the over-shot wad (left).

I tried to duplicate the results that I had gotten earlier with both simple nitro card over-powder wads and also with a single nitro card wad and a single fiber wad. In both cases, the FFFg patterns *were* blown. However, this time around I checked for spent wads and it was a case (I'm quite sure) of wad destruction which caused the blown patterns, and not a case of too much velocity.

All the same, I would still strongly urge the black powder shotgunner to stay with Fg and FFg black powders in the larger bores, since this fuel works fine, produces plenty of velocity, is somewhat easier on some particular types of wad columns, namely those made of paper products, and FFg or Fg powders will deliver less pressure than FFFg black powders. Whenever we can obtain useful ballistics with lower pressures, that's the way to go.

Two means of carrying shotgun loads are shown here. Above, we have a set of horns, one for shot (right) and one for powder (left). Below, we have a standard 35mm film container which has been pre-loaded with shot. In the container we also have placed an over-powder wad, a felt wad and an over-shot wad.

The slower-burning granules of Fg or FFg over FFFg, we believe, will affect the pressure curve by reducing the ultimate peak pressure and elongating the curve.

Shot Variations

Without a doubt, various shotguns in the modern world will produce quite different patterns with different size of shot when the choking is different—that is, from Full to Improved Cylinder. We did not find all that much variation among shot changes in the black powder shotgun. However, it was interesting to note that in these chokeless arms, the nickel-plated No. 4 shot that we tried produced the very best patterns in terms of "holes." The shot was actually better distributed (in our test guns) than was No. 7½ shot.

We also found that in using 7½ Magnum shot from Lawrence the patterns seemed to be better distributed. They were not tighter in terms of percentage; however, they were better in terms of evenness of density. The nickel-plated No. 4 shot from Ballistic Products, Inc., created patterns in both the 12-gauge and the 10-gauge that I would prefer to use on ducks over other brands or types of shot that I have tried before. In the no-choke bore, the larger shot probably does better, on the average, than the smaller shot, too. At least we try to make such a judgement in the modern shotgun when we suggest that some Improved Modified chokes actually throw tighter big shot patterns than some Full chokes toss. I have witnessed this in *some* cases.

And so we will leave our black powder shotgun patterns. I think we have some data indicating that the black powder shotgun is a totally viable tool for modern day gunning in both the raw ballistic sense and the pattern department as well. I think we can also see that there was indeed a good reason for the invention of choke. History has shown us that the original black powder shotgun did indeed get the job done. History also suggests that the scattergun fan wanted better patterns, hence gunmakers went to choke.

If we keep our black powder scatterguns in operation at reasonable ranges, trying for 30-yard shots instead of 45-yard shots, I think our success ratio will be a good one. Though it is a bit more difficult to load a choked black powder frontstok-

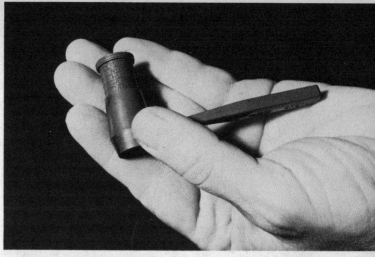

A dipper was used to toss the shot charge. Such a dipper can also be used with modest shot charges for a volume-to-volume ratio of powder/shot, using only Fg or FFg black powder. The author considered this arrangement a maximum load.

ing shotgun, there are a few gunsmiths around who can produce a choke within these bores. That might not be a bad idea for the enthusiast who wants to try for the fast flying ducks in a pass-shooting situation. For the closer targets, however, the open-bore guns are quite good.

Finally, the shooter owes it to himself and his shotgun to individually pattern his own loads. For example, further work with the sophisticated Ballistic Products wads may give us some very useful patterns for longer range work. There is no doubt in my mind that each shotgun can produce a workable load if the owner of that shotgun will safely experiment with wad columns. Remember, as the wad column becomes tighter-fitting to the bore, with less and less leakage, powder charges need not be great. The volume-for-volume load is, in fact, all the powder I will ever use. A shooter will also find that patterns can be improved in some cases by using less powder, not more powder, in the load.

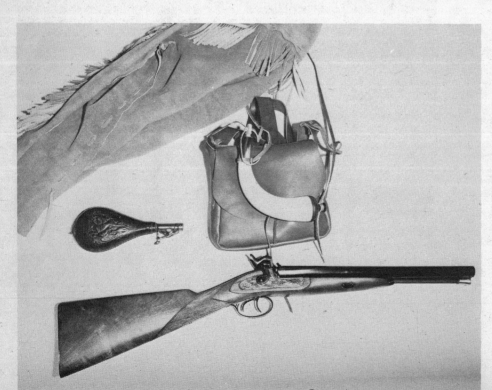

For quick work at close range, Navy Arms offers the Texas Terry Ranger shotgun in 12-gauge with 14-inch barrels. The outfit shown above the shotgun includes a full grain leather shooting bag from Michaels of Oregon with a powder horn from K-W Company. On the left is an original shot pouch from the 19th century.

chapter 11

Loading the Black Powder Cartridge

POPULARITY of the black powder cartridge is, on the one hand, astounding, and on the other hand, we have to question whether or not black powder metallics loaded with smokeless powder are any longer in the class of black powder metallics. That's a question of philosophy, not shooting, and it really means nothing to us. What does mean something to us is the fact that a rather large number of shooters are enjoying black powder cartridge firearms, using black powder.

After all, the historical Sharps, as one example, was made around the black powder mode. Though hundreds of shooters use the Sharps calibers today with smokeless powder loads, many, if not most of these same shooters all stuff 'em full of black powder at least now and then. Also, there is the safety factor with the originals. A friend of mine has a Sharps original, and he will not allow smokeless powder in it. That may be a fetish. However, he feels that the rifle was intended for black powder, that black powder delivers plenty of ballistics with *low* pressures, and that black powder is historically correct for this firearm.

Those who own originals of the black powder world which were a bridge between the muzzleloader and the smokeless powder round may also wish to load these with black powder only. I am speaking of many of the older Winchester, Remington and Marlin models which certainly were designed for black powder rounds, not smokeless. Many of these cartridges lived not only through the advent of the hot smokeless numbers, but they survive today. They survive because shooters still want them.

We could spend the rest of our allotted space discussing these rounds, such as the 45-70, thought dead, while it was only playing possum. It sprang up out of its dormant state to be chambered in a number of modern rifles, most of them commercial, and a few of them custom or commemorative rifles. The 38-55 never did die out totally. Winchester still offers the round in factory form. The 32-40 is back. The 44-40 never died out. It is still loaded by Winchester and Remington. The 38-40 is still loaded. Why? Why are these rounds still with us? I suppose the simplest answer is that they are still performing for enough people to warrant their survival. I'm sure that these would be defunct as garter belts if they did not work for

shooters in some capacity. I have an editor friend who shoots a 32-20 with regularity. Ask him why, and he'll just say he likes the round. And the fellow striking these typewriter keys is a 25-20 fan. I know that there are many rounds which will do a multitude of tasks better and the 25-20 will do them. On the other hand, I just took possession of 200 new shiny Winchester/Western cartridge cases all ready to load up!

This chapter is not geared to justify the continued existence of these famous old rounds. They don't need my help, and are doing fine all by themselves. Instead, this chapter is a basic, and I do mean basic, discussion of loading the cartridges with black powder. Certainly, a whole book could be written on the subject of black powder cartridges. There's a magazine devoted soley to this topic, that being *Black Powder Cartridge Rifles,* published at POB 789, Big Timber, MT 59011. Our interest here is to share with the reader our basic findings, and to warn the reader in strong language that while the process of putting black powder metallics together is a safe one, and while it closely follows many of the same steps associated with smokeless cartridge case loading, there are some totally unique aspects of this involvement, and the shooter had best take these "wrinkles" very seriously. When the basics are all understood and internalized, then our black powder metallic shooter can turn to the literature which delves more deeply into this hobby, and he can learn how to coax the most possible accuracy and safe power from his black powder breechloaders.

Using Old Data

The shooter is better off to forget using old black powder data for one major reason—the cartridge cases of yore and the modern brass cases of today are different in design, and therefore different in *capacity*. Just about anyone involved in firearms knows that the numbers used to designate cartridges in the "old days" had specific meanings. These numbers were not always true to life; however, they did tell the shooter something. For example, a 44-40 supposedly accepted a 44-caliber bullet and burned 40 grains of black powder as a capacity load. In real life, the 44-40 did not accept a true 44-caliber bullet—the bullet it used had a diameter of .427″. It did,

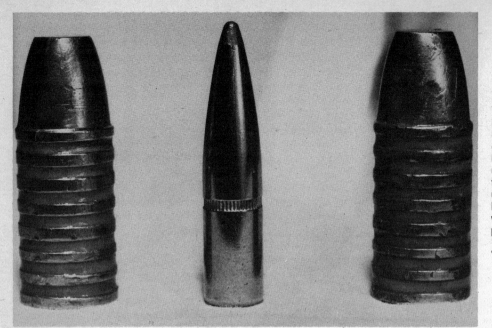

The black powder cartridge deals in bullets, not Minies, Maxis or round balls. Here, we have a modern bullet for comparison, flanked by two 45-caliber bullets which we used in the Sharps rifle. Incidentally, this same bullet was also used very successfully in a muzzleloader, the Navy Arms Whitworth. A bullet of about 490 grains propelled in the neighborhood of 1500 fps at the muzzle, is a real "contender."

however, accept about 40 grains of black powder—about.

Today, a shooter will not get 40 grains of black powder into a modern 44-40 case because our new cases have better designed head areas. That is, there is a lot more brass in the crucial head area of the modern pistol case. The older balloon-head case had much less brass in the head area, therefore, the case volume was greater. I was lucky to get 35 grains of FFFg into my own modern 44-40 cases. I was equally lucky to get 67 grains of FFg in the 45-70 case. (Naturally, that "70" stood for 70 grains of black powder, but no more.)

The bullet used will make a difference in case capacity, too. The 45-70, as an example, was once called a 45-70-500, the last figure designating the weight of the bullet. So, by using a shorter, lighter bullet which does not take up as much case capacity as a longer, heavier bullet (provided the shooter seats it to normal overall length), there might be more room in the boiler for powder. This latter situation depends upon several variables, and I do not want the reader to assume that we were interested in boosting the powder charge, because we were not. The aim was a good safe load, and hang a few grains of powder.

So, to summarize, the powder charges commonly associated with the older cartridges are not useful in modern, web-head cases. But what about using the old cases, if indeed any can be found. Would that not give us full case capacity?

Using Old Cases

Just so we are not misunderstood on the subject, it is my opinion, and I'm sure some will argue with me strongly, that the old balloon-head cases should be kept as relics and left the heck out of modern use altogether. I am fully aware that brass lasts a very long time. I'm also aware of a few other things. Brass can get brittle with age, and something else—we have no way of knowing just how much tender love and care those old cases had, or whether they were fired, left dirty and then cleaned when the shooter had the time and inclination to do so. I have a few old cases around, and I enjoy looking at them, but never will one find its way into a firearm I am responsible for loading.

Trimming Cases

Cases should be faithfully trimmed to length, especially after the initial firing. Brass, even in the mild black powder loadings, does flow, and the case will extend after firing. If the case is left in an elongated state, there is a chance that the forward portion ("mouth") of the case, which holds the bullet, will pinch off in the throat of the chamber.

This condition can cause a substantial increase in pressure. The shooter knows, for example, that if a wad in a shotgun shell or load does not move forward upon the firing of the gun, there is going to be trouble. The entire principle of the contained load is based upon moving energy in a prescribed direction—out of the muzzle, in other words. When that long case pinches up in the chamber, it retards the motion of the bullet and pressures rise. Cases must be trimmed to length, and we should at all times make certain that they stay trimmed.

Cleaning Cases

The best time to clean a fired black powder cartridge case is sooner than later, such as right after the shooter reaches home and deprimes/sizes it, or in the situation of using one or only a few cases on the range and reloading these over and over, then the case should be cleaned between shots. It's so simple. It takes so little effort, and yet it is highly important. I have tested with my own 38-55 cases and found a *decrease* in case capacity of 4 to 6 grains volume when those cases were dirty. In other words, the residue clinging to the walls of the case will take up space, and then the shooter is in the situation of having to force a charge of powder into a case capacity that is actually *reduced* in volume.

I have seen shooters clean cases with soapy water. I have used several things, to include isopropyl and ethyl rubbing alcohols, standard cleaning agents made especially for black powder, such as J&A Old Slickum and water soluble machinist oil mixed 10 percent oil to 90 percent water, or as much as 20 percent oil and 80 percent water. I use a swab, such as a Hoppes standard bore swab, and I simply douse the case out totally and dry it with paper towel until "squeaky clean." Also be sure to solvent-clean the inside of your sizing dies after loading. This will remove any black powder residue left behind during normal resizing/depriming.

Depriming and Sizing

Yes, the case should be deprimed before cleaning. Knock out the old used primer so that the important primer pocket can be cleaned along with the interior of the case itself. This is important, because we want to retain the strength of the primer pocket and case head area, and black powder residue can cause a weakening of this area if left to settle there. Black powder of itself is not highly corrosive. I mean, it will not eat the skin off your body or etch metals just by being around in a light coating, but it can and does attract moisture. We call this condition hygroscopic, *not* hydroscopic, as I see often in print, but hygroscopic with a "g," the meaning being, "Able to absorb or condense moisture from the atmosphere," according to my dictionary, the *Standard College* by Harcourt, Brace.

Cases will last a very long time if cared for, and the primary care centers around cleaning them up. Some shooters like to use very hot, but not boiling water to clean the cases. Some will dry the cases for a short period of time in a very low oven. Remember, subjecting cases to prolonged or excessive heat can change the molecular structure of the case. Sometimes this is just what we want, because the first portion of the case, about to the point where a bullet would normally be seated, can be annealed by dipping the cases briefly in molten lead— set the thermostat of the melting pot to around 700 degrees F. After the case mouths are dipped in the molten lead, they can be quenched in water. The reason for annealing is to retard brittleness and to actually soften the brass.

Of course depriming and resizing are combined in a single operation in most modern die sets. And when it comes to this step in the loading process, I'm in favor of full-length resizing the brass case. This returns the cartridge case to near original, or "spec" dimensions. The case changes somewhat with each firing, and some of this change remains fixed. In fact, I know of shooters who fire a case for the first time for two reasons only: They want to "form the case to the chamber," and they want to check case length after the initial firing. After the case has been used one time in the rifle, you should check it for overall length and trim it to correct length if necessary.

Of course, even when full-length resized, a once-fired or often fired case will still retain some of the dimensions it attained by being used in the chamber of your firearm. Everyone knows of instances where one modern firearm will not accept cases fired in another, even after full-length resizing. Neck size if you will— I'll stay with the full-length approach for most of my sizing chores.

Loading Black Powder in Metallic Cases

For my tests, I used a powder scale for the black powder loads only and a powder measure for Pyrodex so that I would attain about an equal *volume* of Pyrodex and black powder. There are a few cautions to be observed in the loading of the powder charge, and these are important ones. The powder should either fill the case to the point where the base of the bullet comes to rest when normally seated, or the powder should be retained at the rear of the case; in other words, the powder charge, when under capacity, should be confined in the rear of the cartridge case. *Do not use single wads!* I am

The author regularly uses an old favorite, the 45-90 Winchester Model 1886 lever action rifle. Black powder cartridge rifles such as this one are very strong tools in the hands of the hunter willing to get close.

Warning: A recent study has indicated that the use of corn meal, Kapok or any other "filler" can be unsafe in metallic cartridges. While the data may suggest the use of such a filler, we must warn against such practice. Air space in a black powder loaded metallic catridge may be reduced by going to a coarser granulation of black powder and/or a heavier, safe, black powder charge. Space may also be taken up by deeper bullet seating or the use of a longer/heavier bullet. At least 90 percent of the case space available should be filled with either powder or projectile.

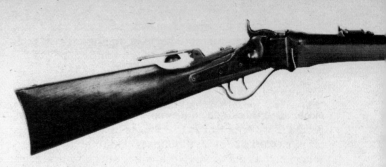

well aware that some shooters retain the powder at the rear of the case by making up a single small cardboard wad which they neatly press down upon the powder charge to hold the charge at the back of the case. In my opinion, this is a poor practice. The *single* wad with an air space in front of it is not, in my opinion, a wise load. If wads fill all the space in the case, then the idea is practical.

I am also sure that there is a *potential* for a problem here. One rifle did show a "ring" in the bore following the use of loads which had a single wad down in the cartridge case to hold the powder in place. I cannot prove that the wad was the problem. But I can guess that it was, and that guess is based upon the notion that the wad could in fact act as a projectile while the bullet takes over the role of being an obstruction in the bore. Sure, a guy could get away with this situation for thousands of rounds, but he might not get away with it even once. To confine a lighter than maximum load of black powder to the rear of a case, use as many cardboard wads as it takes to fill up the air space between the powder charge and the base of the seated bullet. Never use a *single* wad.

Bullet Seating

Bullet seating is the same, be it a black powder or smokeless cartridge. A secure friction-fit is fine for single shots while crimping is recommended for any cartridge to be used in a revolver or tube-fed rifle. The bullet you select should be flat-nosed if you intend to use it in any tube-fed firearm—Winchester 86s and 94s come to mind as good examples. The nose of the bullet rests squarely against the primer of the next round in line, in a tube-fed rifle. When that rifle is fired with a pointed or semi-pointed bullet, the recoil will cause the primers of loaded rounds to be hit sharply by the points of those projectiles. That impact can cause a sympathetic detonation of the rest of the ammo in the tube resulting in an explosion you can live without. Use *only* flat-nosed bullets in tube-fed firearms.

Selection of Powder for the Metallics

I found that FFg and Fg worked well in the larger cases, certainly in all of the calibers which were beyond 32-20 size. In some of the newly manufactured black powder cartridge-type rifles, such as the Ruger, H&R and C. Sharps, I doubt that FFFg black powder loaded so that it filled the case to capacity would harm anything. However, in keeping with the tradition of the old-time loader, I stuck with FFg as my smallest granulation size for these cartridges. It worked well. We can't ask for anything more.

I did use FFFg in maximum 17-grain charges in the 25-20 and the 32-20, but that was about it for FFFg. Even in the 38-40 and the 44-40, I found FFg satisfactory in terms of raw ballistics. I think this is the granulation to use; however, I believe that in some of the big Sharps cases, such as the 45-120, Fg might be good. Also in the 50-140 Sharps, we might consider Fg as a reasonable fuel.

Pyrodex

In the larger cases, Pyrodex in its *cartridge* form was used. This is called CTG, by the way. All Pyrodex was initially loaded *by volume only*. In no load was Pryodex installed into the case by weight. Once a safe weight of a given *black powder* was established then Pryodex was used with a powder measure set to that established number. For example, if we deter-

Many of the old-time black powder cartridge cases were quite large in keeping with the fact that black powder could be burned in safe but somewhat large doses. On the left is a modern 7mm Magnum case, and on the right is a modern 458 Winchester case, and in the middle is a 50-140 Sharps case. The latter, a 19th century round which appeared toward the end of the "buffalo era," was not created by Sharps, but it is still called a Sharps. Its size is apparent, and it was originally made to hold 140 grains of black powder. This case is modern-made by B.E.L.L.

mined that 67 grains of FFg was suitable for the 45-70, then the powder measure was set at 67 and Pyrodex was dumped by volume at that setting, not by weight.

Primers

Standard large rifle primers were used in the rifle cases which accepted large primers, while small rifle primers were used in the cases, such as the 25-20 and 32-20, which demanded small rifle primers. I used only standard primers with my black powder loads. As we know from our Time/Pressure curve in Chapter 4, black powder ignites very easily. I could think of no reason to use magnum type primers with black powder.

Alloy Bullets

As we know, an alloy is the fusion of two or more metals. Brass, for example, is a combination or alloy of copper and zinc. In the case of bullets, we generally add tin and/or antimony to the lead for our alloy. This does one thing, in the main—it results in a *harder* product. In the muzzleloader, we do not want an alloy. Our object in the muzzleloader is to use

This is the Shiloh 1874 Sharps No. 3 Sporting Rifle with optional tang sight offered by the C. Sharps Company of Big Timber, Montana. It is a replica of the "buffalo rifles" of the latter 19th century and it is offered in the popular 45-120-3¼ cartridge. Some shooters, both old-time and new, consider this round the best of the so-called "Sharps" offerings. The rifle is also available in the big 50-140-3¼.

(Left) Three old-time black powder cartridges are the 38-40 (left), and the 45 Colt (right). In the center is a round which was introduced in smokeless powder times, but which still clings to black powder terminology. It's the 25-35 Winchester. One would assume that the 35 meant 35 grains of powder, black powder. It doesn't. The "35" portion of that cartridge designation refers to the grain-weight charge of smokeless powder used at the time of that round's debut. The 38-40 is still dropping deer, though no rifles have been chambered for the round since about 1937. The author ran across an old Winchester Model 92 which was in good, but not perfect condition. He was told by a gunsmith to use black powder cartridges in it. A note on the 45 Colt: Our test loads did not produce ballistics which we felt were commensurate with this caliber. We suspected a problem with the powder charge. Consequently, later testing did improve our velocities. With 35 grains FFg, we obtained 773 fps from the muzzle. This is our recommended charge.

evening, at 50 feet, and they cut into each other nicely. I won a cup and gold medal with .455 commercial round shot at New Breman, Sunday. Got a score of .47 × 50—100 yards, open sights! Recently won a turkey match at 40 yards with .34 'buck shot'. I'm strong for them."

Notice that the author of the letter, Mr. Farris, is speaking of shot, not round ball. And he even refers to buckshot in his letter. So, while we indeed use soft lead for reasons of obturation, we will soon discuss an alloy for the breechloader. But first, we said there were two reasons we preferred soft pure lead for our muzzleloaders. One was obturation, just discussed. The other is molecular cohesion. In other words, pure lead "sticks together" very well, rather than fragmenting. Because it sticks together, it makes a pretty darn good hunting projectile which tends to remain in a single unit for better penetration qualities, since the original mass of the missile is retained, rather than lost through fragmentation. Although pure lead does deform, which is surely not always bad in a hunting missile, the retained mass allows for good penetration.

The alloys used for black powder breechloader cartridges are many. Quite probably, as the black powder cartridge shooter gains in his skills, he will want to try various recommended alloys. However, we used what we knew how to

pure lead for at least two reasons: First, the pure lead will obturate in the bore easily, which we want. It, in short, "form-fits" to the dimensions of the bore. It also changes shape because of obturation, and I'm somewhat convinced at this point that we get away with banged up and somewhat deformed and less than perfect projectiles in our muzzleloaders because of obturation.

In fact, though I have not always gotten the best of results using buckshot or other non-round projectiles in place of true-cast or swaged balls, I think this is more a matter of caliber dimensions than of shape. I've also gotten very good results in the muzzleloader with somewhat misshapen, but well-fitted missiles. And so have others. I recently saw a letter from Mr. E.M. "Red" Farris, then Secretary of the National Muzzle Loading Rifle Association. The letter was written to George Depew on May 25, 1938, and it appeared in *Muzzle Blasts* magazine on page 3 of its March, 1982 issue. The part which interested me went like this:

> We do not furnish moulds . . . find it better and cheaper to get the commercial round shot. The .30 calibre size run 175 to the pound—for all of 20¢! I shot some in a brand new rifle last

make from many years of experience, this being the common Alloy No. 2 from Lyman sources. Alloy No. 2 is 90 parts lead, 5 parts tin and 5 parts antimony. As I say, the shooter may find other alloys more suitable for the bullets used in breech-loading black powder arms; however, for test purposes this alloy was entirely suitable. We did not hunt with any of the breech-loading arms in question here.

As I understand it, the buffalo hunter of our early American West preferred pure soft lead for bullets. At least this is what I have read. And it may be true. My sources state that pure lead was preferred and that if a bullet were recovered from a bison, that bullet went back into the lead pot along with the regular lead ingots, which does make sense.

Duplex Loads

Especially in new and gunsmith-approved firearms, some shooters are using the duplex load which amounts to a small amount of smokeless powder at the bottom of the black powder load and next to the primer area. This smokeless loading "kicks off" the black powder load (so the idea suggests) though that surely has little or nothing to do with it. Proof of oscilloscope readings shows that black powder does *not* have to be kicked off with anything to get it going. However, shooters do report that the use of smokeless with black provides cleaner burning.

I'm aware that this is an accepted practice and highly regarded by many expert shooters of the day. I am, however, going to stick with only black powder in our tests *without* the use of a small charge of smokeless loaded into the case first. Part of my decision came from the fact that black powder alone produces plenty of ballistics. Part of the decision is based on the fact that not all original breechloaders are in perfect repair. We did not use duplex loads.

Lubes

Several bullet styles are fired in the breechloaders. There are the fine paper-patched bullets, which in fact have proved themselves excellent in winning many matches. There are the bullets with grease grooves, and there are the modern jacketed bullets which have been used with success in the old-time black powder breech-loading arms. I have fired all three, and find all three suitable for various applications. Because different bullets are used, then it is obvious that different lubrication styles are in order. I am no expert on paper-patched bullets and would certainly never pretend to be one. I do know that old-time literature speaks of using bear grease or whale oil. The paper patch (and indeed it is a patch) does serve to take up the windage in the bore, much as a round ball patch is supposed to do (gasket arguments notwithstanding). It is lubed with the oil prior to application upon the shank of the bullet where it will remain through the firing process.

Essentially, the paper patch comes between rifling and bullet. There will be no leading of the bore. The patch can be applied lubricated to the bearing surface or shank of the bullet in from one to three strips or it can be affixed by centering the lubed paper over the muzzle and then inserting the bullet downbore, as the paper is forced up and around the bearing surface of the bullet. Various lubes have been used, and Ned Roberts, in his often mentioned book, *The Muzzle Loading Cap Lock Rifle,* suggests Neat's-foot oil as a perfect application for the paper patch.

The grooved bullet, far more familiar to all of us who have cast bullets for modern firearms, is greased as per usual with a waxy type material that will be retained by the grease grooves. The cast bullet which has grease grooves is very easily lubed. I made up a great number of such bullets for tests run in this book, and there was no trouble in terms of lubing. My lube method is simple, old-fashioned and workable. I use 50 percent Alox and 50 percent beeswax melted into a shallow pan. I allow the height of the melted lube to be about shank-high on the bullet. The bullets are set into the warm lube, as many as will fit into the pan without undue crowding. In a short period of time, the grease will cool and harden.

At this point, with a hunk of metal conduit close to caliber size of the bullet, I extract the bullets from the lube. This is done simply by slipping the conduit over the bullets, one at a time. They will fill the tube and soon come out of the top of the tube, one at a time, where they are lifted off and set aside. The conduit cuts the grease neatly, and we have a bullet with grease mainly in the groove though there is often some grease clinging to the driving band(s) as well. If this harms anything, I have yet to discover a problem.

As for the modern bullet, obviously it is not lubed when it is

a jacketed type. I have used these bullets with success, not only in my 45-90 and 45-70, but also in the 38-55, the 32-20 and the 25-20. In the 45-70, I have seen game taken with both the Winchester 405-grain factory bullet and the Remington 405-grain factory bullet. Both worked fine. Where a bit more expansion is desired, the Winchester seems to fill the bill best. Where more penetration is useful, the double-cannelured Remington seems best.

Basic Loading Procedures

While most shooters will know how to create a reload from a new or fired cartridge case, we are going to proceed with a step-by-step approach to the loading process because there are some differences and we want to reiterate a few of the major points made in the text above.

We ask the seasoned veteran of the loading press to travel this short road with us.

Step-By-Step Reloading

1. Depriming and Resizing: With the resizing die in place on your press, the lubed case is raised into the sizing die so that it will be returned to something like original dimensions. We have already noted that a fired case does not jump back to its exact original shape when full-length resized. The first operation, therefore, is designed to return the case to something like "standard specs" so it will easily fit in the chamber of the firearm without getting stuck there. Meanwhile, the decapping pin, which protrudes at the bottom of the sizing die, will punch out the fired primer. Now, clean the case.

2. Priming: Priming can be done with a hand tool. I prefer it. The Lee Auto Prime tool works very well indeed. I prefer the Auto Prime unit to the press-mounted varieties because I can actually "feel" the primer as it seats fully within the primer pocket in the head of the cartridge case. Before priming, however, be sure to clean out the primer pocket with a primer pocket cleaning tool. This will ease the job of seating a fresh primer and also insure that the new primer is firmly seated within the pocket. Removing fired primer residue from the primer pocket is an important step—don't overlook it.

3. Belling/Chamfering the Case Mouth: Three piece die sets will offer an expander plug somewhat like the normal expander plug found on a sizing die. Naturally, we need to expand the mouth of the straight-walled case to accept the bullet. If we do not do this, the bullet may strike the sharp edges of the case mouth, which will either damage the delicate base of a lead bullet and/or crush the mouth of the cartridge case.

Belling should be so slight as to scarcely notice the effect. The shooter should initially set his belling die high enough so that it's beyond the reach of the case when it's fully raised by the ram. Next, screw the die down bit by bit until the expander plug is just touching the mouth of the case. Now it is a simple matter of trial and error until the mouth of the case is belled out just slightly. The idea is to get the base of the bullet to just barely enter the mouth of the properly belled case.

Some shooters prefer to bypass belling altogether and simply chamfer the inside of the case mouth to accomplish the same goal. (This is particularly evident among shooters using 2-die sets.) With some exceptions, most metallic cartridges, in which black powder is often used, are straight walled. And most die sets for straight-walled cases come with a "belling"

(Left) First, we select the proper shell holder for the Pacific 007 press, in this case, a 45-70 shell holder.

(Right) The cartridge case is deprimed and resized in one thrust of the 007 handle.

The case is reprimed with a standard large rifle primer, not a Magnum primer. In this instance, we have used the Lee tool for repriming the case.

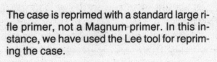

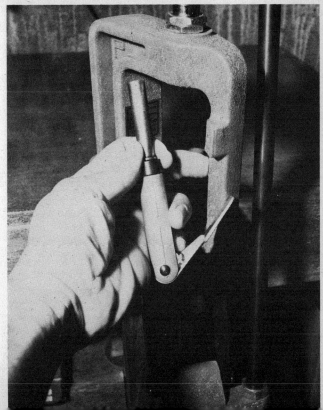

With bullet seating die in place, and after having dropped the appropriate charge of black powder into the resized and reprimed cartridge case, the bullet is not only seated to the correct depth, but it is also crimped in place—in this instance crimping took place on the cannelure of this Remington 405-grain jacketed bullet.

or expanding die. My advice would be to use the belling die, if you have it.

4. Charging Cases Obviously we have to get black powder into the case now. I use a modern powder measure for smokeless powder loads, but I do not use that same powder measure with black powder. I do not recommend its use to anyone. For the tests in this book, I weighed each individual black powder volume charge on a powder/bullet scale. *Warning:* Never use a standard modern powder measure to meter out black powder. The shearing of the powder granules may cause a serious explosion. For our tests, I used a powder/bullet scale to arrive at recommended charges. I've also used, throughout this book, powder measures designed specifically for black powder—I recommend them.

Pyrodex should be loaded by *volume* only, *never* weight. Once a black powder charge is established, the powder measure (that is the hand-held adjustable black powder measures we are familiar with) is used to toss the Pyrodex charge.

5. Bullet Seating I generally follow the bullet seating instructions that come with every set of dies I buy—be they for black powder or smokeless. Seating is an easy step in the loading process; however, don't just slam-bang the bullet into the case. It's a good way to ruin cases (and accuracy). I seat my bullets slowly and deliberately.

Friction-seating bullets for use in single shot firearms is fine; however, take advantage of the crimp ring (built into most modern seating dies) when loading up black powder ammo for revolvers or magazine-fed firearms. A crimped bullet won't recede into the case as a result of recoil. Crimping is especially important when the ammo is to be used in tube-fed rifles like the Model 94 Winchester because the recoil may force friction-seated bullets back into the case. At the least you'll end up with feeding problems. (See our earlier comments in this chapter about the use of flat nosed bullets in cartridges to be used in tube-fed firearms.)

Special Black Powder Loading Instructions

While we have gone over these points to some degree, it is perhaps wise to point out that there are some great differences between modern and black powder cartridge loading. These are well worth looking at again:

1. After the case is sized and deprimed, its primer pocket should be thoroughly cleaned, as mentioned earlier.

2. Trimmed cases are safest. Following depriming, cleaning and drying, the case must be checked for overall length. This is also a perfect time to check for any cracks in the case. A very careful reloader may wish to mike the head of the case after the first shot and keep a record. Serious trouble arises when case heads expand. If a future miking discloses a stretched head (or if visual inspection discovers a crack in the brass), the case should be *discarded* immediately.

3. Single wads should not be used. While this has been mentioned before, it is wise to point out that some readers may feel that there is a gross disagreement between the data presented here and the data offered by C. Sharps. There is no argument! Yes, if the shooter reads the data by C. Sharps, he will find the use of wads offered to keep the black powder at the back of the case and to prevent a partially filled case. *However,* he will also see that a *series* of wads is used. There is *no space* between the top of the wad and the base of the bullet in the C. Sharps suggestion. The wads fill the case, and they use all the space between the powder charge and the base of the bullet.

Special Shooting Instructions

The following are offered for the safety of the shooter who uses the black powder metallic round:

1. Have any original black powder firearm checked by a black powder gunsmith who has knowledge of the firearm type. He must give the firearm a clean "bill of health" or the gun should be considered a wallhanger and never used with ammo.

2. Overall case length should be checked with a caliper, not by "visual" or any other method. Many handbooks give the overall standard case lengths of the old-time rounds. Lyman, for example, shows in its manual that a 32-20 has a case length of 1.315, and at the same time, it tells the reader to trim to 1.305 for full safety.

3. Bore diameters in the old guns were not always held to rigid specs. A shooter should have his own rifle "slugged" by a gunsmith. The lead slug will show the exact dimensions of the bore. If the shooter knows the exact groove to groove diameter of his firearm, he can use an alloy or lead bullet which

runs about .001" oversize, but *no more*.

4. No need to crush the powder charge. In most cases, a recommended black powder load will fill the case so that there is no air space left between the powder charge and the base of the bullet. The reloader should *not* try to squash (or "compress") the powder charge so that a little more powder can be used in the case.

Cleaning the Breechloader

The breechloader is very easy to clean. Some people prefer the use of water, and others do not. A prominent barrelmaker told me that he does not care to use the water method and that he has had no trouble over the years with barrel erosion. He keeps the rifle clean between shots on the range by swabbing the bore with "moose milk" and drying patches. At home, he swabs the bore with moose milk, but he also uses a bristle brush. After he has brushed the bore with moose milk, he dries it totally with cleaning patches and sprays with WD-40. Sometimes, he uses a sophisticated preservative, such as J&A Accragard after the cleaning patches are coming out unsoiled and white.

I have used rubbing alcohol for a solvent first, followed by a bristle brush with moose milk, plenty of drying patches, and finally an application of J&A Accragard—I have been able to detect no problem with this method. There are many shooters who have replaced the older hot-water method with the above for their own muzzleloaders. I am not yet ready to speak as to the rust-prevention qualities of this particular method of black powder cleanup. However, it's probably fine, since the advice comes from a few true experts who have many years' experience.

Summary

This is a look at black powder breechloader shooting. It is not a last word on the subject, nor was it ever intended to be. I am convinced that any shooter who finds a deep interest in the old cartridge guns will explore the topic more fully. There are a number of companies catering to the black powder metallic reloader, and there are cases available from B.E.L.L. (Brass Extrusion Laboratories, Ltd.) for the harder-to-get rounds, as well as the many fine numbers on the shelf from Winchester, Remington and Federal.

Moulds are available in great numbers from commercial sources like Lyman, RCBS, N.E.I. and Lee. There are a few fine custom mould builders around, too, such as Richard Hoch. Dies are offered by all the fine companies such as Pacific, RCBS, Lyman, C&H, and more. And we have, of course, a wealth of loading tools from many of those same companies.

Modern companies make bullets for us, too, in over-the-counter offerings, and they make many which will serve us in the hunting field. In fact, for some of the rifles, either new or in checked-out excellent condition, there are loaded boxes of ammunition waiting. Certainly, the 25-20, 32-20, 44-40 and many others of this type are around.

Things could be much worse for the person interested in black powder metallics. In fact, there are so many fine firearms offered in this area that a shooter's major problem is picking the one he wants. The firearms of the old school were useful in days past, and they are still useful. Loading for them is not only quite rewarding; it is also a lot of fun, and an interesting hobby in itself. There are so many fine points that the shooter can spend a number of years creating loads which will give fine accuracy and very worthwhile ballistics.

These modern day shooters are firing old-style black powder breech-loaders. As George Nonte said, "It is more rewarding to shoot these firearms loaded with the fuel available at the time the rounds were designed." (Photo courtesy Peterson Publishing).

chapter 12

Loading the Black Powder Shotshell

UNFORTUNATELY, we cannot recommend any load whatsoever for the Damascus or "twist steel" shotgun, or any firearm with a barrel of this construction. Yes, they certainly did shoot these fine old guns in days gone by; however, we are forced through an observance of safety factors to deny the use of these great guns today with any loads. We found no loading house which would guarantee any rounds for Damascus "twist steel" barrels.

Loading the shotgun shell, in terms of sheer mechanics, is very simple for the person who already understands the principles of modern shotshell loading. But there are some fine points which must be observed for the sake of safety and performance, as well as shooter understanding of this loading technique and skill. We will talk about two types of black powder shotgun shell reloading. First, we want to discuss the simple hand tool. The simple Lee shotshell loading tool has been around for years. There are thousands of these good little tools around, and we will discuss black powder shotgun shell loading with one of these handy units. Also, we will talk

about how to load shotgun shells with black powder using the more modern bench tool, in this case a MEC 700 model.

First, let us remember that we are talking about *black powder shotgun shells*. Anything said previously about loading the muzzle-loading black powder shotgun may or may not apply here. Certainly, we can absolutely forget about the time-worn, time-tested and time-proved method of volume-for-volume measures of shot and black powder. If the reader will recall, we, going along with tradition and our own tests, allowed for absolute maximum loads by tossing a volume of shot and *volume* (never weight) of powder from the same measure. This *bulk-for-bulk* practice has been used for a very long time as a top end *maximum* load, and we recommend such only in top grade shotguns. However, in discussing muzzleloaders we are not talking about shotgun *shells* loaded with black powder. Please leave the muzzle-loading shotgun data to the muzzleloaders and the shotgun *shell* data with the shotgun shells using black powder. Loading data is, obviously, *not* interchangeable.

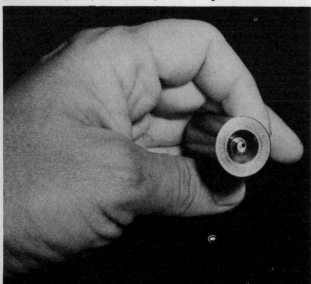

The Sport Specialties instant muzzleloader all-steel unit for shotguns employs a standard No. 11 percussion cap which is fitted over the projection shown here. The flash from the cap flies through the hole (visible in the photo) and into the powder charge within the shell.

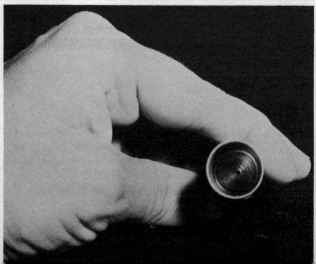

From the inside of the instant muzzleloader shotgun shell from Sports Specialties we see the flashhole. Naturally, powder is poured down into the metal case followed by wads and shot with an over-shot card wad to hold the shot in place in the shell. (In some states this device may not be used to take certain game during "Primitive Hunt" seasons.)

In firing black powder shells in the shotgun, standard loading procedures take place and the Lee handloading tool is perfectly acceptable for such loading techniques. The fired shell is decapped, resized, charged with powder (we simply use a bulk method with a powder horn/volumetric measure), fitted with appropriate wad(s), and the crimp set by the Lee unit itself.

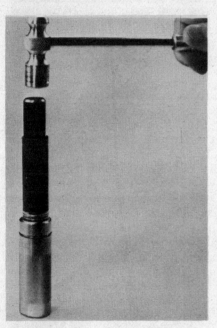

DEPRIMING: Just a light tap will force the old primer out.

PRIMING: A new primer is easily pushed into the shell.

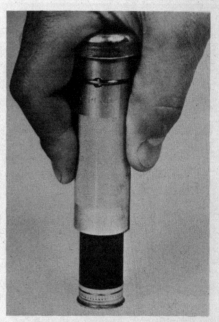

CHARGING/WADDING After powder is added, the wads are correctly seated. (Use bathroom scale to obtain correct wad pressure).

The Lee Tool

With the little Lee tool, here is the procedure for making a round of black powder shotshell ammunition.

1. Depriming

With the tool provided, a metal cylinder with a depriming rod on the end, the old primer is forced out, precisely as it is for a modern shotgun shell.

2. Priming the Shell

Priming the shotgun hull is again the same as in priming the shotgun hull for smokeless powder shooting. The Lee tool comes with a primer seating rod that has a recessed tip. The rod is inserted into the deprimed hull as the hull rests upon a provided platform in the tool and a fresh primer is inserted partially into the shell's primer pocket. With a rap on the rod, the head of the case is forced downward and the new primer is seated. We do *not* need "hot" primers for black powder shooting. Standard shotshell primers are preferred.

3. Charging/Wadding/Adding Shot

The Lee tool comes with a measure for powder. This is *not* to be used for our purposes. Our powder charge in black powder will, indeed, be thrown by volume, but we prefer to use the standard black powder hand-held adjustable measure for this task and no other tool. There are no exceptions in our book. The charge is simply dumped down into the hull as per normal. There is no secret here, other than to remind the reloader to be safety conscious around any powder, smokeless

  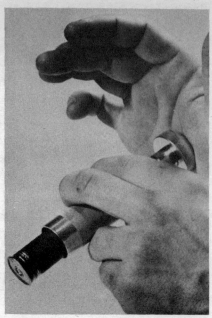

ADDING SHOT: Proper amount of shot is easily added, using adjustable measure.

CRIMPING: Shell is easily crimped and re-sized in one operation.

EJECTING SHELL: The shell that is ejected is comparable to factory loaded ammunition.

or black. No cigars, pipes or cigarettes while loading, please. Just a clear area, alone, where concentration is possible.

Selecting the Powder Charge: We select a black powder charge by first considering *two* other things: We must know the shot charge and the wad column before we can decide upon the powder charge. When we do select the powder charge, our choice is FFg or Fg black powder or RS grade of Pyrodex, in spite of the fact that there are indeed others who use finer granulations in shotgun shells.

If we have selected 1¼ ounces of shot for a 12-gauge hull, for example, we next need to know what the wad column will be comprised of and how high it will stand in the case. Let us suppose that the shooter has decided upon an over-powder wad and one felt wad for his wad column. Now, by trial and error, we come up with our charge. Yes, there are other methods, but this one is useful because it will work with any shotgun shell brand. Again, for the sake of comment, let's say as an example, we start with 70 grains volume of FFg black powder. Remember, we have simply set our black powder measure to "70" on the barrel of the measure, and we dump this charge, period. We fit the over-powder wad and the felt wad and then we dump the shot. At this point, if the shot is too far below the lip of the shotshell and the crimp will be forced down into the body of the hull—the load column is too short.

We do one of two things. If this is the load we want, fine. We can use an inert filler, such as corn meal, over the shot to bring the column up to height. Or, we can add more powder in a second trial run. This time we insert 80 grains volume of FFg and we then drop the over-powder wad into the hull and the felt wad into the hull, followed by the shot charge. It seats perfectly! There is one more thing to do—write it down! In a notebook which will not be lost, write down the exact load chain used—this means the type and brand of shotgun shell, the primer, the exact powder volume tossed, such as 70 or 80 grains of FFg, etc., the brand of powder, the exact wad column and so forth.

4. The Crimp

We have not discussed sizing with the Lee tool because this operation is performed in the normal sequence of operation. The tubular die is pressed down around the hull and the hull, including the head, is resized. In order to crimp the shell, one must force the body of the sizing die around the shell as part of the process. Now, with the shell resting within the body of the sizing die, the crimp is automatically started and a metal rod is forced down through the top of the resizing die to force the crimp into finished form. The shell is crimped.

With this simple hand tool, we have deprimed, primed, sized, charged, fitted the wad column and crimped a spent shotgun shell. We may now bring Grandpa's fine old non-twist-steel barreled shotgun down from the attic, have it approved for safety by a competent professional gunsmith, and perhaps put the gun back into service, using black powder shotgun shells with their low pressures.

The Mec Tool

Once again, the shooter familiar with loading modern shotgun shells is going to have no problem creating good black powder shotgun shells. Before we proceed one step further, however, we sound a warning—we do not under any circumstances recommend or condone the use of a charge bar for tossing a black powder charge of fuel. Period. *In our opinion, the practice is not safe. Therefore, the reader should never load his powder reservoir with black powder and attempt to dump it in this manner into the shell.* Yes, this works with smokeless powder, but we cannot and *do not* recommend the same procedure for black powder

Note: The owner of a shotshell reloading press must follow the instructions which attend that brand or model, keeping in mind our warning *not* to use the charge bar or automatic powder measuring device with black powder. Below, we have listed the process of making a re-loaded black powder shotgun shell with the MEC 700.

1. Depriming/Resizing

Station No. 1 on my unit resizes and deprimes the fired shotgun hull, removing the old (used) primer.

2. Priming

Station No. 2 inserts a new primer. Again, we recommend mild primers for black powder shooting, since black powder ignites readily.

3. Charging

Here, we simply *remove* the shotgun shell from the press and use our hand-held standard adjustable black powder measure to toss the charge by volume. It is that simple. Remember, we have discussed how to find the proper black powder charge and will not explain that process again here. See Step Number Three (3) with the Lee tool.

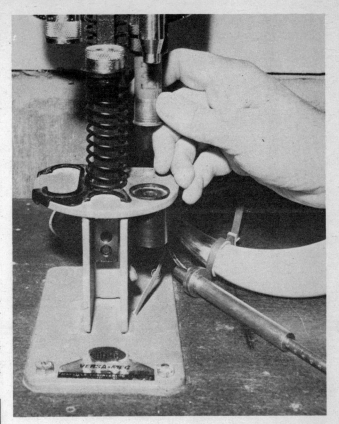

(Right) Using the standard shotshell reloader for loading black powder shotgun shells, we first decap, expelling the spent primer and resizing the body and brass head.

The second step is to replace the spent primer with a fresh one, of course. Again, a standard shotshell primer is used. Black powder is very easily ignited, and we do not require more than a normal primer for the task.

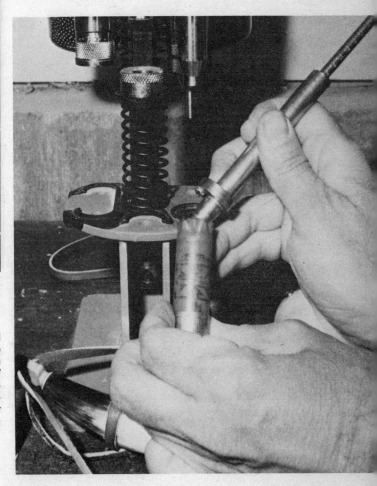

(Right) Now, in step three, we depart from the normal procedure and we turn to the simple volumetric load of Fg or FFg black powder. The author uses a standard powder measure with powder container, such as the Uncle Mike powder measure shown here along with the K-W powder horn. ***Do not use the standard charge bar on any shotshell press or any powder-metering device intended for smokless powder—you may get an explosion.*** Powder (remember, Fg or FFg) is poured down into the primed shotshell. This is a bulk loading.

4. Wads

The wad or wads are inserted into the mouth of the hull and pressed into place via a force of about 30 to 40 pounds pressure. Each individual modern type reloader will offer a specific station for this operation. The reader must check the instructions which came with his loading tool.

5. The Shot Charge

Shot is dumped via the bar now, as it would normally be loaded into the shotgun hull. Or the reloader can use a shot cup such as supplied with the Lee loader.

6. Crimping

On the MEC 700, crimping is accomplished on two stations, a starter and finisher. This may or may not be the situation with the reader's shotgun reloading press, and he must, of course, check his own instruction sheet. However, at this point, the shotgun shell has been reloaded with black powder *without* using the charge bar on the loading tool.

(Right) Wads can be hand-fitted into the mouth of the shotgun shell. Remember, we have already poured home the powder charge.

Shot also may be bulk-loaded into the hull. We simply use the standard shot measure, in this case a measure from Lee.

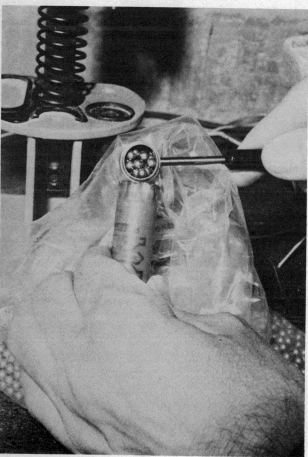

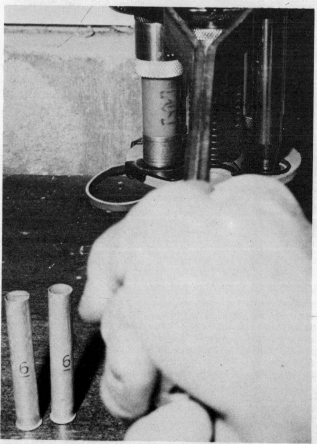

(Right) Now we return in this step to the standard procedure by using the station on the shotshell press which begins the crimp.

98

Note:

We have not discussed resizing of the shotgun hull in depth because this procedure may be achieved at different load stations depending upon the machine used. Let it suffice to say that the modern shotgun reloading tool will provide a station that resizes the shell body and head. However, a hull fired many times may not form to its original head dimensions, but will spring back out and may be sticky in the shotgun. Given this, we suggest you use once or twice fired (only) hulls for black powder shotshell reloading.

Fuels

Our recommendations have been Fg, FFg or Pyrodex RS for shotgun shells. We immediately point out, however, that Pyrodex CTG granulation is considered a very fine fuel for breechloader black powder shotgun shotshells. And we have provided a table which shows the use of Pyrodex CTG—a list of loads recommended by the Hodgdon Powder Company.

(Above and right) The last station completes the crimp. The two shells in the foreground, incidentally, are very old totally brass units in .410 size. All-brass or all-metal shotgun shells are not new; however, they have been very hard to come by the last many years. Sports Specialties, however, is now in the process of building brass shotgun shells once again.

PYRODEX® DATA FOR BREECH LOADING SHOTGUNS*

WARNING: Damascus barrels should be considered unsafe with ANY powder.

ANY TUBE

GAUGE	SHOT WT. OZ.	WAD COLUMN	GR. PYRODEX® "CTG"	VELOCITY	L.U.P.
10-3½	2	Card + Filler	100	1154	6900
10-2⅞	1⅝	Card + Filler	80	1115	4500
12-2¾	1⅛	Card + Filler	72	1043	5700
12-2¾	1¼	Card + Filler	68	1039	5800
12-2¾	1½	Card + Filler	65	1012	5900
16-2¾	1	Card + Filler	65	1128	5600
16-2¾	1⅛	Card + Filler	60	1095	5800
16-2¾	1¼	Card + Filler	56	1040	6000
20-2¾	⅞	Card + Filler	56	1134	5800
20-2¾	1	Card + Filler	52	1090	5900
20-2¾	1⅛	Card + Filler	48	1052	5900
28-2¾	¾	Card + Filler	40	1089	5500
410-3	¾	Card + Filler	24	1038	5800
410-2½	½	Card + Filler	24	1089	5700

*Used with permission from Hodgdon Powder Company

A Few Fine Points

In my tests, I used only the "old fashioned" wad column. These fit the shotshell very well when the bulkier black powder fuel is in use. By using the .135″ nitro card wad from Ballistic Products, Inc., along with felt wads on top of these (same company) in the ½-inch thickness, we were able to produce handsome reloaded shotgun shells which crimped nicely.

The shooter may wish to juggle the wad column, staying with approved components, of course. V.M. Starr, the grand old man of black powder shotgunning, produced 80 percent patterns by juggling components. His shotguns were choked by a master craftsman—himself. The modern shotgun shell with smokeless powder is well suited to the plastic one-piece wad, and in some applications, the one-piece plastic wad is useful with black powder shotshell loads. However, we used, as stated above, the more basic components in our black powder reloaded shotgun hulls.

Our patterning with modern shotguns, by the way, proved excellent with the black powder shotgun shell reload. This simple statement says it all. Due to the high velocity of smokeless loads and the fine wad systems available, the modern shotgunner will no doubt want to stay with the latest in available components for his reloads. We say this to insure that there is no mistake made—nowhere do we suggest that black powder shotgun loads are superior to modern smokeless shotgun loads.

We recommend that shooters carefully mark a box of shells loaded with black powder. No, they will not injure a modern shotgun. In fact, we conducted tests with a Remington 870 Wingmaster using black powder loads. However, in some automatics the black powder load may not provide the necessary impetus to activate the action.

Drams Equivalent

This is a good time to mention drams. Often, we will see shotshell data which speaks in drams or dram equivalents. In smokelesss powder language, we use "dram equivalent," because we most certainly are not going to toss a dram-measured load down into the shell! That would be a lot of powder, far too much in fact. In black powder loading, however, when we say a dram, we mean a dram, but we *never* mean a drachm.

The Dram: A dram is precisely 27.34 grains weight. If one will look into the *Hodgdon Pyrodex/Black Powder Shooters Handbook* on page 66, he will see a listing of black powder loads by both dram and weight in grains. Often, old-time information simply lists the load in drams. But as long as we know that a dram is 27.34 grains of weight, we have no problem turning the dram load into a grains weight load, and then we can simply set the powder measure and actually drop our powder charge by volume.

Let us do one here—we are given a charge of 3 drams of black powder for a 12-gauge shotgun shell using 1⅛ ounces of shot. If we multiply 3 times 27.34 we come up with 82.02 grains, which we obviously call 82 grains and we set our black powder measure at 80, which is certainly close enough. There is also the popular 3¾ drams charge, and here we would have 102.53 grains, which we round off to 102 grains weight, and we set the powder measure for 100 flat.

Now we know what a dram is in actual practice. But what about a "dram equivalent?" As I understand it, when black powder was supplanted by smokeless powder, the manufac-

turers wanted to continue giving the shooter something he could understand, an old familiar term. So the makers of shotgun shells simply put "dram equivalent" on the box to mean that the load, although loaded with smokeless powder, was *equivalent* to an old load holding so many drams of black powder. To this day, we have "dram equivalent" loads still with us, and we certainly do get meaning from them. It takes no great knowledge to realize that a 4-dram load is going to have more punch than a 3-dram load. The shotgun shell manufacturer is telling us about how closely this load matches the old-time black powder charge.

For example, I have before me a brand new box of Federal 2¾″ magnum 12-gauge shotgun shells loaded with 1½ ounces of BB shot. On the box it says "4 DRAM EQ." This means that the shell is loaded with smokeless powder to roughly the same load domain of 109 grains of Fg (probably) or FFg black powder. Of course, the actual charge of smokeless powder in that shell is far below that weight in grains because smokeless powder is much stronger than black powder. Recall that in the Time/Pressure curve in Chapter 4, 82.0 grains of FFFg black powder was used to gain a muzzle velocity of 1200 fps, but it only took 21.0 grains of smokeless to reach the same velocity, albeit with more pressure.

The Drachm

We have to talk about the drachm because in the great sport of black powder shooting, hobbyists enjoy delving back into the old books for information and the drachm will often be encountered. The drachm is *not* a dram. A drachm is 60 grains of weight, while a dram is only 27.34 grains of weight. It is entirely clear to me now that the terms "drachm" and "dram" were interchanged by 19th century English writers, and I am convinced that when the Englishman said drachm he meant dram. If not, some horrendous loads were in use!

Even more modern works may be confusing. In *The Shooter's Handbook* by Richard Arnold, first published in 1955, the author lists some shotgun loads for black powder on page 141. These are no doubt old-time loads which Mr. Arnold is relating in his fine book. One such load is, and I quote, "3 drachms of black powder and 1¼ ounce of shot in a 12 bore." If indeed drachms is meant, then we have a load of 180 grains of powder. I believe drachm has been used for dram here and the real load is about 82 grains of powder, a difference of 100 grains. Do not use drachm loads at face value!

A Word on Heavy Charges

Heavy charges are generally uncalled for in shotgunning, and in the 12-gauge powder shotgun *shell,* my most used charge was 90 volume FFg, which is fairly close to a 3 dram equivalent. Our very heaviest charges in *muzzle-loading* shotguns was the volume-for-volume arrangement. However, this is also limited! We did not, for example, increase shot charges beyond factory recommendations in these loads.

If the shooter will refer to the Winchester Time/Pressure curve which we presented in Chapter 4, he will see that in this test, even though FFFg black powder is used, rather than FFg or Fg, the pressures are quite low as compared with smokeless powder. Looking at the final figures of that test, we find that WC-45-LS ball powder gave a 1⅛ ounce charge of shot a muzzle velocity of 1,202 fps using 21.0 grains of fuel. The pressure for this load was 9,600 PSI (pounds per square inch).

Then the test was run using 82.0 grains weight of du Pont

FFFg black powder with the same shotshell case type and the same 1⅛-ounce charge of shot. This time, velocity was 1,205 fps, or the same, as we round both off to 1,200 fps. But the pressure was much lower, only 4,900 PSI. So, if we do have an old shotgun in the closet, we *might* be able to shoot it with black powder shotshells. I strongly used the word "might" because the condition of the shotgun must be tested by a gunsmith before *any* load is used at all. The shooter is on his own if he wants to rescue an old shotgun from the spider webs in the attic and shoot it without the gun first receiving a good "bill of health" from a competent, professional gunsmith who is familiar with black powder firearms.

Final Points

Cleaning Shotshell Hulls

It isn't a bad idea to wipe out the interior of the shotshell after use. This is not necessarily a soap and water operation. I used a paper towel soaked gently in "moose milk" and wrapped around a wooden dowel. A cloth works even better, as the paper toweling tends to fall apart when wet. The hull is cleaned and then thoroughly dried to help maintain interior dimensions to a standard, and to prevent black powder residue from gathering up moisture and caking the inside of the plastic hull itself.

Cleaning the Shotgun

The double barrel shotgun is very easy to clean and maintain, and I found the use of black powder little to no added problem. Since we are dealing with a breechloader, there is no trouble at all in wiping out any black powder fouling. I can clean the black powder breechloader double barrel shotgun in a few moments.

I prefer to remove the barrels by slipping the fore-end off and levering the barrels free from the rest of the gun. With a bristle brush, I swipe the bores clean by dipping the brush into moose milk and running up and down the bores with several brisk pulls and pushes. Then I simply slip a cleaning patch over the end of the brush and run this up and down the bore.

After a few such patches, the bore will be clean. I like to use patches soaked in solvent if the bores are terribly dirty, this following the brush and moose milk wipe; however, I still apply the patches by merely slipping them over the end of the bristle brush where they remain intact and will not slip off. Obviously, if a patch did slip off, there would be no problem with a breechloader, as the shooter would not have to fish the lost patch out of the bore with a worm, as he would with a muzzleloader.

The standing breech face is wiped down with a clean cloth dipped in J&A (or similar) solvent. And the exterior of the firearm is also wiped down to remove any black powder resi-

BLACK POWDER LOADING DATA FOR BREECHLOADING SHOTGUN SHELLS*
Used with permission from Hodgdon Powder Company

Gauge	Chamber Length in.	Powder	Charge Weight drams	Charge Weight grains	M.V. ft/sec	Shot Weight oz.
10	2⅝	FFg	3½	95	1057	1⅜
	2¾		4	109	1040	1½
	3		4½	123	1060	1¾
12	2½	FFFg	3	82	1069	1⅛
	2¾		3⅜	92	1050	1¼
	3		3¾	102	1044	1½
14	2½	FFFg	2⅞	80	1082	1 1/16
	2¾		3⅛	85	1055	1 3/16
16	2½	FFFg	2¾	75	1010	1
	2¾		3	82	972	1⅛
20	2½	FFFg	2⅜	65	1105	⅞
	2¾		2¾	75	989	1
24	2½	FFFg	2⅛	58	1124	¾
	2¾		2⅜	65	1100	⅞
28	2½	FFFg	1⅞	52	1081	⅝
	2¾		2⅛	58	1104	¾
32	2½	FFFg	1½	41	1080	9/16
	2¾		1¾	48	1065	11/16
.410 in.	2	FFFg	⅞	23	1018	5/16
	2½		1	27	1063	7/16
	1¾		½	13½	980	3/16

*WARNING: Damascus barrels should be considered unsafe with ANY powder.

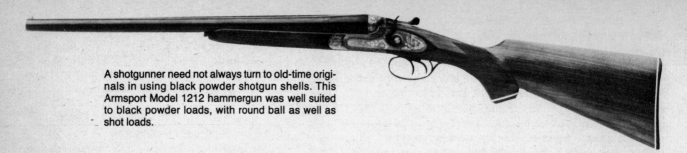

A shotgunner need not always turn to old-time originals in using black powder shotgun shells. This Armsport Model 1212 hammergun was well suited to black powder loads, with round ball as well as shot loads.

due. And that is it, with the exception of lightly coating the bore with an anti-rusting agent of the shooter's choice. As I have stated, keeping the double or single barrel black powder breechloader clean and maintained is not much work.

If you should ever decide to shoot black powder shells in a thoroughly modern, repeating, closed breech shotgun—the Remington 870 is a good example—be sure to thoroughly clean the *entire* gun. This means cleaning not only the barrel and barrel extension, but pulling out the trigger group and cleaning it (and the interior of the receiver) as well.

Autoloaders (gas-operated, especially) and black powder shells don't always mix well as the gases (or recoil energy) may not be sufficient to work the action. Secondly, you will have a real job of cleaning ahead of you because the system of operation is not closed-breech in design. If you ever shoot black powder shotgun shells in a gas-operated autoloader, be certain to *thoroughly* clean the gas system that surrounds the magazine tube and the gas-bleed vents in the barrel. If you don't, rust may form and semiauto function will only be a memory until the local gunsmith has lightened your wallet.

The loading and shooting of breech-loading shotguns with black powder shells does not pose a problem to the modern gunner. As we can see, putting proper black powder shotshells together is not very tricky. A few observations of proper component use is all that is required for success. The reader can see by our chronographed ballistics that the shotgun shell loaded with black powder is certainly adequate enough to bring home the flying suppers and running dinners. Most of our game bird and cottontail/squirrel shooting is done at close range, and while we have not attained the modern ballistic potential of today's smokeless loads with our black powder loads, neither are we stuck with corkgun power loads, because we might be limited to black powder.

With the larger gauges and proper shot, even the waterfowl hunter can enjoy his older black powder breech-loading shotgun, especially if he will limit himself to reasonable ranges by studying hard to become a better hunter, as well as a good shot. Requiring very little care, the black powder breechloading shotgun which may have been gathering dust in a forgotten corner of an out-of-the-way closet might have a new lease on life if its owner will try loading black powder shotgun shells.

Loading Data

CAUTION: The data shown here is the most accurate data we are able to furnish. However, you must apply it with caution and understanding if you wish to assemble safe loads or reloads. It is important for you to realize that no loading or reloading data is an absolute. Maximum charges, along with their velocities and pressures, can and do vary considerably. The maximum charge for your firearm will depend in part on the specific components you use, your specific assembly methods and equipment, and your specific firearm. A maximum load in one firearm can be quite dangerous if used in another firearm. In that neither the author nor the publisher has any control over components used, the assembly of the load or reload, the firearm used, the degree of knowledge of the loader/reloader, or how the resulting charges may be used, we therefore assume no responsibility, either implied or expressed, for the use of this data. It was safe in the test firearms. However, it could prove otherwise in your gun or with your components. Use this data entirely at your own risk. No warranty or guarantee is implied or expressed. The author and publisher assume no responsibility for the use of this data in any way.

Introduction

THE LOADING DATA section, to include muzzle-loading rifles and handguns, the black powder metallics and shotguns, is organized first alphabetically by manufacturer and second by caliber or gauge, from the largest to the smallest. The following loading data will give the shooter a very good idea of the potential of his own black powder firearm. But there may be a few questions about this information, and we hope to clear up a couple of points here.

Powder Charges

Why not use a wider range of powder charges? This is a question which is bound to show up. In other words, instead of using 60 FFg in all 45-caliber rifles for our tests, why not use 57 or 59 grains, or 62.5 grains? The answer lies in the nature of black powder. We did try varying our loads, and the results were virtually without value. For example, we found that when we used 60 grains FFg and then 63 grains FFg in a 45-caliber (as an example) the resulting velocities were in the same domain.

In short, small changes in the actual black powder charge, in the larger calibers especially, made only minor differences, certainly not valuable differences. We agreed early on that a change in powder charge of at least 5 grains was necessary in the 45-caliber and up to make any measurable difference in velocity. Therefore, we used a *standard* set of loads based upon our experience with the firearm, our own tests with black powder arms and the recommendations of the manufacturers.

In the smaller calibers, such as the 32- to 36-caliber class, a little bit of powder makes more of a ballistic difference than it does in the larger calibers. In the first place, we are using FFFg in the smaller calibers for optimum loads. We tend to use FFFg in the bigger calibers only for the target loads in this text. Since FFFg is more "powerful" than FFg in charge-for-charge comparisons, changes in weight for FFFg are more marked and pronounced in their results.

All the same, even in the sub-bores, we still felt that it took 5 grains of powder to truly make a ballistic difference. Finally, let's not misconstrue our meaning here. We are not, under any circumstances, suggesting that black powder is some sooty old charcoal and any dumped amount is just fine. We believe strongly in careful measurement and *safe* loads and we think that overloads of any fuel, black or smokeless, is a sucker's game. We simply state the facts—and our machinery showed small value in charges such as 62.5 instead of 60.0.

Ball or Minie Weights

The reader may also notice that we sometimes list a .530" ball at 224 grains and then call it a 225-grain another time. This was not a typographical error. We found that there was amazing closeness in weight-to-weight precision for our Hornady, Speer and Denver Bullet Company test projectiles, as well as our own cast missiles. However, we did actually weigh a test run of projectiles, and of course, we had some slight variation, no more than a grain from the "standard." Therefore, we might find a

.530" projectile going 224 grains one time and 225 another. In terms of pure lead figures for a sphere, a .530" ball would go 223.99 grains in weight (remember, 7,000 grains of weight to a pound). We, of course, would call this a 224-grain ball. In real life measurements, however, a .530" ball might actually "mike out" at .531", which would give us a weight of 225.27 grains or 225 rounded off. Therefore, since we weighed our projectiles, then we did have to record these minute differences.

As for elongated projectiles, some moulds did not toss a "bullet" exactly as prescribed on the box. The Lyman 570-grain made a 600-grain missile for us and the Lyman 500-grain made a 525-grain missile in pure lead. Again, these fine moulds are not at fault in any way. The fact is, all moulds vary to some degree as a result of the manufacturing process. When that is coupled with varying casting techniques and melt purity, you can end up with variations in the weight of the projectile being tossed. This is no problem whatsoever and we bring it up only for the reader's interest.

Lubes and Velocity Readings

While it is true that we have detected minute differences in velocity among various lubes, these differences have always been very small for us and of no consequence whatsoever in terms of useful ballistics. However, we can support the rule that a grease will generally give small (and at times unmeasurable) gains over a liquid in *some* rifles in terms of raw muzzle velocity.

We detected minor differences in accuracy using various lubes, and we urge the shooter to try different lubes until he finds the most compatible for his own uses. For target shooting and range work, modern lubes such as Young Country No. 103, Hoppes, J&A Old Slickum, Old Grizz and many others were fine. For the field we preferred a grease such as RIG or 103. Moose milk also worked well.

Most important was the condition of the bore due to lube. We did find that a damp or oily or greasy bore often shot to a different point of impact. The degree varied among different firearms. In our own Hatfield 36-caliber rifle, for example, we found that at 50 yards the slightly damp bore did not affect our groups nor our point of impact. Accuracy remained high with a *slightly* damp bore and the balls struck the same point on the target at 50 yards. But with a custom rifle we found that a greasy bore put the balls high and to the left at 50 yards. Therefore, we always mopped the bore dry with a swipe or two from a cleaning patch *after* the ball was rammed home. Naturally, a mopping with a cleaning patch will not totally dry the bore, which is fine. We want a light protective coat of lubricant downbore while hunting, but we do not want so much bore dampness or grease that the point of impact is changed.

Why the Same Calibers in Different Brands?

One may wonder why we have several 36-caliber rifles tested for our book. Wouldn't one 36-caliber rifle give us all we need to know about that caliber? The answer is *no*, it would not. In the first place, we set out to help the shooter with data for *his own personal firearm*. Naturally, we could not include every black powder gun ever made. However, we did manage, we feel, to test-fire a wide range of arms available over the counter for the American and Canadian muzzleloader fan as well as the black powder shooter abroad.

Secondly, contrary to our own early opinions, we did indeed find significant differences in barrel length and velocity. We even detected some differences in actual minute bore variations and velocity. In other words, testing the various arms in the same caliber paid off. This is not to suggest that one should buy a rifle soley on velocity. That would be foolish. However, it is nice to know that barrel length can make a difference. We once felt that black powder was consumed in the first few inches of bore. So, this indicated that the rest of the barrel would give us "bore drag" only. Not true. The time/pressure curve from Chapter 4 shows us that black powder ignites easily and that initial pressure does shoot up rapidly, but is also shows a smooth burning curve.

While we, again, are not ballistically concerned with a few feet per second, we are concerned with knowing what we can about the great shooting sport of muzzle-loading. Certainly, getting rid of misinformation is a goal for all of us who enjoy black powder. Knowing that barrel length did matter to some degree in terms of raw velocity was and is one more bit of useful information for the shooter.

Black Powder Standard Deviation

We were so amazed at the very low (excellent) standard deviation from the mean velocity in our shooting program that we halted all tests for a 10-day period and called upon the advice of other ballistics students and experts. In fact, we had a few tests run by our peers located in various parts of the country to verify or refute our own findings. In fact, the test results from our constituents proved to be "right on the money" as compared with our own run.

We were still surprised at the low standard deviations, but our two machines continued to show these excellent results, as did the machines of similar sophistication owned by other testers. In the main, our standard deviations fell into a general realm which matched over-the-counter factory ammo *at worst*, but which was usually in the same numerical area as our best custom handloads with modern ammo. A large number of our loads went into a classification which we thought virtually out of the question prior to testing.

Let's face it—there are many variables in a black powder load. The powder is bulk-loaded. The patches are not always identical in nature. The lube can vary. Powders vary. Ignition is not always the same. However, in using our carefully concocted loads, these variables did not interfere with reliability. Many times we had standard deviation figures of 5 or 6! These were not flukes. They occurred time and again. And they happened for other shooters, *provided* that the shooters followed a method of using uniform components in a uniform manner.

In our loads, we stayed with top grade patch material, for example. We used Ox-Yoke Precision Blue-Striped pillow ticking and the best pure Irish linen money could buy.

We lubed as closely to the same as possible each time. Our powder was from GOEX, Inc., fresh (though that seemed not to matter much, as our older GOEX powder was also excellent). We did find that when our Pyrodex "cured," it was more powerful. But our Pyrodex loads were extremely uniform and produced equally excellent low standard deviation figures.

Below, just for the reader's interest, we have presented two 10-shot strings as a sample of standard deviation in 22 Long Rifle high velocity (not match grade) ammunition. Remember, we felt that anything in the range of 5 or 6 was a miracle when we started our testing. Later on, we called these standard deviation figures "excellent," but dropped the idea of their being impossible. In the range of 20 standard deviation, we felt that this was an expected and possible figure. Up to 29 we called "good;" above 29, we re-tested the load.

22 Long Rifle Data (10-shot string)

STRING A				
Lowest Velocity	Highest Velocity	Extreme Spread	Average	Standard Deviation
1161	1249	88	1205	28
STRING B				
1162	1234	72	1207	21

For our reader's interest, here is a run with the Ozark Mountain Arms Muskrat rifle. We have, of course, selected this run because of the superbly low standard deviations, and we did not always achieve this level with all loads, primarily because the constants could not always be held in check to such a high level. However, we feel the following data is entertaining at the very least.

Muskrat (caliber .40) Rifle Data
5-shot strings, .395" round ball, Lyman cast

Charge	Lowest Velocity	Highest Velocity	Extreme Spread	Average	Standard Deviation
20 FFFg	1290	1298	8	1294	4
30 FFFg	1574	1590	16	1584	8
40 FFFg	1805	1826	21	1813	11
50 FFFg	1989	1998	9	1993	6

We felt that cleaning between shots was helpful in obtaining such a high degree of consistency. At this point in time, we believe that it is wise to clean between shots when a shooter is trying for a fine group. However, we do not mean a hot water cleanup. We found that a few swipes with a saturated patch followed by a mopping with a dry patch was sufficient to give us the level of standard deviation from the mean (or the average velocity) as seen above.

In some test runs, we purposely prepared loads carelessly, slopping on the lube, with mismatched patches, and inconsistent cleaning methods. Even when we kept the pressure on the loading rod fairly uniform, the standard deviation fell off with these sloppy loads. And when we were sloppy, plus putting inconsistent pressure upon the loading rod, the spread from shot-to-shot velocity fell off badly. This is our belief: **"Consistency of components and loading methods in black powder shooting translates into reliable loads and loading information."**

INDEX TO BLACK POWDER LOADING DATA

Loading Data

MUZZLE-LOADING RIFLES

INTRODUCTION

THE MAJOR GOAL of this section is the same as the others in this book—*reliable safe* loads. By reliable, we mean, of course, optimum hunting loads, along with low level, accurate target loads. Hopefully, the shooter will take a long look at those lower end offerings. For example, take a look at the load data for the 36-caliber Muskrat rifle from Ozark Mountain Arms. The hottest loads listed here are 40 grains of FFFg GOI or 50 grains of FFg GOI. The first load gives the .350" lead pill a starting velocity of 2,015 fps while the second provides a starting velocity of 1,975 fps.

Even though the wild turkey hunter may feel a need for this much punch, most of the shooting done with a 36-caliber is neatly accomplished with only 20 to 30 grains of FFFg. Therefore, the shooter must look at the loading data with several things in mind: First, what am I trying to do with this rifle, handgun or shotgun? Do I need true flatness of trajectory? Do I need as much energy as I can safely obtain? If the answer is yes, then the optimum safe load is called for. But if the goal is to enjoy an afternoon of informal paper punching, the answer is to look into the low-end loads.

The second criterion is a rather obvious one—*accuracy.* If the rifle won't shoot well with the "hotter" loads, then the answer is to cut back and look for a load which is accurate. All too often, I'm afraid, the shooter feels that the lowest possible charge must always deliver the best accuracy. That simply is not true. It is not the situation with many tested rifles. However, I much prefer the lowest *accurate* charge in a rifle when everyday shooting is the goal. I wish I could list an accurate load for every rifle and sidearm in this book; however, here is where the individual shooter takes over. It's up to him to head for the bench, get a solid rest, and try out his rifle with his own load chain, provided he is within the confines of safety.

Safety

I am well aware that this topic seems to be overstressed. It seems to be overstressed even though black powder is a terrifically safe shooting fuel and the accidents are few. But, there are numerous instances of misloaded arms which did, for reasons we do not know, go to Hades in a handbasket. As a result I feel that the true *fun* of black powder shooting rests within the confines of *safety.*

Furthermore, as we hope our loads will show, a suitable velocity is often reached with rather mild charges of powder. It is a false notion that black powder firearms require huge doses of black powder just to get a tiny bit of velocity. Using our little 36-caliber rifle as an example one more time, the 20-grain charge at 1,477 fps will do all the cottontail harvesting ever required of a rifle, either new-style or old-style for that matter. A 22 Long Rifle round fires a 22-caliber 40-grain bullet at something like 1250-1300 fps, depending upon rifle, brand of ammo and many other factors.

The .350" lead ball from the above rifle weighs 65 grains, and even though the ball slows down greatly at 50 or 75 yards, most of our small game hunting is at very close range and a starting velocity of 1400 to 1500 fps with a 65-grain ball is all we need. So, though criticism is bound to fall on me, I recommend that the shooter remain safety-conscious by selecting accuracy as his prime goal. In other words, if accurate, always use the lower end loads for the small game and target work.

Standard Deviations

All loads listed here met my own requirements for a standard deviation from the mean which showed reliability. Remember, we can have precision without accuracy, and it is possible for a load to be wrong time after time in its readings. But when a shooter is consistently using standard loads to verify the data that he is receiving, the chances of a 50-caliber rifle firing a .490" ball at 2500 fps with 80 grains of FFg being accepted as the truth are nil. Example: The shooter knows from his standard body of data that 50-caliber rifles using FFg black powder in 80-grain charges do not drive .490" round balls at 2500 fps, and he will immediately search out the reason for such an erroneous figure.

In short, our loads were put to the test in two ways: First, they had to meet my own standard deviation requirements or they were tossed out and retested with new load chains. This did happen, by the way, in the course of gathering the data. And I did have as much as 150 to even 200 fps difference in some rifles by going to different patch/ball/lube combinations. Often, I found that the standard loads, however, held up to scrutiny. When using good patching material that provided a tight fit between ball and bore, and a ball of proper diameter, with standard lubes and standard black powder, I got "standard" and reliable velocities, considering altitude, atmospheric temperature and other variables.

Second, we took the rifle out on two occasions. Thus we could see immediately if there was disparagement between the first and second sets of chronographed results. Actually, there was not a single time that the results were spread far apart. In fact, it was more amazing to see how close the results were. I contacted a friend who is a professional ballistician, and he was amazed at the small (excellent) standard deviations resulting from tossing black powder charges. In fact, quite often the Sd was a tiny 5 or 7, and on a few occasions, it was lower yet.

Calibers

We all have seen the charts put out by loading companies and other sources which give general indications of what shot size or calibers to use on what game. This is always a very tenuous proposition, of course. One man's squirrel rifle is another man's venison-getter. But with the risks in mind, we'll try to give the reader a general view of calibers as we see them for black powder shooting. Mainly, we'll talk hunting because *all* the calibers are fine for target work, assuming the rifle is accurate. Even a 58-caliber rifle makes a good target rifle, stable as a rock, as long as the shooter can handle it well. So, our inclinations are toward hunting considerations. I'm sure there are a number of hunters who will disagree with me. I have a friend who hunts geese with 7½ shot. He's successful. But I don't think that makes 7½ shot ideal for geese.

32-Caliber

This little gem fires a .310" or .315" ball of about 45 or 47 grains of weight respectively. It's dandy for small game, and it will take a wild turkey to task at the higher-end loadings. Shooting across a windy draw, even at only 75 yards will, however, often cause this little ball to blow off course, but it is still a fine choice for the small game opportunity. Target shooters might want a little more missile stability, i.e., larger caliber and bullet mass.

36-Caliber

A 36-caliber rifle usually shoots a .350" ball that weighs 65 grains. It is a bit more stable in terms of sensitivity to the wind, but all the small calibers are wind-shy. Round balls, even of larger caliber, often drift quite a bit in the wind. The 36 is mainly a small game number; however, I have taken many a wild turkey with the 36 with no problem at all.

38-Caliber

Although we usually seize upon the 38-caliber as the all-round "average" for our eastern seaboard adventurers who settled America with the longrifle, this caliber is not widely seen today. The Plainsman rifle, however, is 38-caliber, and this longarm uses the standard swaged .375" round ball, which weighs in at about 80 grains.

The .375" ball will certainly take small game neatly, and it is sufficient for wild turkey without a doubt, and in the hands of a good shot, the 38 will harvest game up to javelina size. The 38 will also shoot nicely at the rendezvous or other target meet. It's a viable caliber, in spite of the fact that it is not currently offered in many firearms. Balls and bullets in 38-caliber are available over the counter due to the popularity of this caliber in handguns.

40-Caliber

Not offered in the *average* over-the-counter rifle, this caliber still maintains high popularity with many shooters. An example would be the accurate Muskrat rifle from Ozark Mountain Arms. The .395" ball weighs about 93 grains. I have friends who hunt deer and antelope successfully with the 40, and we can't even guess at the number of medium-sized game animals that ended up in the pots of the early pioneers who used 38- or 40-caliber firearms.

In the hands of a cool shot who will place his ball just so, there is no doubt that a 40-caliber rifle will take deer and similar game. (In the hands of a hasty shot, no firearm, modern or early-style, will do the job.) For small game, the 40 is quite useful. As the reader can see from our data, light loads are available for 40-caliber rifles. In all truth, even the little 32 and 36 are devastating to tender small game with body shots. So, the 40 is actually quite a useful caliber, at home in the game fields, and very much at home at the target range where recoil is light and the ball is fairly stable.

45-Caliber

I like to think of the 45 as the starting point for deer-sized caliber rifles. I say this in hopes that crack shots with the 40s will allow me to do this. A 45 ball weighs 128 grains in the .440" size and about 133 grains in the .445" size. Lots of deer have been brought to bag with these pills. The small game hunter using head shots is also going to experience success with the 45 and, if he wants to use a conical, several weights are available. Our tests show results using a 220-grain Maxi. Considering that a 220-grain projectile is pretty hefty, the 45-caliber rifle is not underpowered for deer.

50-Caliber

I think of the 50 as a "separation point" in that my son, Bill Fadala, uses one successfully on elk, and I have several friends who have collected bison and other large game with 50-caliber rifles firing the round ball. I took a big bear with a 50-caliber Hurricane from Navy Arms using a 367-grain Maxi, and I have dropped several deer and antelope with the same caliber of rifle firing the 177-grain, .490" round ball.

The hunter is free to choose his own projectile style for the 50 (both ball and bullet are available), and he should select his projectile based upon the accuracy and stability of the missile from his personal rifle. As far as "killing power" is concerned, a .490" ball is quite good, and I am speaking from field experience, not a whim, guess or mathematical computation. For me, I prefer a rifle larger than 50-caliber for elk. That is my opinion.

53-Caliber

The 53 is found today in the Allen Fire Arms Santa Fe Hawken rifle, a very accurate replica of an original plains rifle. The reason for the existence of the 53-caliber falls into two different spheres: First, the 53-caliber is to the western plains rifle what the 38-caliber was to the eastern longarm; both are "averages" based upon the experiences of gun collectors. Just as a 38 is considered the "average" bore size for the longarm of the East, the 53 is considered the "average" bore size of the plains rifle.

Second, the original rifle used in creating the Santa Fe Hawken was of 53-caliber, so in copying other details, the manufacturers also copied the bore size.

The 53, using the Lyman .520" mould, will toss a sphere that goes about 211 grains in weight. It is enough larger than the .490" (177-grain) or .495" (182-grain) 50-caliber balls to make it a viable increase in bore size. I would consider it adequate for elk with well-placed shots only. I consider no rifle good for elk with poorly placed shots, however, with the possible exception of super large caliber high velocity numbers of modern times.

54-Caliber

The 54 is a great favorite of many black powder riflemen. It is large enough for elk in the hands of a careful shot. It is not too large for deer. The .530" ball will weigh about 224 grains, sometimes 225 depending on mould. The .535" will go about 230 grains. At 1900+ fps from the muzzle, the 54 is strong. I have, with witnesses to verify it, driven a .530" ball through the chest of a bull bison from side-to-side.

In the Maxi numbers, a weight of 400 to 430 grains is not hard to locate. In one special custom rifle with a barrel width across the flats of 1¼ inches, the 400-grain Maxi attained a velocity of about 1700 fps, which gave it about 2,568 foot-pounds of muzzle energy. In either round ball or conical configuration the 54 is a winner.

58-Calibers

The 58 and its big brothers are very useful hunting numbers, and these calibers come in *big* round balls of the 280-grain class and even heftier Maxis and Minies running into the 600-grain domain. Custom moulds can produce even larger conicals for the 58 in terms of mass weight. There is not much which needs to be said about the 58 and larger calibers. *They are big!* And that's about it. Of course, an accurate 58 is a fine target rifle if a fellow does not mind the recoil. However, the 58 is mainly for hunting big game.

The reader can see from the data that follows the vast range of ballistic variation possible among the many black powder calibers. And he can see something else, too. The muzzleloader can be turned into a fire-breathing dragon or purring pussycat by switching from a big charge to a small charge of powder. Of course, the modern handloader has the same option in his cartridges. But the muzzleloader has the capacity to change and adapt to the conditions at any given time. I think the shooter should take advantage of this fact. He should pay as much attention to those useful low end loads as he pays to the higher end optimum hunting loads.

ALLEN
Santa Fe Hawken (53-cal.)

Caliber: 53
Barrel Length: 32"
Barrel Dim: 1" across flats
Rate of Twist: 1:66"
Depth of Groove: .010"—.012"

Powder: GOI, Pyrodex (RS)
Patch: Ox-Yoke Wonder .015"/
Ox-Yoke Precision
Blue-Striped .015"*
Ignition: CCI No. 11
Lube: Wonder patch self-lubed;
Precision patch with Hoppes
No. 9 Plus
Powd. Meas.: Tresco 200
Powd. Temp.: 70° F.

LOAD DATA

Projectile/.520" Weight/211-gr. Type/Lyman round ball Mould/No. 520**

Powder Charge (Volume)	Powder Charge (Approx. gr. wt.)	Muzzle Velocity FPS.	Muzzle Energy Ft. Lbs.	Velocity 100 yds.	Energy 100 yds.
40 FFFg	41.5	1322	819	886	368
60 FFFg	61.4	1578	1167	1025	492
50 FFg	50.2	1291	781	865	351
70 FFg	70.1	1396	913	977	447
90 FFg	90.0	1529	1096	993	462
110 FFg*	109.7	1873	1644	1123	591
Pyrodex (RS)					
100 RS	72.5	1683	1327	889	370
110 RS	79.3	1712	1374	1061	528

▶ **110 FFg or 110 RS maximum recommended load**

* This load shot with .015" Ox-Yoke Blue-Striped patch.

** A slight change in bore diameter was recently made on this rifle. Older Santa Fe Hawkens will produce best accuracy with a .520" ball while current rifles will (may) do better with a .526" ball (Lyman mould Nos. 520 and 526). Have your bore slugged to determine exact dimension.

COMMENTS

As for an *optimum hunting load,* the 110 volume charge of FFg with its muzzle velocity of 1,873 fps is impressive and should serve well for big game within black powder ranges. Naturally, the owner of the Santa Fe will want to start with the 40 FFFg charge and see how it groups for target work. Remember, such a load is also useful for small game hunting if ball placement is precise.

See the caution that precedes this section. Note: Maximum load listed in bold should be used with caution.

ARMSPORT

Tryon Trailblazer (54-cal.)

Caliber: 54
Barrel Length: 32"
Barrel Dim: 1" across flats
Rate of Twist: 1:63"
Depth of Groove: .015"

Powder: GOI, Pyrodex (RS)
Patch: .010" Ox-Yoke Wonder
Ignition: CCI No. 11
Lube: Self-lubed
Powd. Meas.: Tresco 200
Powd. Temp.: 75° F.

LOAD DATA

Projectile/.530" Weight/225-gr. Type/Denver Bullet Co. round ball

Powder Charge (Volume)	Powder Charge (Approx. gr. wt.)	Muzzle Velocity FPS.	Muzzle Energy Ft. Lbs.	Velocity 100 yds.	Energy 100 yds.
40 FFFg	41.5	1207	728	845	357
60 FFFg	61.4	1470	1080	926	429
50 FFg	50.2	1181	697	827	342
70 FFg	70.1	1414	999	919	422
90 FFg	90.0	1562	1219	984	484
100 FFg	99.7	1649	1359	1022	522
120 FFg	119.6	1815	1646	1071	573
Pyrodex (RS) 130 RS	94.0	1663	1382	978	478

▶ **120 FFg or 130 RS maximum recommended load**

COMMENTS

While there is not too much difference in remaining energy at 100 yards between the 100 FFg load the 120 FFg load, there are sufficient power differences at closer ranges to allow us the 120 FFg choice as our *optimum load* and maximum big game load. We might call the 90 FFg load an optimum, too, as in most cases, especially at woods ranges, that charge is ample for deer hunting. Obviously, the little 40 FFFg charge is sufficient for target work, but the shooter will have to try his own personal rifle at the bench with loads from 40 to 60 FFFg to find the best accuracy.

Although this rifle will handle a Minie or Maxi, none was used, as we felt the 1:63 twist was best suited to the round ball.

See the caution that precedes this section. Note: Maximum load listed in bold should be used with caution.

ARMSPORT

Hawkentucky No. 5146 (50-cal.)

Caliber: 50

Barrel Length: 28″

Barrel Dim: 13⁄16″ across flats

Rate of Twist: 1:48″

Depth of Groove: .003″—.005″

Powder: GOI

Patch: .015″ Ox-Yoke Precision Blue-Striped

Ignition: CCI No. 11

Lube: RIG

Powd. Meas.: Uncle Mike 120

Powd. Temp.: 75° F.

LOAD DATA

Projectile/.490″ Weight/177-gr. Type/Speer round ball

Powder Charge (Volume)	Powder Charge (Approx. gr. wt.)	Muzzle Velocity FPS.	Muzzle Energy Ft. Lbs.	Velocity 100 yds.	Energy 100 yds.
40 FFFg	41.2	1396	766	879	304
50 FFFg	51.7	1509	895	920	333
50 FFg	49.5	1330	695	865	294
60 FFg	59.5	1408	779	887	309
70 FFg	70.1	1498	882	914	328

▶ **70 FFg maximum recommended load**

COMMENTS

In this instance, our maximum load is also our *optimum load* for close-range deer hunting with this lightweight rifle—70 volume FFg and the 177-grain .490″ Speer projectile.

ARMSPORT

Hawken 5102-V (36-cal.)

Caliber: 36

Barrel Length: 28″

Barrel Dim: 1″ across flats

Rate of Twist: 1:48″

Depth of Groove: .003″—.005″

Powder: GOI, Pyrodex (RS)

Patch: .015″ Ox-Yoke Precision Blue-Striped

Ignition: CCI No. 11

Lube: Whale oil

Powd. Meas.: Uncle Mike 120

Powd. Temp.: 70° F.

LOAD DATA

Projectile/.350″ Weight/65-grs. Type/Speer round ball

Powder Charge (Volume)	Powder Charge (Approx. gr. wt.)	Muzzle Velocity FPS.	Muzzle Energy Ft. Lbs.	Velocity 100 yds.	Energy 100 yds.
20 FFFg	20.7	1520	334	821	97
30 FFFg	30.9	1827	482	895	116
40 FFFg	41.2	2087	629	981	139
Pyrodex (RS) 50 RS	36.1	1897	520	967	135

▶ **40 FFFg or 50 RS maximum recommended load**

COMMENTS

The *optimum load* is 30 FFFg. The accuracy is excellent. For wild turkey hunting, however, I would suggest going to the 40 FFFg charge. If you are unable to locate any sperm whale oil, J&A Old Slickum may be used as a substitute.

See the caution that precedes this section. Note: Maximum load listed in bold should be used with caution.

Jonathan Browning Mtn. Rifle (54-cal.)

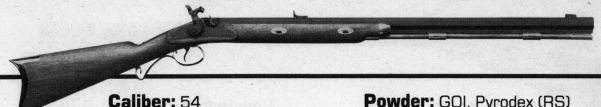

Caliber: 54
Barrel Length: 30"
Barrel Dim: 1" across flats
Rate of Twist: 1:66"
Depth of Groove: .012"—.014"

Powder: GOI, Pyrodex (RS)
Patch: .015" Ox-Yoke Precision Blue-Striped
Ignition: CCI No. 11
Lube: Young Country No. 103
Powd. Meas.: Tresco 200
Powd. Temp.: 70° F.

LOAD DATA

Projectile/.530" Weight/225-gr.* Type/Denver Bullet Co. round ball

Powder Charge (Volume)	Powder Charge (Approx. gr. wt.)	Muzzle Velocity FPS.	Muzzle Energy Ft. Lbs.	Velocity 100 yds.	Energy 100 yds.
40 FFFg	41.5	1221	745	842	354
50 FFFg	51.6	1391	967	899	404
50 FFg	50.2	1276	814	867	376
70 FFg	70.1	1496	1118	942	443
90 FFg	90.0	1644	1351	993	493
120 FFg	119.6	1845	1701	1089	593
130 FFg	129.6	1909	1821	1126	634
140 FFg	139.5	1965	1930	1159	671
150 FFg	149.6	1970	1939	1162	675
Pyrodex (RS) 150 RS	108.0	1940	1881	1145	655

▶ **150 FFg or 150 RS maximum recommended load**

* Round ball miked slightly oversize.

COMMENTS

The Laws of Diminishing Returns showed up in this strongly built rifle. Browning allows as much as 150 grains volume FFg or FFFg in this firearm with a .530" round ball. However, we feel we peaked out at 130 grains volume. Of course, velocity did increase with added powder beyond the 130 FFg range. However, the increase, we felt, was not commensurate with the added charge. We did not use the 150 FFFg charge in our tests, feeling that 130 FFg gave excellent hunting ballistics—it's the *optimum load*. Also note that the little FFFg charges in this rifle are useful for small game and informal work, as well as target shooting. An FFg charge of 90 volume was quite accurate for us.

See the caution that precedes this section. Note: Maximum load listed in bold should be used with caution.

BROWNING
Jonathan Browning Mtn. Rifle (50-cal.)

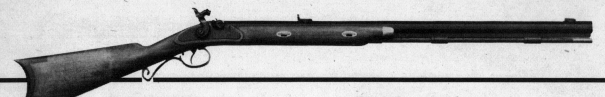

Caliber: 50

Barrel Length: 30″
Barrel Dim: 1″ across flats

Rate of Twist: 1:62″

Depth of Groove: .012″—.014″

Powder: GOI, Pyrodex (RS)

Patch: .015″ Ox-Yoke Precision Blue-Striped

Ignition: CCI No. 11

Lube: Young Country No. 103

Powd. Meas.: Tresco 200

Powd. Temp.: 70° F.

LOAD DATA

Projectile/.490″ Weight/177-gr. Type/Speer round ball

Powder Charge (Volume)	Powder Charge (Approx. gr. wt.)	Muzzle Velocity FPS.	Muzzle Energy Ft. Lbs.	Velocity 100 yds.	Energy 100 yds.
40 FFFg	41.5	1362	729	858	289
50 FFFg	51.6	1495	879	912	327
50 FFg	50.2	1387	756	874	300
70 FFg	70.1	1602	1009	961	363
90 FFg	90.0	1759	1216	1020	409
120 FFg	119.6	1974	1532	1113	487
Pyrodex (RS) 120 RS	87.5	1929	1463	1090	467

▶ **120 FFg or 120 RS maximum recommended load**

COMMENTS

We obtained useful accuracy with the 120 FFg load and can recommend that charge as the *optimum load* for hunting. It is flat-shooting and at close range would cleanly harvest deer-sized game and perhaps larger game as well in the hands of a good shot. We noted an increased performance with Pyrodex in this rifle. The particular batch of Pyrodex used in our tests was somewhat less dense than usual, and the moisture content slightly higher than usual. The fuel could probably be used in larger volumes to make up for this situation; however, we elected to stay within or near the *recommended volumetric charges*, even with Pyrodex. We surmised that the Pyrodex lot may have slightly dried by the time we tested this rifle (toward the end of the data gathering), giving the more usual power found in this fuel.

See the caution that precedes this section. Note: Maximum load listed in bold should be used with caution.

BROWNING

Jonathan Browning Mtn. Rifle (45-cal.)

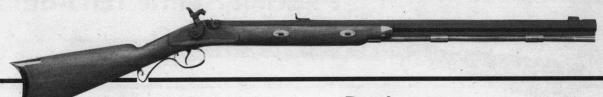

Caliber: 45

Barrel Length: 30″

Barrel Dim: 1″ across flats

Rate of Twist: 1:56″

Depth of Groove: .012″—.014″

Powder: GOI, Pyrodex (RS)

Patch: .015″ Ox-Yoke Precision Blue-Striped

Ignition: CCI No. 11

Lube: RIG

Powd. Meas.: Tresco 200

Powd. Temp.: 70° F.

LOAD DATA

Projectile/.445″ Weight/133-gr. Type/Denver Bullet Co. round ball

Powder Charge (Volume)	Powder Charge (Approx. gr. wt.)	Muzzle Velocity FPS.	Muzzle Energy Ft. Lbs.	Velocity 100 yds.	Energy 100 yds.
40 FFFg	41.5	1608	764	917	248
50 FFFg	51.6	1727	881	967	276
50 FFg	50.2	1571	729	895	237
70 FFg	70.1	1828	987	1005	298
90 FFg	90.0	2025	1211	1069	338
Pyrodex (RS) 90 RS	66.7	1902	1069	1027	312

▶ **90 FFg or 90 RS maximum recommended load**

COMMENTS   The most accurate load in our gun was 50 FFFg; however, we would opt for 90 FFg as *optimum load* for hunting.

See the caution that precedes this section. Note: Maximum load listed in bold should be used with caution.

C.V.A.

Frontier Rifle (50-cal.)

Caliber: 50

Barrel Length: 28″

Barrel Dim: ¹⁵⁄₁₆″ across flats

Rate of Twist: 1:66″

Depth of Groove: .010″

Powder: GOI, Pyrodex (RS)

Patch: .015″ Ox-Yoke Precision Blue-Striped

Ignition: CCI No. 11

Lube: Young Country No. 103

Powd. Meas.: Tresco 200

Powd. Temp.: 78° F.

LOAD DATA

Projectile/.490″ Weight/177-gr. Type/Speer round ball

Powder Charge (Volume)	Powder Charge (Approx. gr. wt.)	Muzzle Velocity FPS.	Muzzle Energy Ft. Lbs.	Velocity 100 yds.	Energy 100 yds.
40 FFFg	41.5	1366	734	874	300
50 FFFg	51.6	1548	942	937	345
50 FFg	50.2	1348	714	816	262
60 FFg	60.2	1479	860	909	325
70 FFg	70.1	1588	991	954	358
80 FFg	80.1	1700	1136	997	391
90 FFg	90.0	1785	1253	1035	421
Pyrodex (RS) 90 RS	66.7	1735	1183	1015	405

▶ **90 FFg or 90 RS maximum recommended load**

COMMENTS

We found the slight variations among different rifles of the same caliber interesting. No two rifles shot with the same velocity readings despite being the same caliber. We also found that in some rifles, a specific charge of powder gained a reasonable velocity, while more or less powder was not as good. In this rifle, 80 FFg seemed to do quite well, and we'd call that one our *optimum* hunting *load* for up to deer-sized game.

See the caution that precedes this section. Note: Maximum load listed in bold should be used with caution.

Hawken Rifle (50-cal.)

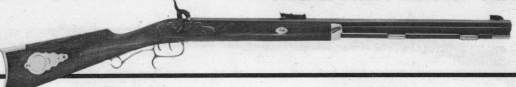

Caliber: 50

Barrel Length: 28″

Barrel Dim: 1″ across flats

Rate of Twist: 1:66″

Depth of Groove: .010″

Powder: GOI, Pyrodex (RS)

Patch: .015″ Ox-Yoke precision Blue-Striped

Ignition: CCI No. 11

Lube: Young Country No. 103

Powd. Meas.: Tresco 200

Powd. Temp.: 78° F.

LOAD DATA

Projectile/.490″ Weight/177-gr. Type/Hornady round ball

Powder Charge (Volume)	Powder Charge (Approx. gr. wt.)	Muzzle Velocity FPS.	Muzzle Energy Ft. Lbs.	Velocity 100 yds.	Energy 100 yds.
40 FFFg	41.5	1371	739	758	226
50 FFFg	51.6	1569	968	883	307
50 FFg	50.2	1351	718	838	276
60 FFg	60.2	1481	862	873	300
70 FFg	70.1	1592	996	923	335
80 FFg	80.1	1705	1143	955	359
90 FFg	90.0	1793	1264	986	382
Pyrodex (RS) 90 RS	66.7	1744	1196	968	368

▶ **90 FFg or 90 RS maximum recommended load**

COMMENTS

The prescribed load of 90 FFg for the 177-grain round ball is also the charge we recommend as an *optimum load* for hunting where shots will exceed 50 yards. For those who hunt in very tight brush or forest, where shots seldom exceed 50 yards, the 50 FFFg load might be considered. Remember, we recommend FFg in most rifles of 45-caliber or larger and for heavy hunting charges. However, FFFg is also useful for the lower-end loads in the same rifles.

See the caution that precedes this section. Note: Maximum load listed in bold should be used with caution.

C.V.A.

Kentucky Rifle (45-cal.)

Caliber: 45

Barrel Length: 33½"

Barrel Dim: ⅞" across flats

Rate of Twist: 1:66"

Depth of Groove: .010"

Powder: GOI

Patch: .015" Ox-Yoke Precision Blue-Striped

Ignition: FFFFg pan powder

Lube: Young Country No. 103

Powd. Meas.: Tresco 200

Powd. Temp.: 79° F.

LOAD DATA

Projectile/.440" Weight/128-gr. Type/Speer round ball

Powder Charge (Volume)	Powder Charge (Approx. gr. wt.)	Muzzle Velocity FPS.	Muzzle Energy Ft. Lbs.	Velocity 100 yds.	Energy 100 yds.
40 FFFg	41.5	1561	693	882	221
50 FFFg	51.6	1767	888	981	274
50 FFg	50.2	1577	707	908	234
60 FFg	60.2	1754	875	973	269
70 FFg	70.1	1803	924	992	280
75 FFg	75.1	1856	979	1012	291

▶ **75 FFg maximum recommended load**

COMMENTS The rifle shot well with the 75 FFg charge, and we'd consider that load an *optimum load* for our deer hunting number. However, we also found that 50 FFFg was a useful load in timber or brush. With close shots the rule (50 yards or less), this load would be a winner.

See the caution that precedes this section. Note: Maximum load listed in bold should be used with caution.

Brown Bess Musket (74-cal.)

Caliber: 74

Barrel Length: 41¾"

Rate of Twist: Smoothbore

Powder: GOI

Patch: .015" Ox-Yoke Precision Blue-Striped with one over-powder wad, one felt wad and one over ball wad

Ignition: FFFFg pan powder

Lube: RIG

Powd. Meas.: Tresco 200

Powd. Temp.: 60° F.

LOAD DATA

Projectile/.690" Weight/494-gr. Type/Denver Bullet Co. round ball

Powder Charge (Volume)	Powder Charge (Approx. gr. wt.)	Muzzle Velocity FPS.	Muzzle Energy Ft. Lbs.	Velocity 100 yds.	Energy 100 yds.
80 Fg	79.9	809	718	680	507

▶ **80 Fg maximum recommended load***

* Dixie Gun Works has a standing policy against recommending loads for their rifles. The charges are left up to the discretion of the shooter. Charges were determined by the author.

COMMENTS

Only one load was chronographed for the big Brown Bess 74. Because this load worked quite well in terms of accuracy as well as recoil, it's our *optimum load*. The loading procedure included a card wad compressed upon the powder charge, followed by a single felt wad well soaked in liquified RIG. The .690" ball was then patched with a .015" Ox-Yoke Precision patch; however, with other smoothbores when the ball fitted well to the bore, no patch was used. We found no greater accuracy with or without a patch. A patch, of course, might be useful to totally prevent leading, should there be any leading at such very low velocities. Over the ball, we placed a single thin wad such as normally used as an overshot wad, just to insure that the ball remained on the powder charge.

See the caution that precedes this section. Note: Maximum load listed in bold should be used with caution.

Zouave Carbine (58-cal.)

Caliber: 58

Barrel Length: 26"

Barrel Dim: 1 1/8" breech, 7/8" muzzle

Rate of Twist: 1:56"

Depth of Groove: .006"

Powder: GOI, Pyrodex (RS)

Patch: None

Ignition: Navy Arms Musket Cap

Lube: RIG

Powd. Meas.: Tresco 200

Powd. Temp.: 70° F.

LOAD DATA

Projectile/.575" Weight/460-gr. Type/Lyman Minie Mould/No. 575 213-OS

Powder Charge (Volume)	Powder Charge (Approx. gr. wt.)	Muzzle Velocity FPS.	Muzzle Energy Ft. Lbs.	Velocity 100 yds.	Energy 100 yds.
50 FFg	50.2	799	652	711	516
70 FFg	70.1	1026	1152	882	795
90 FFg	90.0	1154	1361	935	893
100 Fg	99.8	1088	1209	903	833
Pyrodex (RS)					
70 RS	51.8	826	697	735	552
100 RS	72.5	1064	1157	883	797

▶ **90 FFg or 100 RS maximum recommended load***

* Dixie Gun Works has a standing policy against recommending loads for their rifles. The charges are left up to the discretion of the shooter. Charges were determined by the author.

COMMENTS

The *optimum load* settled upon here was 70 FFg. As the velocity seemed rather on the high side for the powder charge, considering the projectile mass, this load was triple-tested before publication, and it was also verified by an independent source for further convincing. The 460-grain Minie at a bit over 1000 fps is certainly ample for big game at close range, and the 70 FFg charge was milder in recoil than the 90 FFg charge. A good look at the 100 Fg charge shows that this larger granulation would also be a wise choice when Fg is available to the shooter. As we know, Fg gives less pressure than FFg.

See the caution that precedes this section. Note: Maximum load listed in bold should be used with caution.

Tennessee Squirrel Rifle (32-cal.)

Caliber: 32

Barrel Length: 41½"

Barrel Dim: 13/16" across flats

Rate of Twist: 1:56"

Depth of Groove: .008"

Powder: GOI

Patch: .015" Ox-Yoke Precision Blue-Striped

Ignition: CCI No. 11

Lube: J&A Old Slickum

Powd. Meas.: Uncle Mike 120

Powd. Temp.: 68° F.

LOAD DATA

Projectile/.310" Weight/48-gr. Type/Hornady round ball

Powder Charge (Volume)	Powder Charge (Approx. gr. wt.)	Muzzle Velocity FPS.	Muzzle Energy Ft. Lbs.	Velocity 100 yds.	Energy 100 yds.
10 FFFg	10.5	1263	170	720	55
20 FFFg	20.7	1776	336	852	77
25 FFFg*	25.8	1941	402	893	85
30 FFFg	30.9	2081	462	936	93

▶ **30 FFFg maximum recommended load****

* At 25 volume FFFg, the Uncle Mike 120 measure was set between the 20 and 30 setting, as there is no mark at that point.

** Dixie Gun Works has a standing policy against recommending loads for their rifles. The charges are left up to the discretion of the shooter. Charges were determined by the author.

COMMENTS

The 20 FFFg charge was ample for the intended use of the rifle—squirrel, rabbit, other small game, and plinking, with occasional calm-day target work. However, the 25 FFFg charge was also accurate and acceptable. The 30FFFg charge is shown for its informational value; however, it has no practical increase in trajectory over the 25 FFFg charge. The 30 FFFg charge is *not* recommended. Our *optimum load* is 20 to 25 FFFg. The author's 22-grain spout for the CVA flask also provided an accurate load, in fact. At 20 to 25 FFFg, noise was modest, and there was not sufficient recoil to raise the muzzle of the Dixie Squirrel Rifle.

See the caution that precedes this section. Note: Maximum load listed in bold should be used with caution.

GARRETT

Replica Purdey Rifle (54-cal.)

Caliber: 54

Barrel Length: 27"

Barrel Dim: 1" across flats

Rate of Twist: 1:66"

Depth of Groove: .008"

Powder: GOI

Patch: .020+" (see comments)

Ignition: CCI No. 11

Lube: Whale oil

Powd. Meas.: Tresco 200

Powd. Temp.: 61° F.

LOAD DATA

Projectile/.526" Weight/219-gr. Type/Lyman round ball Mould/No. 526

Powder Charge (Volume)	Powder Charge (Approx. gr. wt.)	Muzzle Velocity FPS.	Muzzle Energy Ft. Lbs.	Velocity 100 yds.	Energy 100 yds.
50 FFFg	50.2	1317	844	872	370
70 FFg	70.1	1367	909	902	396
90 FFg	90.0	1532	1142	962	450
110 FFg	109.7	1649	1323	998	484

▶ **110 FFg maximum recommended load**

COMMENTS

This English-style rifle was tested with the .526" ball and a heavy .020+" patching material backed by a single ¹⁄₁₆" thick cork wad cut to bore size and placed on top of the powder charge. The cork, incidentally, was recovered intact even with the 110 charge of FFg. And the patch was also intact, showing that the cork did its job. Accuracy with the .526" round ball and heavy material was excellent and there was no appreciable difference between the 90 and 110 charges (our *optimum load* recommendation) at the bench. Incidentally, a .535" ball with .013" Irish linen patch was also bench-tested and accuracy was equal to the above ball/patch combo. Velocity with the .535" ball and patch was very much on par with the .526" ball and patch in the 110 FFg charge, which was the only one tested. With 110 FFg and the .535" ball, velocity was 1,612 fps at the muzzle. Note: If you are unable to locate any sperm whale oil, J&A Old Slickum will serve well as a substitute.

See the caution that precedes this section. Note: Maximum load listed in bold should be used with caution.

Replica Purdey Sporting Rifle (50-cal.)

Caliber: 50

Barrel Length: 27"

Barrel Dim: 15/16" across flats

Rate of Twist: 1:48"

Depth of Groove: .008"

Powder: GOI, Pyrodex (RS)

Patch: .015" Ox-Yoke Precision Blue-Striped

Ignition: CCI No. 11

Lube: Young Country No. 103

Powd. Meas.: Tresco 200

Powd. Temp.: 77° F.

LOAD DATA

Projectile/.490" Weight/177-gr. Type/Speer round ball

Powder Charge (Volume)	Powder Charge (Approx. gr. wt.)	Muzzle Velocity FPS.	Muzzle Energy Ft. Lbs.	Velocity 100 yds.	Energy 100 yds.
40 FFFg	41.5	1381	750	877	302
50 FFFg	51.6	1541	934	932	341
50 FFg	50.2	1452	829	900	318
70 FFg	70.1	1696	1131	1009	400
90 FFg	90.1	1776	1240	1057	439
100 FFg	99.7	1873	1379	1070	450
Pyrodex (RS) 100 RS	72.5	1687	1119	1004	396

▶ **100 FFg or 100 RS maximum recommended load**

COMMENTS

The Purdey shot well with 70 FFg. In close cover, this charge with the .490" ball would be sufficient for deer. We recommend it as our *optimum load.* The shooter may wish to try over 70, but not more than 100 FFg in his own replica Purdey 50-caliber to see how his personal rifle reacts to the various charges.

See the caution that precedes this section. Note: Maximum load listed in bold should be used with caution.

GARRETT
Santfl-Schuetzen Free-Style (45-cal.)

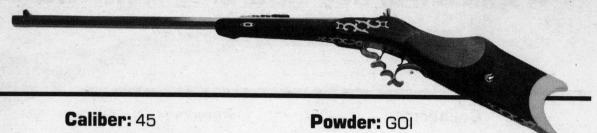

Caliber: 45

Barrel Length: 29"

Barrel Dim: 15/16" across flats

Rate of Twist: 1:47"

Depth of Groove: .005"

Powder: GOI

Patch: None

Ignition: CCI No. 11

Lube: Alox 2138F/bee's wax 50/50

Powd. Meas.: Uncle Mike 120

Powd. Temp.: 80° F.

LOAD DATA—A

Projectile/.463" Weight/185-gr. Type/R.E.A.L. bullet

Powder Charge (Volume)	Powder Charge (Approx. gr. wt.)	Muzzle Velocity FPS.	Muzzle Energy Ft. Lbs.	Velocity 100 yds.	Energy 100 yds.
30 FFg	29.6	1067	468	806	267
40 FFg	39.5	1192	584	859	303

▶ **40 FFg maximum recommended load**

COMMENTS

The Santfl is not a hunting rifle. We got good accuracy with the ball; however, we also wanted to test one "bullet," and we selected the 185-gr. R.E.A.L. for our test. Two loads were considered, both shown above. The 40 FFg charge is considered our *optimum load*.

See the caution that precedes this section. Note: Maximum load listed in bold should be used with caution.

▶ All pertinent data for Load Data—B is the same as for Load Data—A except the following

Patch: .015" Ox-Yoke Precision Blue-Striped

Lube: RIG

LOAD DATA—B

Projectile/.445" Weight/133-gr. Type/Speer round ball

Powder Charge (Volume)	Powder Charge (Approx. gr. wt.)	Muzzle Velocity FPS.	Muzzle Energy Ft. Lbs.	Velocity 100 yds.	Energy 100 yds.
40 FFg	39.5	1465	634	908	244

▶ **40 FFg maximum recommended load**

COMMENTS We decided on the 40 FFg charge as our only chronographed load because we obtained excellent results with it, not only from the bench, but also in the offhand stance, which is the forte of this rifle. The above charge is considered our *optimum load*.

See the caution that precedes this section. Note: Maximum load listed in bold should be used with caution.

127

GREEN MOUNTAIN

Barrel Drop-In (50-cal.)*

Caliber: 50

Barrel Length: 32"

Barrel Dim: 1" across flats

Rate of Twist: 1:70"

Depth of Groove: .010"—.011"

Powder: GOI

Patch: .015" Ox-Yoke Precision Blue-Striped

Ignition: CCI No. 11

Lube: RIG

Powd. Meas.: Uncle Mike 120

Powd. Temp.: 75° F.

*This barrel is a drop-in unit for Thompson/Center rifles. This unit is constructed of 1137 steel and rifled for round-ball shooting only.

LOAD DATA

Projectile/.495" Weight/182-gr. Type/Speer round ball

Powder Charge (Volume)	Powder Charge (Approx. gr. wt.)	Muzzle Velocity FPS.	Muzzle Energy Ft. Lbs.	Velocity 100 yds.	Energy 100 yds.
40 FFFg	41.2	1376	765	881	314
50 FFFg	51.7	1547	967	936	354
50 FFg	49.5	1253	635	814	268
60 FFg	59.5	1450	850	906	332
70 FFg	70.1	1515	928	924	345
80 FFg	81.0	1627	1070	976	385
90 FFg	90.2	1710	1182	1000	404
100 FFg	99.3	1809	1323	1038	436
110 FFg	110.3	1890	1444	1070	463

▶ **110 FFg maximum recommended load**

COMMENTS

In cursory accuracy tests, this barrel seemed to prefer the .495" ball over the .490" ball, using the Ox-Yoke .015" patch. The Green Mountain Barrel was made to give the T/C shooter an option. Note, it is a round-ball barrel, using a 1:70" twist with deep grooves. It is not intended for conicals. Our recommended *optimum* accuracy *load* is 80 volume FFg. For deer hunting we would go to the 110 FFg volume charge.

See the caution that precedes this section. Note: Maximum load listed in bold should be used with caution.

GREEN MOUNTAIN

Barrel Drop-In (36-cal.)*

Caliber: 36

Barrel Length: 28"

Barrel Dim: 1" across flats

Rate of Twist: 1:48"

Depth of Groove: .010"—.011"

Powder: GOI

Patch: .020" Ox-Yoke Wonder

Ignition: CCI No. 11

Lube: Self-lubed

Powd. Meas.: Uncle Mike 120

Powd. Temp.: 75° F.

*This barrel is a drop-in unit for Thompson/Center rifles. This unit is constructed of 1137 steel and rifled for round-ball shooting only.

LOAD DATA

Projectile/.350" Weight/65-gr. Type/Speer round ball

Powder Charge (Volume)	Powder Charge (Approx. gr. wt.)	Muzzle Velocity FPS.	Muzzle Energy Ft. Lbs.	Velocity 100 yds.	Energy 100 yds.
20 FFFg	20.7	1514	331	816	96
30 FFFg	30.9	1736	435	894	115
40 FFFg	41.2	2000	577	946	129
50 FFFg	51.8	2115	646	992	142

▶ **50 FFFg maximum recommended load**

COMMENTS

The 36-caliber squirrel rifle class seems to continually show plenty of small game ballistics with the 20 FFFg charge. And with a flat 2000 fps earned with the 40 FFFg charge, it is certain that this rifle requires no more than that for anything a 36-caliber rifle would be called upon to perform. I would call the 20 FFFg charge the small game choice depending upon individual rifle accuracy, and the 40 FFFg charge the wild turkey or varmint load for longer range shooting. These are our *optimum loads*.

See the caution that precedes this section. Note: Maximum load listed in bold should be used with caution.

HATFIELD

Squirrel Rifle (36-cal.)

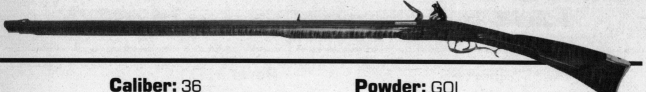

Caliber: 36

Barrel Length: 39½"

Barrel Dim: ¹³⁄₁₆" across flats

Rate of Twist: 1:40"

Depth of Groove: .010"—.012"

Powder: GOI

Patch: .017" Ox-Yoke Precision Blue-Striped

Ignition: FFFFg pan powder

Lube: J&A Old Slickum

Powd. Meas.: Uncle Mike 120

Powd. Temp.: 66° F.

LOAD DATA

Projectile/.350" Weight/65-gr. Type/Speer round ball

Powder Charge (Volume)	Powder Charge (Approx. gr. wt.)	Muzzle Velocity FPS.	Muzzle Energy Ft. Lbs.	Velocity 100 yds.	Energy 100 yds.
20 FFFg	20.7	1471	312	794	91
25 FFFg	25.8	1653	394	851	105
30 FFFg	30.9	1799	467	882	112
40 FFFg	41.2	2023	591	956	132

▶ **40 FFFg maximum recommended load***

* This maximum charge is based upon accuracy recommendations and is not a reflection on the strength of this steel barrel.

COMMENTS

Note the more rapid twist here because of the smaller ball of less mass, which is a correct way to handle the round ball twist of course. Accuracy levels tied at 25 and 30 FFFg, both being better than either 20 or 40 FFFg in our test rifle. We add the latter, since we have witnessed many individual differences in black powder arms. We would also like to point out that even greater accuracy was obtained with 30 FFFg and a .355" ball with .015" patch.

As for an *optimum load*, the author's own Hatfield is used with different powder charges for different tasks. At 20 FFFg, the rifle is a rabbit/squirrel tool. With 30, it becomes a target/jackrabbit rifle. And the author would use either 30 or 40 FFFg with the .350" or .355" ball for wild turkey hunting.

See the caution that precedes this section. Note: Maximum load listed in bold should be used with caution.

HOPKINS & ALLEN

Pennsylvania Hawken Rifle, M29 (50-cal.)

Caliber: 50

Barrel Length: 29″

Barrel Dim: 15/16″ across flats

Rate of Twist: 1:66″

Depth of Groove: .006″

Powder: GOI

Patch: .015″ Ox-Yoke Precision Blue-Striped

Ignition: FFFFg pan powder

Lube: Young Country No. 103

Powd. Meas.: Tresco 200

Powd. Temp.: 80° F.

LOAD DATA

Projectile/.490″ Weight/177-gr. Type/Speer round ball

Powder Charge (Volume)	Powder Charge (Approx. gr. wt.)	Muzzle Velocity FPS.	Muzzle Energy Ft. Lbs.	Velocity 100 yds.	Energy 100 yds.
40 FFFg	41.5	1317	682	856	288
50 FFFg	51.6	1482	863	908	324
50 FFg	50.2	1361	728	871	298
60 FFg	60.2	1491	874	910	326
70 FFg	70.1	1600	1006	960	362
80 FFg	80.1	1721	1164	1002	395
85 FFg	85.0	1787	1255	1036	422

► **85 FFg maximum recommended load**

COMMENTS The 70 FFg load was accurate in our specific test arm; however, we would elect for the 80 or 85 FFg charge as the *optimum loads* for hunting because of the slight advantage in trajectory and ball impact.

See the caution that precedes this section. Note: Maximum load listed in bold should be used with caution.

HOPKINS & ALLEN
Heritage Underhammer M32 (45-cal.)

Caliber: 45

Barrel Length: 24"

Barrel Dim: 15/16" across flats

Rate of Twist: 1:66"

Depth of Groove: .008"

Powder: GOI, Pyrodex (RS)

Patch: .015" Ox-Yoke Precision Blue-Striped

Ignition: CCI No. 11

Lube: Young Country No. 103

Powd. Meas.: Uncle Mike 120

Powd. Temp.: 78° F.

LOAD DATA

Projectile/.445" Weight/133-gr. Type/Hornady round ball

Powder Charge (Volume)	Powder Charge (Approx. gr. wt.)	Muzzle Velocity FPS.	Muzzle Energy Ft. Lbs.	Velocity 100 yds.	Energy 100 yds.
40 FFFg	41.2	1488	654	893	236
50 FFFg	51.7	1658	812	937	259
60 FFFg	62.5	1776	932	980	284
70 FFFg	72.1	1866	1029	1011	302
75 FFg	75.6	1768	923	978	283
Pyrodex (RS) 75 RS	56.1	1732	886	961	273

▶ **70 FFFg or 75 RS maximum recommended load.**

COMMENTS

The range of accuracy with this rifle was good. That is, loads on both the low and high ends rendered good accuracy. There was a tendency for the patch to be cut upon short-starting the .445" ball. The shooter may wish to try a .440" ball in his rifle, or he may wish to use the .445" ball with a patch under .015" thickness, such as the Irish linen(.013") which we had on hand for some of our tests. We selected 70 FFFg as our *optimum* hunting *load*. Velocity was very good. While our usual recommendation for calibers 45 and up is FFg granulation, FFFg was selected as the main fuel due to the max rating on this rifle, and due to the recommendations of the manufacturer. Incidentally, higher charges of FFg would of course render no more pressure than encountered with the top end FFFg charges here. However, accuracy and power were both good at the manufacturer's levels, and we chose 70 FFFg as our own *optimum load* due to its fine accuracy and velocity.

See the caution that precedes this section. Note: Maximum load listed in bold should be used with caution.

LYMAN

Great Plains Rifle (50-cal.)

Caliber: 50

Barrel Length: 32"

Barrel Dim: ¹⁵⁄₁₆" across flats

Rate of Twist: 1:66"

Depth of Groove: .010"

Powder: GOI

Patch: .013" Irish linen

Ignition: CCI No. 11

Lube: RIG

Powd. Meas.: Uncle Mike 120

Powd. Temp.: 75° F.

LOAD DATA

Projectile/.490" Weight/177-gr. Type/Speer round ball

Powder Charge (Volume)	Powder Charge (Approx. gr. wt.)	Muzzle Velocity FPS.	Muzzle Energy Ft. Lbs.	Velocity 100 yds.	Energy 100 yds.
60 FFg	59.5	1135	506	806	255
60 FFFg	62.5	1692	1125	989	385
90 FFFg	90.2	1930	1464	1092	469

▶ **90 FFFg maximum recommended load**

COMMENTS

With 60 FFFg, accuracy was quite good, and not at all out of the realm of small game work using head shots. Likewise, 60 FFg, with a lower velocity, was a useful load. Under 60 FFFg in this particular test rifle was less accurate *in our tests*, and with our specific test rifle. The 90 FFFg load was also accurate, and we recommend it as our *optimum load* for hunting. However, accuracy was acceptable with 100 FFg, though that load was not chronographed. The 100 FFg load would give less pressure than the 90 FFFg for those who prefer this situation.

See the caution that precedes this section. Note: Maximum load listed in bold should be used with caution.

LYMAN

Trade Rifle (50-cal.)

Caliber: 50

Barrel Length: 28"

Barrel Dim: 15/16" across flats

Rate of Twist: 1:48"

Depth of Groove: .005"

Powder: GOI, Pyrdoex (RS)

Patch: .017" Ox-Yoke Precision Blue-Striped

Ignition: CCI No. 11

Lube: RIG

Powd. Meas.: Tresco 200

Powd. Temp.: 69° F.

LOAD DATA—A

Projectile/.490" Weight/177-gr. Type/Speer round ball

Powder Charge (Volume)	Powder Charge (Approx. gr. wt.)	Muzzle Velocity FPS.	Muzzle Energy Ft. Lbs.	Velocity 100 yds.	Energy 100 yds.
40 FFFg	41.5	1395	765	879	304
50 FFFg	51.6	1545	938	916	330
70 FFg	70.1	1598	1004	959	362
80 FFg	80.1	1680	1110	996	390
90 FFg	90.0	1737	1186	1009	400
Pyrodex (RS) 90 RS	66.7	1606	1014	964	365

▶ **90 FFg or 90 RS maximum recommended load**

COMMENTS

The 90 FFg load, recommended by Lyman, is also our choice as an *optimum load* for hunting with the Trade Rifle. As usual, we again found that the lower-end loadings were quite useful, such as the 40 FFFg above. This load provided good accuracy in the Trade Rifle. The most accurate load in our own specific model was 70 FFg, with 50 FFFg a very close second, almost identical in accuracy.

See the caution that precedes this section. Note: Maximum load listed in bold should be used with caution.

LYMAN

Trade Rifle (50-cal.)

▶ All pertinent data for Load Data—B is the same as for Load Data—A except the following:

Patch: None

LOAD DATA—B

Projectile/.497" Weight/358-gr.* Type/Lee Minie Mould/No.497-350

Powder Charge (Volume)	Powder Charge (Approx. gr. wt.)	Muzzle Velocity FPS.	Muzzle Energy Ft. Lbs.	Velocity 100 yds.	Energy 100 yds.
60 FFg	60.2	1154	1059	860	588
70 FFg	70.1	1235	1213	932	691
80 FFg	80.1	1311	1367	957	728
Pyrodex (RS) 80 RS	58.1	1187	1120	914	664

▶ **80 FFg or 80 RS maximum recommended load**

* Mould modified by author—see Comments

COMMENTS

With a conical from 350 to 370 grains, the 80 FFg load seems most useful and is our *optimum load* for hunting. We could detect no differences in accuracy between this and the 70 or 60 FFg charge, with the exception that the 60 FFg charge was more pleasant to shoot from the bench than the other two. The Lee 50-caliber Minie mould used in these tests was modified by turning down the base pin, thereby producing a projectile that's 8 grains heavier than what that mould would normally throw. The loads listed here are suitable for the same Lee mould mentioned, in unmodified form.

See the caution that precedes this section. Note: Maximum load listed in bold should be used with caution.

MOWREY

Ethan Allen Plains Rifle (54-cal.)

Caliber: 54

Barrel Length: 32″

Barrel Dim: 1″ across flats

Rate of Twist: 1:60″

Depth of Groove: .012″

Powder: GOI, Pyrodex (RS)

Patch: .015″ Ox-Yoke Precision Blue-Striped

Ignition: CCI No. 11

Lube: RIG

Powd. Meas.: Tresco 200

Powd. Temp.: 70° F.

LOAD DATA

Projectile/.530″ Weight/225-gr. Type/Speer round ball

Powder Charge (Volume)	Powder Charge (Approx. gr. wt.)	Muzzle Velocity FPS.	Muzzle Energy Ft. Lbs.	Velocity 100 yds.	Energy 100 yds.
40 FFFg	41.5	1269	805	847	359
50 FFFg	51.6	1419	1006	917	420
50 FFg	50.2	1228	754	860	370
70 FFg	70.1	1448	1049	913	417
90 FFg	90.0	1571	1233	977	477
110 FFg	109.7	1699	1417	1019	519
Pyrodex (RS) 120 RS	87.5	1586	1257	967	467

▶ **110 FFg or 120 RS maximum recommended load**

COMMENTS

This is another powerful black powder rifle, and it would be useful on big game beyond the deer class. Note that the little 40 FFFg load would be at home in informal target shooting. As for an *optimum load*, there is no doubt that the 70 FFg charge with the 225-grain ball would suffice for deer, but there is extra punch in the 110 FFg load for big game, and it is a recommended load. The shooter can try the various charges for ultimate accuracy before deciding upon his personal load. Anywhere from 70 to 110 FFg would fall into the deer category with ease.

See the caution that precedes this section. Note: Maximum load listed in bold should be used with caution.

MOWREY

Ethan Allen Squirrel Rifle (36-cal)*

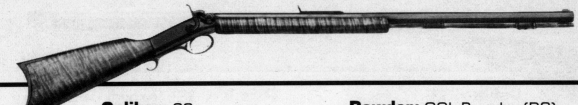

Caliber: 36

Barrel Length: 28"

Barrel Dim: 13/16" across flats

Rate of Twist: 1:60"

Depth of Groove: .012"

Powder: GOI, Pyrodex (RS)

Patch: .015" Ox-Yoke Precision Blue-Striped

Ignition: CCI No. 11

Lube: RIG

Powd. Meas.: Uncle Mike 120

Powd. Temp.: 75° F.

*All steel version.

LOAD DATA

Projectile/.350" Weight/65-gr. Type/Denver Bullet Co. round ball

Powder Charge (Volume)	Powder Charge (Approx. gr. wt.)	Muzzle Velocity FPS.	Muzzle Energy Ft. Lbs.	Velocity 100 yds.	Energy 100 yds.
20 FFFg	20.7	1416	289	765	84
30 FFFg	30.9	1681	408	841	102
40 FFFg	41.2	1826	481	913	120
50 FFFg	51.8	1981	567	932	125
Pyrodex (RS) 60 RS	44.5	1802	469	919	122

▶ **50 FFFg or 60 RS maximum recommended load**

COMMENTS

Although the manufacturer vouched for a full 75 GOI FFFg black powder in this rifle, the author ceased testing at 50 FFFg, having previously found that the velocity increase beyond 50 grains was not necessary. The 36 is a squirrel/rabbit number. One can see that as little as 20 grains is plenty for such game, which is taken at close range. If medium-sized varmints are hunted, the 50 FFFg charge is sufficiently powerful. The *optimum load* here was 40 FFFg due to fine accuracy at that level. However, the 20 and 30 FFFg charges were also accurate; the latter was used to harvest a wild turkey. There would seldom be a reason to load beyond 40 grains of powder.

See the caution that precedes this section. Note: Maximum load listed in bold should be used with caution.

MOWREY

Squirrel Rifle (32-cal.)

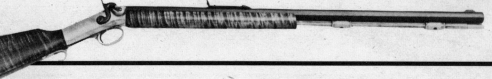

Caliber: 32

Barrel Length: 29″

Barrel Dim: 13⁄16″ across flats

Rate of Twist: 1:60″

Depth of Groove: .010″

Powder: GOI, Pyrodex (RS)

Patch: .015″ Ox-Yoke Precision Blue-Striped

Ignition: CCI No. 11

Lube: J&A Old Slickum

Powd. Meas.: Uncle Mike 120

Powd. Temp.: 70° F.

LOAD DATA

Projectile/.310″ Weight/48-gr. Type/Hornady round ball

Powder Charge (Volume)	Powder Charge (Approx. gr. wt.)	Muzzle Velocity FPS.	Muzzle Energy Ft. Lbs.	Velocity 100 yds.	Energy 100 yds.
10 FFFg	10.5	1220	159	660	46
15 FFFg	15.6	1517	245	819	72
20 FFFg	20.7	1725	317	880	83
25 FFFg	25.8	1861	369	903	87
30 FFFg	30.9	1878	376	909	88
Pyrodex (RS) 30 RS	21.0	1734	321	886	84

▶ **30 FFFg or 30 RS maximum recommended load**

COMMENTS

As one can see, our test rifle did not gain appreciable velocity beyond the 25 FFFg charge. Round-ball accuracy was fine with all of the above charges; however, accuracy was better with 15-25 FFFg than with the 10 and the 30 FFFg charge. The author decided upon a spout tossing 22 grains of FFFg as his own personal *optimum load* for this squirrel rifle. Note that only 20 grains of FFFg gave over 1700 fps, and 25 grains was not far under 1900 fps, which shows how small caliber arms using FFFg gain rapidly in velocity per added amount of fuel.

See the caution that precedes this section. Note: Maximum load listed in bold should be used with caution.

1853 3-Band Enfield (58-cal.)

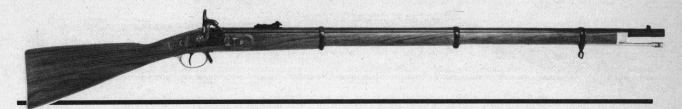

Caliber: 58

Barrel Length: 39″

Barrel Dim: Tapered

Rate of Twist: 1:48″

Depth of Groove: .005″

Powder: GOI, Pyrodex (RS)

Patch: None

Ignition: Navy Arms Musket Cap

Lube: RIG

Powd. Meas.: Tresco 200

Powd. Temp.: 70° F.

LOAD DATA

Projectile/.577″ Weight/530-gr. Type/Lyman Minie Mould/No. 577611

Powder Charge (Volume)	Powder Charge (Approx. gr. wt.)	Muzzle Velocity FPS.	Muzzle Energy Ft. Lbs.	Velocity 100 yds.	Energy 100 yds.
60 FFg	60.2	934	1027	852	854
70 FFg	70.1	1092	1404	950	1062
80 FFg	80.1	1157	1576	995	1165
Pyrodex (RS) 90 RS	66.7	1037	1266	923	1003

▶ **80 FFg or 90 RS maximum recommended load**

COMMENTS

We found that 70 FFg was sufficient charge to give the big 530-grain Lyman-moulded Minie a velocity near the speed of sound. Also, 100-yard retained velocity would be close enough to the 80 FFg charge to make little difference in big game effect or target trajectory. Our *optimum load*, then, is 70 FFg.

See the caution that precedes this section. Note: Maximum load listed in bold should be used with caution.

NAVY ARMS

Hawken "Hunter" Rifle (58-cal.)

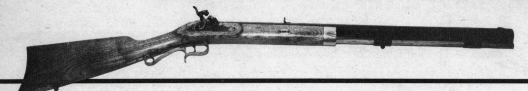

Caliber: 58

Barrel Length: 26"

Barrel Dim: 1" across flats

Rate of Twist: 1:60"

Depth of Groove: .003"—.005"

Powder: GOI

Patch: .015" pillow ticking/one cotton or linen patch over powder

Ignition: Navy Arms Musket Cap

Lube: RIG

Powd. Meas.: Tresco 200

Powd. Temp.: 80° F.

LOAD DATA—A

Projectile/.570" Weight/278-gr. Type/Hornady round ball

Powder Charge (Volume)	Powder Charge (Approx. gr. wt.)	Muzzle Velocity FPS.	Muzzle Energy Ft. Lbs.	Velocity 100 yds.	Energy 100 yds.
100 FFg	99.3	1288	1024	773	369
110 FFg	110.3	1331	1094	900	500
120 FFg	121.5	1401	1212	911	512
130 FFg	129.6	1440	1280	929	533
140 FFg	139.5	1550	1483	977	589

▶ **140 FFg maximum recommended load**

COMMENTS   We recommend the 130 FFg load as our *optimum load* for hunting.

See the caution that precedes this section. Note: Maximum load listed in bold should be used with caution.

NAVY ARMS

Hawken "Hunter" Rifle (58-cal.)

► All pertinent data for Load Data—B is the same as for Load Data—A except the following:

Powder: Pyrodex (RS)
Patch: None

LOAD DATA—B

Powder Charge (Volume)	Powder Charge (Approx. gr. wt.)	Muzzle Velocity FPS.	Muzzle Energy Ft. Lbs.	Velocity 100 yds.	Energy 100 yds.
Projectile/.575" Weight/460-gr. Type/Lyman Minie Mould/575213-OS					
100 RS	76.0	1369	1915	1082	1196
Projectile/.575" Weight/525 (500)* gr. Type/Lyman Minie Mould/No. 575213					
120 RS	88.0	1397	2276	1140	1515
Projectile/.575" Weight/470-gr. Type/Lee Minie Mould/No. 575-470M					
120 RS	88.0	1470	2256	1103	1270
Projectile/.577" Weight/600 (570)* gr. Type/Lyman Minie Mould/No. 57730					
120 RS	88.0	1358	2458	1109	1639
Projectile/.575" Weight/625 (610)* gr. Type/Shiloh Minie Mould/"Stakebuster 610"					
120 RS	88.0	1313	2393	1079	1616
150 RS	108.0	1403	2732	1150	1836

*See Comments for explanation of Minie weights.

COMMENTS

This big strong 58-caliber rifle was tested with various conicals and rather modest powder charges. The charges were considered ample for close-range hunting on game even larger than deer. The 525-gr. Lyman Minie is from the Lyman 500-gr. mould, which actually threw a 525-gr. projectile. The 600-gr. Lyman is from the 570-gr. mould, which actually cast a 600-grain projectile. The 625-gr. Shiloh is from the 610-gr. mould, which actually gave a 625-grain missile. Accuracy with the Lyman 570-gr. mould and 120 grs. of Pyrodex RS was the best. We recommend it as the *optimum load.*

See the caution that precedes this section. Note: Maximum load listed in bold should be used with caution.

NAVY ARMS

J.P. Murray Artillery Carbine (58-cal.)

Caliber: 58

Barrel Length: 23½"

Barrel Dim: Round tapered

Rate of Twist: 1:48"

Depth of Groove: .003"—.005"

Powder: GOI

Patch: None

Ignition: Navy Arms Musket Cap

Lube: Young Country No. 103

Powd. Meas.: Tresco 200

Powd. Temp.: 63° F.

LOAD DATA

Projectile/.577" Weight/530-gr. Type/Lyman Minie Mould/No. 577611

Powder Charge (Volume)	Powder Charge (Approx. gr. wt.)	Muzzle Velocity FPS.	Muzzle Energy Ft. Lbs.	Velocity 100 yds.	Energy 100 yds.
50 FFg	50.2	764	687	714	600
60 FFg	60.2	905	964	828	807
70 FFg	70.1	980	1131	882	916

▶ **70 FFg maximum recommended load**

COMMENTS

The 70 FFg charge with the big 58-caliber, 530-grain Minie, produced plenty of "punch." We tried this load out of the little carbine at 100-yard targets and found no difference in accuracy between it and the 60 FFg load. Both the 60 and 70 FFg loads slightly edged the 50 FFg in our single test run off the bench. Our recommendation for "everyday" use would be the 60 FFg charge, with the 70 FFg charge used for hunting—they are our *optimum loads*.

See the caution that precedes this section. Note: Maximum load listed in bold should be used with caution.

Mississippi Rifle of 1841 (58-cal.)

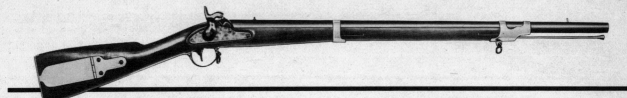

Caliber: 58

Barrel Length: 33″

Barrel Dim: Round tapered

Rate of Twist: 1:48″

Depth of Groove: .003″—.005″

Powder: GOI

Patch: None

Ignition: Navy Arms Musket Cap

Lube: Young Country No. 103

Powd. Meas.: Tresco 200

Powd. Temp.: 60° F.

LOAD DATA

Projectile/.577″ Weight/530-gr. Type/Lyman Minie Mould/No. 577611

Powder Charge (Volume)	Powder Charge (Approx. gr. wt.)	Muzzle Velocity FPS.	Muzzle Energy Ft. Lbs.	Velocity 100 yds.	Energy 100 yds.
50 FFg	50.2	853	857	785	725
60 FFg	60.2	975	1119	882	916
70 FFg	70.1	1034	1259	931	1020
80 FFg	80.1	1102	1430	959	1083

▶ **80 FFg maximum recommended load**

COMMENTS The standard deviations in all of the 58-caliber rifles followed the rather remarkable trend established with the round-ball shooters. When we cleaned between shots, our standard deviations with this rifle ran from a low of 3 to a high of 11, which is superb. The 70 FFg charge was our favorite thus our *optimum load*. We have no doubts about the lethal punch of this load.

See the caution that precedes this section. Note: Maximum load listed in bold should be used with caution.

NAVY ARMS

Zouave Rifle (58-cal.)

Caliber: 58

Barrel Length: 32½"

Barrel Dim: Round tapered

Rate of Twist: 1:48"

Depth of Groove: .003"—.005"

Powder: GOI

Patch: None

Ignition: Navy Arms Musket Cap

Lube: Young Country No. 103

Powd. Meas.: Tresco 200

Powd. Temp.: 64° F.

LOAD DATA

Projectile/.577" Weight/530-gr. Type/Lyman Minie Mould/No. 577611

Powder Charge (Volume)	Powder Charge (Approx. gr. wt.)	Muzzle Velocity FPS.	Muzzle Energy Ft. Lbs.	Velocity 100 yds.	Energy 100 yds.
50 FFg	50.2	850	850	782	720
60 FFg	60.2	971	1110	879	910
70 FFg	70.1	1035	1261	932	1023
80 FFg	80.1	1095	1411	953	1069

▶ **80 FFg maximum recommended load**

COMMENTS The Zouave rifle has been used for hunting from the very early days of the rebirth of black powder firearms. We found the 70 FFg charge the best in this particular rifle, and certainly it produces sufficient force to take on big game. Therefore, that is our recommended *optimum load* for hunting.

See the caution that precedes this section. Note: Maximum load listed in bold should be used with caution.

Hawken Hurricane (50-cal.)

Caliber: 50

Barrel Length: 28"

Barrel Dim: 1" across flats

Rate of Twist: 1:48"

Depth of Groove: .003"—.005"

Powder: GOI

Patch: None

Ignition: Navy Arms Musket Cap

Lube: RIG

Powd. Meas.: Tresco 200

Powd. Temp.: 75° F.

LOAD DATA

Projectile/.503" Weight/367-gr. Type/Lyman Maxi Mould/No. 504617

Powder Charge (Volume)	Powder Charge (Approx. gr. wt.)	Muzzle Velocity FPS.	Muzzle Energy Ft. Lbs.	Velocity 100 yds.	Energy 100 yds.
60 FFg	60.2	988	796	810	535
70 FFg	70.1	1040	882	848	586
80 FFg	80.1	1212	1197	921	691
90 FFg	90.0	1384	1561	983	788
100 FFg	99.7	1444	1700	1025	856
110 FFg	109.7	1541	1936	1056	909
120 FFg	119.6	1600	2087	1088	965

▶ **120 FFg maximum recommended load**

COMMENTS

The *optimum load* was set at 110 FFg with the 367-grain Maxi. Even though 100 FFg gave plenty of velocity in our test rifle, the more accurate load was the 110. The 120 does not offer enough extra velocity to merit its use. With its 1137 steel barrel, this rifle was rated at a capacity of 140 grains volume of FFFg; however, the tests with FFg proved totally acceptable, and the 110 volume load was more than sufficiently powerful for big game.

See the caution that precedes this section. Note: Maximum load listed in bold should be used with caution.

NAVY ARMS

Ithaca Hawken Flintlock (50-cal.)

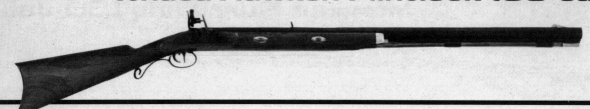

Caliber: 50

Barrel Length: 32"

Barrel Dim: 1" across flats

Rate of Twist: 1:66"

Depth of Groove: .010"

Powder: GOI

Patch: .015" pillow ticking on powder/.015"Ox-Yoke Precision Blue-Striped on ball

Ignition: FFFFg pan powder

Lube: RIG

Powd. Meas.: Uncle Mike 120

Powd. Temp.: 85° F.

LOAD DATA

Projectile/.490" Weight/177-gr. Type/Speer round ball

Powder Charge (Volume)	Powder Charge (Approx. gr. wt.)	Muzzle Velocity FPS.	Muzzle Energy Ft. Lbs.	Velocity 100 yds.	Energy 100 yds.
60 FFFg	62.5	1692	1125	998	392
60 FFg	59.5	1499	883	914	328
70 FFg	70.1	1507	893	919	332
80 FFg	81.0	1717	1159	999	392
90 FFg	90.2	1892	1407	1078	457
100 FFg	99.3	1916	1443	1083	461
110 FFg	110.3	1977	1537	1111	485

▶ **110 FFg maximum recommended load**

COMMENTS Our *optimum load* recommendation for hunting is 110 FFg. For target work we would recommend the 60 FFg load—it's very accurate.

See the caution that precedes this section. Note: Maximum load listed in bold should be used with caution.

NAVY ARMS

New Model Ithaca Hawken (50-cal.)

Caliber: 50

Barrel Length: 34"

Barrel Dim: 1" across flats

Rate of Twist: 1:66"

Depth of Groove: .010"
(approx.)

Powder: GOI

Patch: Loads 50-80 FFg: .013" Irish linen ball patch
Loads 90-110 FFg: ball patch above plus pillow ticking patch over powder

Ignition: CCI No. 11

Lube: RIG

Powd. Meas.: Uncle Mike 120

Powd. Temp.: 80° F.

LOAD DATA

Projectile/.490" Weight/177-gr. Type/Speer round ball

Powder Charge (Volume)	Powder Charge (Approx. gr. wt.)	Muzzle Velocity FPS.	Muzzle Energy Ft. Lbs.	Velocity 100 yds.	Energy 100 yds.
50 FFg	49.5	1355	722	879	304
60 FFg	59.5	1493	876	911	326
70 FFg	70.1	1505	890	919	332
80 FFg	81.0	1712	1152	1002	395
90 FFg	90.2	1889	1403	1069	449
100 FFg	99.3	1912	1437	1082	460
110 FFg	110.3	2000	1572	1120	493

▶ **110 FFg maximum recommended load**

COMMENTS

Since there was a jump in velocity between the 70 FFg charge and the 80 FFg charge, this test run was performed three different times over three different test sessions; however, the data repeated each time. The manufacturer allows for as much as 110 volume of FFg behind the 177-grain round ball, and since a flat 2000 fps was reached with this load, we accepted it as our *optimum* hunting *load*. However, the 70 FFg load was very accurate and is a good one for general work, and for target shooting.

See the caution that precedes this section. Note: Maximum load listed in bold should be used with caution.

NAVY ARMS

Morse Rifle (45-cal.)

Caliber: 45

Barrel Length: 26"

Barrel Dim: ⅞" across flats

Rate of Twist: 1:22"

Depth of Groove: .003"—.005"

Powder: GOI

Patch: None

Ignition: Navy Arms No. 11

Lube: RIG

Powd. Meas.: Uncle Mike 120

Powd. Temp.: 75° F.

LOAD DATA

Projectile/.455" Weight/220-gr. Type/Denver Bullet Co. Maxi

Powder Charge (Volume)	Powder Charge (Approx. gr. wt.)	Muzzle Velocity FPS.	Muzzle Energy Ft. Lbs.	Velocity 100 yds.	Energy 100 yds.
30 FFFg	30.9	899	395	733	263
40 FFFg	41.2	1101	593	837	342
50 FFFg	51.8	1300	826	910	405
60 FFFg	62.5	1498	1096	980	469
70 FFFg	72.1	1554	1180	1010	498

▶ **70 FFFg maximum recommended load**

COMMENTS

The 60-grain FFFg charge was considered the *optimum load* here. Accuracy was still very good at 60 grains, and the velocity was sufficient for flatness of trajectory and reasonable energy. Remaining velocity at 100 yards was also good. The most *accurate load* in this particular test rifle was 50 FFFg, which rendered consistent 1½-inch groups for 5 shots at 50 yards from the bench.

See the caution that precedes this section. Note: Maximum load listed in bold should be used with caution.

Parker Hale Whitworth Rifle (45-cal.)

Caliber: 45

Barrel Length: 36"

Barrel Dim: 1" breech/
¾" muzzle

Rate of Twist: 1:20"

Depth of Groove: N.A.

Powder: GOI

Patch: None

Ignition: Navy Arms Musket Cap

Lube: 50% bee's wax/50% RIG

Powd. Meas.: Tresco 200

Powd. Temp.: 75° F.

LOAD DATA

Projectile/.457" Weight/490-gr. Type/Lyman bullet Mould/No. 457121

Powder Charge (Volume)	Powder Charge (Approx. gr. wt.)	Muzzle Velocity FPS.	Muzzle Energy Ft. Lbs.	Velocity 100 yds.	Energy 100 yds.
50 FFg	50.2	971	1026	892	866
70 FFg	70.1	1161	1467	999	1086
90 FFg	90.0	1306	1856	1112	1346

▶ **90 FFg maximum recommended load**

COMMENTS Superb accuracy was attained with this rifle and bullet combination for all of the powder charges listed. All of these loads could be considered *optimum loads* depending upon the type of shooting you intend to do—the choice is yours.

See the caution that precedes this section. Note: Maximum load listed in bold should be used with caution.

NUMRICH ARMS

Buggy Rifle (45-cal.)

Caliber: 45

Barrel Length: 20"

Barrel Dim: 15/16" across flats

Rate of Twist: 1:66"

Depth of Groove: .008"

Powder: GOI, Pyrodex (RS)

Patch: .015" Ox-Yoke Precision Blue-Striped

Ignition: CCI No. 11

Lube: J&A Old Slickum

Powd. Meas.: Uncle Mike 120

Powd. Temp.: 80° F.

LOAD DATA

Projectile/.445" Weight/133-gr. Type/Hornady round ball

Powder Charge (Volume)	Powder Charge (Approx. gr. wt.)	Muzzle Velocity FPS.	Muzzle Energy Ft. Lbs.	Velocity 100 yds.	Energy 100 yds.
40 FFFg	41.2	1453	624	872	225
50 FFFg	51.8	1596	752	910	245
60 FFFg	62.5	1742	896	967	276
70 FFFg	72.1	1803	960	992	291
75 FFg	75.6	1713	867	859	272
Pyrodex (RS) 75 RS	56.1	1663	817	940	261

▶ **70 FFFg or 75 RS maximum recommended load**

COMMENTS

This handy short-barreled rifle was tested with FFFg as the main fuel. With 70 FFFg, velocity was slightly over 1800 fps as an average. One may note that its brother (the 45-caliber Underhammer) with the 24" barrel averaged 1866 fps with the same charge. Patches were often cut upon entry to the muzzle crown, and we had to be very careful in short-starting our loads. The shooter may wish to try the .440" ball with the .015" patch, or stay with the .445" ball and go to a thinner than .015" patch, perhaps a linen patch of .013", which we used with some of our rifles. Although the most accurate load in this rifle was 50 grains of FFFg, we're going to recommend the 75 FFg charge as the *optimum* hunting *load.*

See the caution that precedes this section. Note: Maximum load listed in bold should be used with caution.

OZARK

Muskrat Rifle (40-cal.)

Caliber: 40

Barrel Length: 36"

Barrel Dim: 13⁄16" across flats

Rate of Twist: 1:42"

Depth of Groove: .012"

Powder: GOI

Patch: .017" Ox-Yoke Precision Blue-Striped

Ignition: CCI No. 11

Lube: J&A Old Slickum

Powd. Meas.: Uncle Mike 120

Powd. Temp.: 70° F.

LOAD DATA

Projectile/.395" Weight/93-gr. Type/Lyman round ball Mould/Part No. 2645395

Powder Charge (Volume)	Powder Charge (Approx. gr. wt.)	Muzzle Velocity FPS.	Muzzle Energy Ft. Lbs.	Velocity 100 yds.	Energy 100 yds.
20 FFFg	20.7	1294	346	828	142
30 FFFg	30.9	1584	518	927	177
40 FFFg	41.2	1813	679	981	199
50 FFFg	51.7	1993	820	1017	214
60 FFg*	59.5	1886	735	999	206

▶ **50 FFFg maximum recommended load**

* Up to a 50 volume charge, we recommend FFFg. For anything over a 50 volume charge, we recommend FFg which will provide lower pressures in this small-bore rifle.

COMMENTS For best accuracy, the 30 FFFg load was a winner. The *optimum* *load* for hunting would be the 50 FFFg charge.

See the caution that precedes this section. Note: Maximum load listed in bold should be used with caution.

OZARK

Muskrat Rifle (36-cal.)

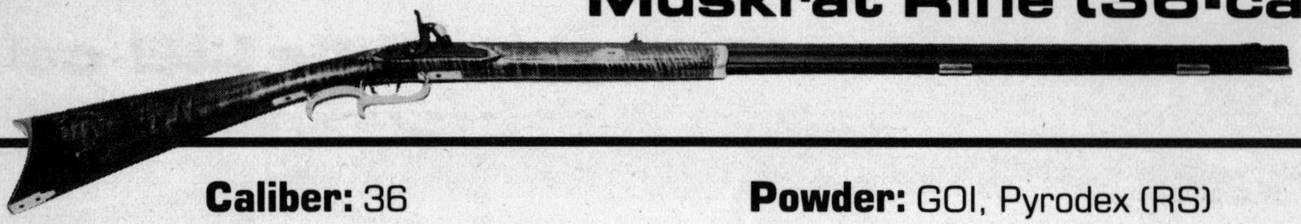

Caliber: 36

Barrel Length: 36"

Barrel Dim: 13/16" across flats

Rate of Twist: 1:42"

Depth of Groove: .012"

Powder: GOI, Pyrodex (RS)

Patch: .020" Ox-Yoke Wonder

Ignition: CCI No. 11

Lube: Self-lubed

Powd. Meas.: Uncle Mike 120

Powd. Temp.: 70° F.

LOAD DATA

Projectile/.350" Weight/65-gr. Type/Hornady round ball

Powder Charge (Volume)	Powder Charge (Approx. gr. wt.)	Muzzle Velocity FPS.	Muzzle Energy Ft. Lbs.	Velocity 100 yds.	Energy 100 yds.
20 FFFg	20.7	1477	315	798	92
30 FFFg	30.9	1721	428	878	111
40 FFFg	41.2	2015	586	949	129
40 FFg	39.5	1751	443	893	115
50 FFg	49.5	1975	563	928	124
Pyrodex (RS) 50 RS	36.1	1943	545	913	120

▶ **40 FFFg or 50 RS maximum recommended load**

COMMENTS

The establishment of a very low extreme spread/Sd followed after the first set of velocity figures was abandoned because of a rather high Sd/extreme spread. The only change from Test One to Test Two (the published data) was the use of constant pressure from a loading rod on the second test, while the first test used the ramrod and varying pressures on the powder charge. (See Chapter 7, Loading for Accuracy.)

The rifle was tested for accuracy and was found to be highly accurate with the 20 and 30 FFFg loads, while accuracy fell off with the 40 FFFg load. Since this is a small game rifle, it would seem wise to stay with the 20 and 30 FFFg loads. The 45 FFFg load was recommended by the manufacturer but not used. In this particular rifle, very high velocity per charge was established, and it was not deemed necessary to go beyond the 40 FFFg charge. At over 2000 fps from the muzzle, this 36-caliber rifle is capable of harvesting wild turkeys, and the 40 FFFg load provides for that. The 40 FFg load was also very accurate. It is our *optimum load* for hunting.

See the caution that precedes this section. Note: Maximum load listed in bold should be used with caution.

RICHLAND

Plainsman Rifle (38-cal.)

Caliber: 38

Barrel Length: 37"

Barrel Dim: ¾" across flats

Rate of Twist: 1:60"

Depth of Groove: .007"

Powder: GOI, Pyrodex (RS)

Patch: .015" Ox-Yoke Wonder

Ignition: CCI No. 11

Lube: Self-lubed

Powd. Meas.: Uncle Mike 120

Powd. Temp.: 70° F.

LOAD DATA

Projectile/.375" Weight/80-gr. Type/Speer round ball

Powder Charge (Volume)	Powder Charge (Approx. gr. wt.)	Muzzle Velocity FPS.	Muzzle Energy Ft. Lbs.	Velocity 100 yds.	Energy 100 yds.
20 FFFg	20.7	1418	357	851	129
30 FFFg	30.9	1686	505	944	158
40 FFFg	41.2	1876	625	1013	182
50 FFFg	51.7	1930	662	1051	196
Pyrodex (RS) 50 RS	36.1	1763	552	969	167

▶ **50 FFFg or 50 RS maximum recommended load**

COMMENTS

This was the only 38-caliber rifle tested, and the viability of the ball size is apparent. As a small game number, along with wild turkeys and possibly javelina, the 80-grain ball with an optimum hunting charge of about 40 FFFg should get the job done. The 50 FFFg charge did not offer much better ballistics, not for the work the 38 was cut out to perform. So, we will call the 40 FFFg charge our *optimum load.*

See the caution that precedes this section. Note: Maximum load listed in bold should be used with caution.

Hawken Hunter Carbine (50-cal.)

Caliber: 50

Barrel Length: 22"

Barrel Dim: 15/16" across flats

Rate of Twist: 1:48"

Depth of Groove: .006"

Powder: GOI

Patch: .010" Ox-Yoke Master Patch

Ignition: CCI No. 11

Lube: RIG

Powd. Meas.: Uncle Mike 120

Powd. Temp.: 71° F.

LOAD DATA

Projectile/.495" Weight/182-gr. Type/Speer round ball

Powder Charge (Volume)	Powder Charge (Approx. gr. wt.)	Muzzle Velocity FPS.	Muzzle Energy Ft. Lbs.	Velocity 100 yds.	Energy 100 yds.
40 FFFg	41.2	1392	783	877	311
60 FFFg	62.5	1616	1056	970	380
60 FFg	59.5	1427	823	899	327
110 FFg	110.3	1801	1311	1034	432

▶ **110 FFg maximum recommended load**

COMMENTS

This handy little carbine, with its 22-inch barrel, and its hard chrome easy-to-clean bore, is a natural for hunting in close cover. The 110 FFg load would be advisable for the longer range work. We tried the manufacturer's recommended load of 100 FFFg for a velocity of 1,818 fps, and this load, even though 10 grains less than the 110 FFg load, would give more pressure for very little added velocity. Therefore, we recommend 110 FFg as the *optimum load*.

See the caution that precedes this section. Note: Maximum load listed in bold should be used with caution.

Hawken (Double Key) Rifle (45-cal.)

Caliber: 45

Barrel Length: 28½"

Barrel Dim: ¹⁵⁄₁₆" across flats

Rate of Twist: 1:48"

Depth of Groove: .006"

Powder: GOI

Patch: .015" Ox-Yoke Precision Blue-Striped

Ignition: Navy Arms No. 11

Lube: J&A Old Slickum

Powd. Meas.: Uncle Mike 120

Powd. Temp.: 62° F.

LOAD DATA

Projectile/.445" Weight/133-gr. Type/Speer round ball

Powder Charge (Volume)	Powder Charge (Approx. gr. wt.)	Muzzle Velocity FPS.	Muzzle Energy Ft. Lbs.	Velocity 100 yds.	Energy 100 yds.
40 FFFg	41.2	1561	720	882	230
50 FFFg	51.7	1702	856	953	268
50 FFg	49.5	1566	724	885	231
60 FFg	59.5	1699	853	951	267
70 FFg	70.1	1749	904	971	279
90 FFg	90.2	1903	1070	1028	312

▶ **90 FFg maximum recommended load**

COMMENTS While the 90 FFg charge showed impressive ballistics, and while we would opt for this charge for some hunting situations, the 70 FFg was the more accurate load, shooting very much the same groups as the 50 FFFg charge. The 40 FFFg charge was also accurate. Depending upon the type of shooting you are doing, any one of these loads could serve as your *optimum load.*

See the caution that precedes this section. Note: Maximum load listed in bold should be used with caution.

THOMPSON/CENTER

Renegade Rifle (54-cal.)

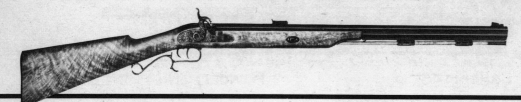

Caliber: 54

Barrel Length: 26″

Barrel Dim: 1″ across flats

Rate of Twist: 1:48″

Depth of Groove: .006″

Powder: GOI, Pyrodex (RS)

Patch: .015″—.016″ Ox-Yoke Precision Blue-Striped

Ignition: CCI No. 11

Lube: RIG

Powd. Meas.: Tresco 200

Powd. Temp.: 80° F.

LOAD DATA—A

Projectile/.530″ Weight/225-gr. Type/Denver Bullet Co. round ball

Powder Charge (Volume)	Powder Charge (Approx. gr. wt.)	Muzzle Velocity FPS.	Muzzle Energy Ft. Lbs.	Velocity 100 yds.	Energy 100 yds.
40 FFFg	41.5	1245	775	834	348
60 FFFg	61.4	1463	1070	922	429
60 FFg	60.2	1260	793	832	346
70 FFg	70.1	1538	1182	970	470
90 FFg	90.0	1579	1246	980	480
100 FFg	99.7	1648	1357	989	489
120 FFg	119.6	1748	1527	1079	582
Pyrodex (RS) 120 RS	87.5	1600	1279	987	487

▶ **120 FFg or 120 RS maximum recommended load**

See the caution that precedes this section. Note: Maximum load listed in bold should be used with caution.

THOMPSON/CENTER

Renegade Rifle (54-cal.)

▶ All pertinent data for Load Data—B is the same as for Load Data—A except the following:

Patch: None
Lube: CVA "Grease Patch" (Maxi grooves only)

LOAD DATA—B

Projectile/.530" Weight/400-gr. Type/Denver Bullet Co. Maxi

Powder Charge (Volume)	Powder Charge (Approx. gr. wt.)	Muzzle Velocity FPS.	Muzzle Energy Ft. Lbs.	Velocity 100 yds.	Energy 100 yds.
80 FFg	80.1	1219	1320	1000	888
100 FFg	99.7	1375	1680	1100	1075
120 FFg	119.6	1499	1996	1137	1149
Pyrodex (RS) 120 RS	87.5	1363	1650	1095	1065

▶ **120 FFg or 120 RS maximum recommended load**

COMMENTS
(Load Data A&B)

Due to twist being 1:48", the 100 FFg load with the round ball was more accurate than the 120 FFg load with the same projectile. Therefore, this load was selected for hunting, especially since it was within 100 fps of the 120 FFg load. While 100 fps would not make that much difference in practical hunting terms, the added 100 fps with the 120 FFg charge did cut back on accuracy in the specific test rifle.

However, with the Maxi ball, accuracy with the 120 and 100 FFg loads was very similar, and since the 120 FFg load is deemed safe by the manufacturer, a hunter would be advised to use this charge for large game, although the 80 FFg charge would certainly be adequate for any deer. In terms of a ballistically *optimum load*, the 120 FFg charge is elected; however, in practical terms, the 80 FFg charge is more than sufficient for deer hunting purposes. The most accurate load in our test rifle was 90 grains of FFg with the 225-grain Denver Bullet Company round ball.

Pyrodex, used in our Tresco 200 powder measure, turned in adequate velocity when one considers the actual charge in terms of grain weight. If a full 100-grains weight of Pyrodex were employed (20 percent below the weight of the black powder charge), the velocity with Pyrodex would equal that of black powder.

See the caution that precedes this section. Note: Maximum load listed in bold should be used with caution.

THOMPSON/CENTER

Hawken Rifle (50-cal.)

Caliber: 50

Barrel Length: 28″

Barrel Dim: 15/16″ across flats

Rate of Twist: 1:48″

Depth of Groove: .006″

Powder: GOI, Pyrodex (RS)

Patch: .015″ Ox-Yoke Wonder

Ignition: CCI No. 11

Lube: Self-lubed

Powd. Meas.: Tresco 200

Powd. Temp.: 72° F.

LOAD DATA—A

Projectile/.490″ Weight/177-gr. Type/Hornady round ball

Powder Charge (Volume)	Powder Charge (Approx. gr. wt.)	Muzzle Velocity FPS.	Muzzle Energy Ft. Lbs.	Velocity 100 yds.	Energy 100 yds.
40 FFFg	41.5	1384	753	875	301
50 FFFg	51.6	1552	947	939	347
50 FFg	50.2	1453	830	908	324
70 FFg	70.1	1646	1065	979	377
90 FFg	90.0	1860	1360	1060	442
110 FFg	109.7	1998	1569	1123	496
Pyrodex (RS) 110 RS	79.3	1803	1278	1035	421

▶ **110 FFg or 110 RS maximum recommended load**

COMMENTS   Since the rifle is rated for 110 FFg, the hunter may wish to use this charge for its near 2000 fps muzzle velocity and flat trajectory. Of course, the 90 FFg charge is also very useful, and in our test rifle, that charge was more accurate than the 110, with the 70 FFg charge the most accurate of the bunch. For this reason we consider the 70 FFg charge the *optimum load.*

See the caution that precedes this section. Note: Maximum load listed in bold should be used with caution.

THOMPSON/CENTER

Hawken Rifle (50-cal.)

▶ All pertinent data for Load Data—B is the same as for Load Data—A except the following:

Patch: None

LOAD DATA—B

Projectile/.497" Weight/358-gr.* Type/Lee Minie Mould/No. 497-350M

Powder Charge (Volume)	Powder Charge (Approx. gr. wt.)	Muzzle Velocity FPS.	Muzzle Energy Ft. Lbs.	Velocity 100 yds.	Energy 100 yds.
70 FFg	70.1	1310	1365	956	727
90 FFg	90.0	1404	1567	997	790
100 FFg	99.7	1456	1686	1019	826
Pyrodex (RS) 100 RS	72.5	1368	1488	990	779

▶ **100 FFg or 100 RS maximum recommended load**

* Modified Lee mould—see comments.

COMMENTS

Accuracy with the 90 FFg charge was good, and we would recommend this load for hunting. It seemed in our test rifle that the additional powder charge (from 90 to 100 FFg) did not give sufficient velocity to merit the additional powder increase. Certainly, the 70 FFg charge would serve on deer-sized game in close cover where shots would be short.

The Minie was produced from a modified Lee 350-grain 50-caliber mould. By turning down the base plug, a thicker skirt was produced, and the additional lead in the skirt increased total projectile weight to 358 grains in pure lead. We have used the 370-grain Maxi with good results in this rifle, again with the 70 and 90 FFg charges. Both were accurate. Both the 70 and 90 FFg loads serve as *optimum loads*.

See the caution that precedes this section. Note: Maximum load listed in bold should be used with caution.

THOMPSON/CENTER

Hawken Rifle (45-cal.)

Caliber: 45

Barrel Length: 28"

Barrel Dim: 15/16" across flats

Rate of Twist: 1:48"

Depth of Groove: .006"

Powder: GOI, Pyrodex (RS)

Patch: .015" Ox-Yoke Wonder

Ignition: Navy Arms No. 11

Lube: Self-lubed

Powd. Meas.: Tresco 200

Powd. Temp.: 70° F.

LOAD DATA—A

Projectile/.440" Weight/128-gr. Type/Hornady round ball

Powder Charge (Volume)	Powder Charge (Approx. gr. wt.)	Muzzle Velocity FPS.	Muzzle Energy Ft. Lbs.	Velocity 100 yds.	Energy 100 yds.
40 FFFg	41.5	1553	686	901	231
50 FFFg	51.6	1750	871	971	268
50 FFg	50.2	1547	680	897	229
60 FFg	60.2	1714	835	960	262
70 FFg	70.1	1772	893	975	270
80 FFg	80.1	1919	1047	1036	305
90 FFg	90.0	1982	1117	1050	313
100 FFg	99.7	2021	1161	1065	322
110 FFg	109.7	2095	1248	1110	350
Pyrodex (RS) 120 RS	87.5	1951	1082	1044	310

▶ **110 FFg or 120 RS maximum recommended load**

COMMENTS

The *optimum load* here would be 90 FFg for deer hunting, since that is close to 2000 fps, provided that the individual rifle obtains good accuracy with that load. We got better results in accuracy with 70 FFg, and certainly that load would be enough for deer at close range. The test rifle was amply accurate for informal targeting with the mild 40 FFFg load.

See the caution that precedes this section. Note: Maximum load listed in bold should be used with caution.

THOMPSON/CENTER

Hawken Rifle (45-cal.)

▶ All pertinent data for Load Data—B is the same as for Load Data—A except the following:

Patch: None
Ignition: CCI No. 11
Lube: RIG

LOAD DATA—B

Projectile/.445" Weight/220-gr. Type/Denver Bullet Co. Maxi

Powder Charge (Volume)	Powder Charge (Approx. gr. wt.)	Muzzle Velocity FPS.	Muzzle Energy Ft. Lbs.	Velocity 100 yds.	Energy 100 yds.
70 FFg	70.1	1482	1073	969	459
80 FFg	80.1	1557	1185	996	485
90 FFg	90.0	1661	1348	1038	526
100 FFg	99.7	1748	1493	1093	584
Pyrodex (RS) 110 RS	79.3	1678	1376	1049	538

▶ **100 FFg or 110 RS maximum recommended load**

COMMENTS

Certainly the 90 FFg charge will suffice for deer, and it's a toss-up between that or the 80 FFg charge. For the hunter who insists upon the extra velocity, the full 100 FFg charge could be used, of course, but the 80 and 90 FFg charges suffice. The hunter should test his individual 45-caliber T/C Hawken for accuracy before he decides upon his own *optimum load*.

See the caution that precedes this section. Note: Maximum load listed in bold should be used with caution.

Loading Data

MUZZLE-LOADING HANDGUNS

INTRODUCTION

THE RANGE of loads and loading techniques in the black powder handguns is not as wide as it is in the rifles, but there are many applications for the black powder sidearm, and I have been sufficiently enthused and enthralled with this type of firearm to put a book together on the subject, *The Black Powder Handgun* (DBI Books, Inc.). Most of us, I think, will use the black powder handgun as an adjunct to the rifle.

This is not abnormal, for most of us use the modern handgun as an adjunct to the modern rifle. Whether we like it or not, the rifle is first. But the handgun is second, and second place is not so bad. The reader looking over the section on black powder handgun loads will find fewer offerings here than in the rifle section due to the fact that rifle interest is highest, and the lion's share of the book was devoted to that firearm type.

But the black powder handgunner can have a world of enjoyment with his favorite hand-held smokepole in at least three ways: First, in a safe place, with informal targets backed up by a big sand hill, plinking with the smokepole sidearm is not exactly a bad way to spend a little time. Many of these firearms are quite accurate and certainly capable of making a tin can jump off its roost and roll down the hill. Second, serious target work with the muzzle-loading handgun is perfectly viable and practiced daily in this country.

A good many of the modern day black powder handguns are quite accurate, and they will create a worthy group at normal handgun ranges. Third, there are a few hunters who use the black powder handgun in the field to harvest game, both small and large. No one is going to argue, I'm sure, with the idea of bagging small game with the black powder sidearm, but a few might think it unwise to use that type of firearm on big game.

It all depends. I think that some of the lesser black powder handguns are, in general, too small for big game hunting. I do not consider myself a good enough shot to use 36-caliber handguns and the like for big game of the deer class or larger, and I would not, myself, use them on javelina-sized game even if legal to do so. The 36-caliber handgun, firing a .375″ ball, will give an 80-grain projectile usually not over 1000 fps at the muzzle with a muzzle energy in the 177+ foot-pounds rank. In one 36-caliber handgun, I got a muzzle velocity of 1100 fps for a foot-pounds rating of about 218.

In spite of the fact that KE figures do not tell all in terms of "killing power," I think that 218 foot-pounds is too little energy for big game. After all, the 9mm Luger with a 115-grain bullet (which I do not believe to be big game medicine), will attain an energy of over 400 foot-pounds at the muzzle. With that in mind, the general 44-caliber black powder load with a 141-grain ball at about 1000 fps will only yield 313 foot-pounds.

However, we have been talking about the revolvers. There are still the pistols to consider, but before going on to those, and before the readers start buying expensive stamps to mail me letters, I know that the 44-caliber ball in the handgun has taken big game clean as spring rain. But we have to talk in *averages*, I think, and on the average, the old-time revolver does not produce powerhouse big game ballistics. It sure had enough snort to bag a lot of bad (and good) guys in the West. But on a buck running through the brush, I'm not so sure.

I am certain that if a fellow considers the 357 Magnum a deer caliber, then some of our big black powder pistols are also deer numbers as well. The 44 Magnum with its 240-grain bullet at about 1300 fps earns a KE of 901 foot-pounds. The 58-caliber Navy Arms Horse Pistol with a 525-grain Minie at 900 fps earns about 945 foot-pounds. With good sights and in the hands of a good shot, it's going to be hard to convince me that a 58-caliber 525-grain slug is not good for deer, but a 240-grain 44-caliber slug is.

Our introduction to the handguns is, as we have stated, a bit less involved than was the rifle section, but this is not to slight this type of firearm. Today, a shooter can buy a wonderfully accurate black powder handgun, as proven by the Thompson/Center Patriot, the Ruger Old Army, some of the Remington copies and a number of pistols in many calibers. The shooter can also mate a sidearm with his rifle, keeping the two matched in style as well as caliber, by selecting a plains pistol of the Lyman, CVA or Navy Arms types, often in precisely the same caliber shooting precisely the same ball as the rifle. Simply put, the smaller caliber black powder sidearms are a great deal of fun to own. While some are not in the target shooting domain, they are good enough to plink with.

Calibers

We will not entertain each black powder handgun caliber separately because, in this one person's opinion, at least, there are only three "schools" of muzzleloader sidearm bore sizes. We have first the smaller calibers. These, such as the 31 and 36, were far more than adequate to put a few of the boys into Boot Hill, but they are not viable, again in my opinion, for game past the small variety. But some certainly will punch accurate groups in paper.

The middle ground is occupied by the 44 calibers. In the hands of good shots, deer, boars and black bear, not to mention a variety of other game, have been felled with these calibers, mainly in revolvers. Fitted with a telescopic sight, one noted handgunner, the late Al Georg, did very well with such a handgun. And these middle-roaders are also good small game meat-potters, as well as being capable of winning shooting matches.

As for the 44s, on the whole, being adequate for big game in the hands of that mythical "average shot," I am skeptical. I do feel that if the hunter had the practice, it could make a difference. And circumstances also matter a good deal. Given a boar in the closeness of a briar patch and a 44-caliber ball in the head, the middle-sized handgun would probably suffice.

Finally, there are the big bore handguns, and I usually think of the 50, 53 and 58 calibers when I think of this category. Because of bore size and mass, regardless of the modest velocities, I think these numbers might be all right for deer-sized game in the hands of cool shots. But having no experience in actually taking big game with them, I only speak from ballistics knowledge.

C.V.A.

Hawken Pistol (50-cal.)

Caliber: 50

Barrel Length: 9¾″

Barrel Dim: 1″ across flats

Rate of Twist: 1:66″

Depth of Groove: .010″

Powder: GOI

Patch: .015″ Ox-Yoke Precision Blue-Striped

Ignition: FFFFg pan powder

Lube: Young Country No. 103

Powd. Meas.: Uncle Mike 120

Powd. Temp.: 80° F.

LOAD DATA

Projectile/.490″ Weight/177-gr. Type/Speer round ball

Powder Charge (Volume)	Powder Charge (Approx. gr. wt.)	Muzzle Velocity FPS.	Muzzle Energy Ft. Lbs.	Velocity 100 yds.	Energy 100 yds.
30 FFFg	30.9	887	309	754	223
40 FFFg	41.2	1019	408	856	288
60 FFFg	62.5	1159	528	956	359

▶ **60 FFFg maximum recommended load**

COMMENTS

While some shooters may wonder about the 1:66″ twist in this handgun, there are many who contend that this is very ample in terms of stabilizing the round ball over handgun distances. Our informal shooting was certainly satisfactory. And no one can argue with the power of this 50-caliber sidearm. The manufacturer's recommendation of 60 FFFg develops over 1150 fps at the muzzle with the 177-grain round ball. The *optimum load* is 40 FFFg.

See the caution that precedes this section. Note: Maximum load listed in bold should be used with caution.

C.V.A.

Colonial Pistol (45-cal.)

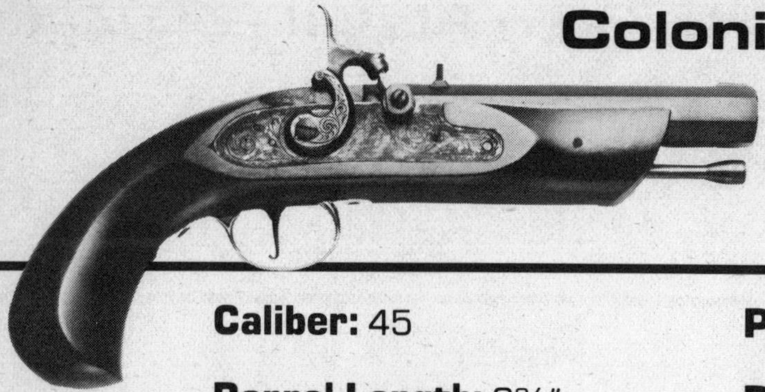

Caliber: 45

Barrel Length: 6¾"

Barrel Dim: ⅞" across flats

Rate of Twist: 1:66"

Depth of Groove: .010"

Powder: GOI

Patch: .013" Irish linen

Ignition: CCI No. 11

Lube: RIG

Powd. Meas.: Uncle Mike 120

Powd. Temp.: 70° F.

LOAD DATA

Projectile/.440" Weight/129-gr. Type/Hornady round ball

Powder Charge (Volume)	Powder Charge (Approx. gr. wt.)	Muzzle Velocity FPS.	Muzzle Energy Ft. Lbs.	Velocity 50 yds.	Energy 50 yds.
20 FFFg	20.7	791	179	676	131
40 FFFg	41.2	1012	293	830	197

▶ **40 FFFg maximum recommended load**

COMMENTS

The 40 FFFg charge was more accurate in this pistol; however, the 20 FFFg charge, or something between 20 and 40, might be considered if the sidearm is used as a companion piece to the rifle, such as in a small game capacity. The *optimum load* is a matter of choice based on intended use.

See the caution that precedes this section. Note: Maximum load listed in bold should be used with caution.

Kentucky Pistol (45-cal.)

Caliber: 45

Barrel Length: 10¼"

Barrel Dim: ⅞" across flats

Rate of Twist: 1:66"

Depth of Groove: .010"

Powder: GOI

Patch: .013" Irish linen

Ignition: CCI No. 11

Lube: RIG

Powd. Meas.: Uncle Mike 120

Powd. Temp.: 70° F.

LOAD DATA

Projectile/.440" Weight/129-gr. Type/Hornady round ball

Powder Charge (Volume)	Powder Charge (Approx. gr. wt.)	Muzzle Velocity FPS.	Muzzle Energy Ft. Lbs.	Velocity 50 yds.	Energy 50 yds.
20 FFFg	20.7	859	211	713	146
40 FFFg	41.2	1153	381	911	238

▶ **40 FFFg maximum recommended load.**

COMMENTS

Depending upon the use, either of the above charges will serve the shooter well in this pistol. If the shooter is interested in plinking, the 20 FFFg charge is preferred. The 40 FFFg charge, however, was the more accurate one. As to *optimum load*, the choice is yours, and should be made based upon the type of shooting you are doing.

See the caution that precedes this section. Note: Maximum load listed in bold should be used with caution.

GARRETT

Napolean Le Page Pistol (45-cal.)

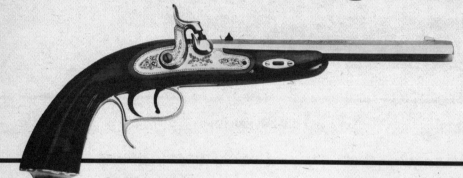

Caliber: 45

Barrel Length: 9¾"

Barrel Dim: 13⁄16" across flats

Rate of Twist: 1:18"

Depth of Groove: .008"

Powder: GOI, Pyrodex (P)

Patch: .015" Ox-Yoke Wonder

Ignition: CCI No. 11

Lube: Self-lubed

Powd. Meas.: Uncle Mike 120

Powd. Temp.: 78° F.

LOAD DATA

Projectile/.440" Weight/128-gr. Type/Hornady round ball

Powder Charge (Volume)	Powder Charge (Approx. gr. wt.)	Muzzle Velocity FPS.	Muzzle Energy Ft. Lbs.	Velocity 50 yds.	Energy 50 yds.
20 FFFg	20.7	859	210	730	151
30 FFFg	30.9	1014	292	831	196
Pyrodex (P) 30 P	24.0	959	261	796	180

▶ **30 FFFg or 30P maximum recommended load**

COMMENTS   The 30 FFFg charge was useful in this firearm, but since the gun's function is informal target work and enjoyment at the range or plinking ground, the 20 FFFg charge seemed totally sufficient and an *optimum load* for this pistol.

See the caution that precedes this section. Note: Maximum load listed in bold should be used with caution.

Rochatte Dueling Pistol (45-cal.)

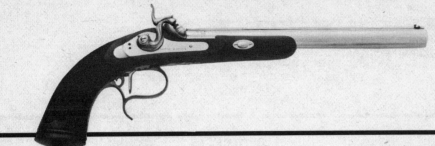

Caliber: 45

Barrel Length: 9¾"

Barrel Dim: 1³⁄₁₆" round

Rate of Twist: 1:18"

Depth of Groove: .008"

Powder: GOI, Pyrodex (P)

Patch: .015" Ox-Yoke Precision Blue-Striped

Ignition: CCI No. 11

Lube: Young Country No. 103

Powd. Meas.: Uncle Mike 120

Powd. Temp.: 79° F.

LOAD DATA

Projectile/.440" Weight/128-gr. Type/Denver Bullet Co. round ball

Powder Charge (Volume)	Powder Charge (Approx. gr. wt.)	Muzzle Velocity FPS.	Muzzle Energy Ft. Lbs.	Velocity 50 yds.	Energy 50 yds.
20 FFFg	20.7	946	254	785	175
30 FFFg	30.9	1047	312	848	204
Pyrodex (P) 30 P	24.0	1031	302	840	201

▶ **30 FFFg or 30 P maximum recommended load**

COMMENTS

Firearm individuality showed up among the various pistols as well as rifles which we tested. A group of handsome 45-caliber pistols proved to be unique in the velocities they gained using the same load chain, although these differences would not be at all important to the function of any of the sidearms tested. With plinking and informal target fun in mind, all of the above loads worked well, and proved to be *optimum loads* for the Rochatte Dueling Pistol.

See the caution that precedes this section. Note: Maximum load listed in bold should be used with caution.

GARRETT

William Parker Pistol (45-cal.)

Caliber: 45

Barrel Length: 10⅝"

Barrel Dim: 1³⁄₁₆" across flats

Rate of Twist: 1:18"

Depth of Groove: .008"

Powder: GOI, Pyrodex (P)

Patch: .015" Ox-Yoke Precision Blue-Striped

Ignition: FFFFg pan powder

Lube: Young Country No. 103

Powd. Meas.: Uncle Mike 120

Powd. Temp.: 77° F.

LOAD DATA

Projectile/.440" Weight/128-gr. Type/Hornady round ball

Powder Charge (Volume)	Powder Charge (Approx. gr. wt.)	Muzzle Velocity FPS.	Muzzle Energy Ft. Lbs.	Velocity 50 yds.	Energy 50 yds.
20 FFFg	20.7	799	181	683	133
30 FFFg	30.9	937	250	784	175
Pyrodex (P) 30 P	24.0	901	231	757	163

▶ **30 FFFg or 30 P maximum recommended load**

COMMENTS

The 20 FFFg charge seemed sufficient for the short-range target and plinking work this pistol was intended for. However, the 30 volume FFFg and 30 volume Pyrodex P loads were also fine. Any would be more than sufficient for small game as well as target work; they should be considered *optimum loads*.

See the caution that precedes this section. Note: Maximum load listed in bold should be used with caution.

HOPKINS & ALLEN

Boot Pistol, Model 133 (36-cal.)*

Caliber: 36

Barrel Length: 6″

Barrel Dim: 13/16″ across flats

Rate of Twist: 1:15″

Depth of Groove: .006″

Powder: GOI, Pyrodex (P)

Patch: .013″ Irish linen

Ignition: CCI No. 11

Lube: RIG

Powd. Meas.: Uncle Mike 120

Powd. Temp.: 80° F.

*Also known as Ashabell Cook underhammer

LOAD DATA

Projectile/.350″ Weight/65-gr. Type/Denver Bullet Co. round ball

Powder Charge (Volume)	Powder Charge (Approx. gr. wt.)	Muzzle Velocity FPS.	Muzzle Energy Ft. Lbs.	Velocity 50 yds.	Energy 50 yds.
20 FFFg	20.7	987	141	755	82
30 FFFg	30.9	1128	184	835	101
Pyrodex (P)					
20 P	15.3	684	68	554	44
30 P	24.0	745	80	596	51

▶ **30 FFFg or 30 P maximum recommended load**

COMMENTS

This little single-shot pistol was very comfortable to shoot with either the 20 or 30 volume FFFg load. In our short tests, and with our load chain, the 20 FFFg load (very pleasant to shoot), was the more accurate of the two; however, the shooter would be urged to try loads from 15 to 30 FFFg volume in his personal H&A before settling on an *optimum load* for accuracy.

See the caution that precedes this section. Note: Maximum load listed in bold should be used with caution.

LYMAN

Plains Pistol (54-cal.)

Caliber: 54

Barrel Length: 8″

Barrel Dim: 15/16″ across flats

Rate of Twist: 1:30″

Depth of Groove: .0095″

Powder: GOI

Patch: .013″ pure Irish linen

Ignition: CCI No. 11

Lube: RIG

Powd. Meas.: Uncle Mike 120

Powd. Temp.: 65° F.

LOAD DATA

Projectile/.530″ Weight/225-gr. Type/Denver Bullet Co. round ball

Powder Charge (Volume)	Powder Charge (Approx. gr. wt.)	Muzzle Velocity FPS.	Muzzle Energy Ft. Lbs.	Velocity 50 yds.	Energy 50 yds.
30 FFFg	30.9	860	370	753	283
40 FFFg	41.2	952	453	819	335
30 FFg	29.6	743	258	650	211
40 FFg	39.5	856	366	749	280
50 FFg	49.5	926	429	803	322

▶ **40 FFFg or 50 FFg maximum recommended load**

COMMENTS

Although we were allowed as much as 50 FFFg in the Lyman Plains Pistol, I stopped at 40 FFFg and used a 50 volume charge only with FFg granulation. The velocity with 50 FFg, it seems to me, is gratifying, and so is the velocity with 40 FFFg. Considering the nature of this handgun, I would look at 30 FFFg as my *optimum load* dropping in 50 FFg when the pistol is used as a backup for rifle hunting, and using 40 FFFg for a hunting load.

See the caution that precedes this section. Note: Maximum load listed in bold should be used with caution.

NAVY ARMS

Harper's Ferry 1855 (58-cal.)

Caliber: 58

Barrel Length: 11⅞"

Barrel Dim: ¹⁵⁄₁₆"

Rate of Twist: 1:48"

Depth of Groove: .003—.005"

Powder: GOI

Patch: None

Ignition: Navy Arms Musket Cap

Lube: RIG

Powd. Meas.: Uncle Mike 120

Powd. Temp.: 75° F.

LOAD DATA—A

Projectile/.575" Weight/500-gr.* Type/Lyman Minie Mould/No. 575213

Powder Charge (Volume)	Powder Charge (Approx. gr. wt.)	Muzzle Velocity FPS.	Muzzle Energy Ft. Lbs.	Velocity 50 yds.	Energy 50 yds.
30 FFg	29.6	577	388	554	358
40 FFg	39.5	657	503	631	464
50 FFg	49.5	730	621	701	573
60 FFg	59.5	802	750	766	684

▶ **60 FFg maximum recommended load**

* The Lyman mould used for our test actually tossed a projectile weighing 525 grains.

COMMENTS

The *optimum load* for hunting purposes is 60 FFg. This is a powerful pistol.

See the caution that precedes this section. Note: Maximum load listed in bold should be used with caution.

NAVY ARMS

Harper's Ferry 1855 (58-cal.)

▶ All pertinent data for Load Data—B is the same as for Load Data—A except the following:

Projectile: .577" 570-gr. Lyman Minie

LOAD DATA—B

Projectile/.577" Weight/570-gr.* Type/Lyman Minie Mould/No. 57730

Powder Charge (Volume)	Powder Charge (Approx. gr. wt.)	Muzzle Velocity FPS.	Muzzle Energy Ft. Lbs.	Velocity 50 yds.	Energy 50 yds.
50 FFg	49.5	697	647	669	596

▶ **50 FFg maximum recommended load**

* The Lyman mould used for our test actually tossed a projectile weighing 600 grains.

COMMENTS   *Optimum load* is 50 FFg.

▶ All pertinent data for Load Data—C is the same as for Load Data—A except the following:

Patch: .015" Ox-Yoke Precision Blue-Striped
Ignition: CCI No. 11

See the caution that precedes this section. Note: Maximum load listed in bold should be used with caution.

LOAD DATA—C

Projectile/.570" Weight/278-gr. Type/Hornady round ball

Powder Charge (Volume)	Powder Charge (Approx. gr. wt.)	Muzzle Velocity FPS.	Muzzle Energy Ft. Lbs.	Velocity 50 yds.	Energy 50 yds.
30 FFg	29.6	612	231	557	206
40 FFg	39.5	660	269	597	220
50 FFg	49.5	790	385	703	305
60 FFg	59.5	975	587	839	435

▶ **60 FFg maximum recommended load**

COMMENTS

Our loads with this big pistol changed over the course of testing, and we ended up with maximum charges based in part on sheer recoil. If indeed the 44 Magnum, 41 Magnum and 357 Magnum are listed as big game numbers among some hunters and state game departments, which they are, then there can be no doubt that this big-bore handgun is also a big game sidearm.

At 100 yards with the heavier charges and the Minies, the 58 erupted 1-gallon cans filled with water.

See the caution that precedes this section. Note: Maximum load listed in bold should be used with caution.

NAVY ARMS

J&S Hawken Pistol (54-cal.)

Caliber: 54

Barrel Length: 9″

Barrel Dim: 15/16″ across flats

Rate of Twist: 1:36″

Depth of Groove: .010″

Powder: GOI

Patch: .015″ Ox-Yoke Precision Blue-Striped

Ignition: CCI No. 11

Lube: RIG

Powd. Meas.: Uncle Mike 120

Powd. Temp.: 70° F.

LOAD DATA

Projectile/.530″ Weight/225-gr. Type/Speer round ball

Powder Charge (Volume)	Powder Charge (Approx. gr. wt.)	Muzzle Velocity FPS.	Muzzle Energy Ft. Lbs.	Velocity 50 yds.	Energy 50 yds.
30 FFFg	30.9	757	286	685	234
40 FFFg	41.2	988	488	844	356
30 FFg	29.6	632	225	581	169
40 FFg	39.5	727	264	658	216

▶ **40 FFFg maximum recommended load**

COMMENTS

The J&S Hawken pistol is a handmate to the shooter who has a rifle of the same caliber. As one can see by the data, it is a rather powerful handgun for small game use, but with head shots, such loads make no difference. It is also a good Rendezvous sidearm, since it corresponds to the old-time sash gun. As it turns out, we could not see a lot of difference in accuracy between the 30 and 40 FFFg charges, but in terms of recoil, the 30, obviously, was more pleasant to shoot from the bench. For a sidearm used as a companion piece on the backtrail, the 40 FFFg would be a good one. An *optimum load* would be a matter of personal choice, in this case.

See the caution that precedes this section. Note: Maximum load listed in bold should be used with caution.

Buntline Dragoon Revolver (44-cal.)

Caliber: 44

Barrel Length: 18″

Barrel Dim: Round

Rate of Twist: 1:24″

Depth of Groove: .003″—.004″

Powder: GOI, Pyrodex

Patch: None

Ignition: Navy Arms No. 11

Lube: RIG (over ball)

Powd. Meas.: Uncle Mike 120

Powd. Temp.: 70° F.

LOAD DATA—A

Projectile/.454″ Weight/141-gr. Type/Speer round ball

Powder Charge (Volume)	Powder Charge (Approx. gr. wt.)	Muzzle Velocity FPS.	Muzzle Energy Ft. Lbs.	Velocity 50 yds.	Energy 50 yds.
20 FFFg	20.7	658	136	572	102
30 FFFg	30.9	961	289	807	204
40 FFFg	41.2	1192	445	954	285
45 FFFg	46.5	1269	504	1009	319
Pyrodex (P) 20 P	15.3	726	165	632	125
30 P	24.0	1043	341	855	229
40 P	31.0	1180	436	944	279
45 P	36.1	1336	559	1055	349

▶ **45 FFFg or 45 P maximum recommended load**

COMMENTS Best accuracy was with the 30 Pyrodex P charge. We recommend 45 Pyrodex P as the *optimum load* for hunting.

See the caution that precedes this section. Note: Maximum load listed in bold should be used with caution.

NAVY ARMS

Buntline Dragoon (44-cal.)

▶ All pertinent data for Load Data—B is the same as for Load Data—A except the following:

Projectile: .456″ 220-gr.

LOAD DATA—B

Projectile/.456″ Weight/220-gr. Type/Lee bullet Mould/No. 456-220-IR

Powder Charge (Volume)	Powder Charge (Approx. gr. wt.)	Muzzle Velocity FPS.	Muzzle Energy Ft. Lbs.	Velocity 50 yds.	Energy 50 yds.
30 FFFg	30.9	1065	554	980	469
35 FFFg	36.0	1114	606	1019	507
Pyrodex (P) 35 P	27.5	980	469	907	402

▶ **35 FFFg or 35 P maximum recommended load**

COMMENTS

The Buntline Dragoon's chamber capacity was slightly lower than the chamber capacity on the standard Walker we tested; therefore, we show an appropriately lower volume charge. However, the long barrel did appear to be of some value in picking up on velocity. The *optimum load* is 35 of FFFg.

See the caution that precedes this section. Note: Maximum load listed in bold should be used with caution.

NAVY ARMS

Kentucky Pistol (44-cal.)

Caliber: 44

Barrel Length: 10⅛"

Barrel Dim: ⅞" across flats

Rate of Twist: 1:60"

Depth of Groove: .003"—.005"

Powder: GOI, Pyrodex (P)

Patch: .015" pillow ticking

Ignition: FFFFg pan powder

Lube: RIG

Powd. Meas.: Uncle Mike 120

Powd. Temp.: 70° F.

LOAD DATA

Projectile/.440" Weight/129-gr. Type/Hornady round ball

Powder Charge (Volume)	Powder Charge (Approx. gr. wt.)	Muzzle Velocity FPS.	Muzzle Energy Ft. Lbs.	Velocity 50 yds.	Energy 50 yds.
40 FFFg	41.2	1095	344	876	220
40 FFg	39.5	977	274	811	188
Pyrodex (P) 40 P	31.0	979	275	813	189

▶ **40 FFFg or 40 P maximum recommended load**

COMMENTS

We settled upon one *optimum load* for this pistol—40 FFg—which seemed to satisfy both the demands of informal target practice and power. Due, perhaps, to the 10⅛-inch barrel, we found good velocity with FFg in this handgun. Ignition, by the way, was equal with FFFg and FFg in our tests. We had zero misfires or hangfires with either.

See the caution that precedes this section. Note: Maximum load listed in bold should be used with caution.

NAVY ARMS

"Reb" Model 60 Sheriff Revolver (44-cal.)

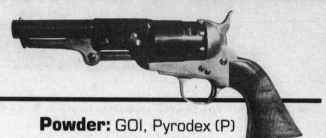

Caliber: 44

Barrel Length: 4⅞"

Barrel Dim: Round tapered

Rate of Twist: 1:24"

Depth of Groove: .003"—.004"

Powder: GOI, Pyrodex (P)

Patch: None

Ignition: Navy Arms No. 11

Lube: RIG (over ball)

Powd. Meas.: Uncle Mike 120

Powd. Temp.: 70° F.

LOAD DATA

Projectile/.451" Weight/138-gr. Type/Hornady round ball

Powder Charge (Volume)	Powder Charge (Approx. gr. wt.)	Muzzle Velocity FPS.	Muzzle Energy Ft. Lbs.	Velocity 50 yds.	Energy 50 yds.
15 FFFg	15.6	450	62	396	48
20 FFFg	20.7	563	97	493	74
25 FFFg	25.8	647	128	563	97
30 FFFg	30.9	694	148	604	112
Pyrodex (P) 15 P	11.5	508	79	447	61
20 P	15.3	699	150	608	113
25 P	19.7	761	178	662	134
30 P	24.0	782	187	679	141

▶ **30 FFFg or 30 P maximum recommended load**

COMMENTS

This is a properly named model, as it would indeed have been fitting for a law officer, being a compact firearm in a good bore size. We found that close-range plinking was definitely a possibility, in spite of the lack of target sights, so our tests included a range of loads. Our recommended *optimum load* is 20 FFFg or Pyrodex P, a satisfying compromise in "authority," shooting fun, and accuracy.

See the caution that precedes this section. Note: Maximum load listed in bold should be used with caution.

Remington 1858 Revolver (44-cal.)

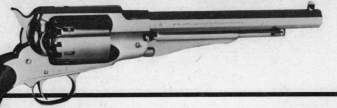

Caliber: 44

Barrel Length: 8"

Barrel Dim: Tapered octagonal

Rate of Twist: 1:12"

Depth of Groove: .003"—.005"

Powder: GOI, Pyrodex (P)

Patch: None

Ignition: Navy Arms No. 11

Lube: RIG (over ball)

Powd. Meas.: Uncle Mike 120

Powd. Temp.: 70° F.

LOAD DATA

Projectile/.454" Weight/141-gr. Type/Speer round ball

Powder Charge (Volume)	Powder Charge (Approx. gr. wt.)	Muzzle Velocity FPS.	Muzzle Energy Ft. Lbs.	Velocity 50 yds.	Energy 50 yds.
20 FFFg	20.7	591	109	514	83
35 FFFg*	36.0	907	258	771	186
Pyrodex (P) 40 P**	31.0	882	244	754	178

▶ **35 FFFg or 40 P maximum recommended loads**

* 35 FFFg with the .454" ball filled the chamber.
**40 Pyrodex P with the .454" ball filled the chamber.

COMMENTS

Accuracy was best with 20 FFFg and corn meal filler. With 35 FFFg, the chambers were easily filled, leaving enough room for the ball and an over-ball daub of grease to prevent chain firing. However, 40 Pyrodex P did fit into the chamber by compressing the charge somewhat. In my opinion, the *optimum load* is the 20 FFFg charge —its accuracy is excellent.

See the caution that precedes this section. Note: Maximum load listed in bold should be used with caution.

NAVY ARMS

Rogers & Spencer Army Revolver (44 cal.)

Caliber: 44

Barrel Length: 7½"

Barrel Dim: Tapered octagonal

Rate of Twist: 1:12"

Depth of Groove: .003"—.005"

Powder: GOI

Patch: None

Ignition: Navy Arms No. 11

Lube: RIG (over ball)

Powd. Meas.: Uncle Mike 120

Powd. Temp.: 66° F.

LOAD DATA

Projectile/.454" Weight/141-gr. Type/Speer round ball

Powder Charge (Volume)	Powder Charge (Approx. gr. wt.)	Muzzle Velocity FPS.	Muzzle Energy Ft. Lbs.	Velocity 50 yds.	Energy 50 yds.
20 FFFg	20.7	586	108	510	81
30 FFFg	30.9	796	198	689	149
35 FFFg*	36.0	901	252	766	184

▶ **35 FFFg maximum recommended load**

 * 35 FFFg with the .454" ball filled the chamber.

COMMENTS

Best accuracy was obtained with 20 FFFg and corn meal filler. In later tests, 25 FFFg proved just as accurate in this handgun as 20 FFFg grains. Using 35 FFFg by volume, which in our measure is also 36.0 by grains weight, there was ample room to seat the ball with enough space above the ball for grease, used to prevent chain firing. My *optimum load* would be 25 FFFg by virtue of its proven accuracy and increased velocity over the 20 FFFg charge.

See the caution that precedes this section. Note: Maximum load listed in bold should be used with caution.

Walker Colt Revolver (44-cal.)

Caliber: 44

Barrel Length: 9"

Barrel Dim: Round tapered

Rate of Twist: 1:24"

Depth of Groove: .003"—.004"

Powder: GOI, Pyrodex (P)

Patch: None

Ignition: CCI No. 11

Lube: RIG (over ball)

Powd. Meas.: Uncle Mike 120

Powd. Temp.: 70° F.

LOAD DATA

Projectile/.454" Weight/141-gr. Type/Hornady round ball

Powder Charge (Volume)	Powder Charge (Approx. gr. wt.)	Muzzle Velocity FPS.	Muzzle Energy Ft. Lbs.	Velocity 100 yds.	Energy 100 yds.
55 FFFg	57.2	1205	455	964	291
Pyrodex (P) 57 P	44.2	1215	462	972	296

▶ **55 FFFg or 57 P maximum recommended load**

COMMENTS

Since this big Walker Colt replica is not meant for target shooting, we worked toward an *optimum load* which would give us the ultimate in *safe* high velocity, and found that we could get 55 grains volume of FFFg in the chambers or 57 volume of Pyrodex P into the chambers. Two notes: 1. The Pyrodex P was a lot which had been resting for 6 months after purchase in a very dry atmosphere. We call this type of powder "cured." 2. Other replicas of the Walker may not have as much chamber capacity (or could have slightly more for that matter). The chambers will sometimes vary according to the manufacturer. Our data, however, is intended to be confined to the Navy Arms Walker Colt covered here.

See the caution that precedes this section. Note: Maximum load listed in bold should be used with caution.

NAVY ARMS

Colt Pocket Police Revolver (36-cal.)

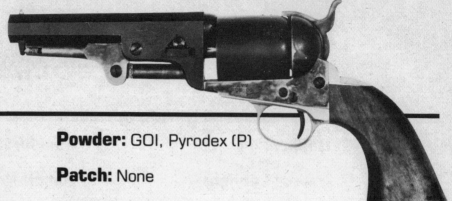

Caliber: 36

Barrel Length: 8"

Barrel Dim: Round tapered

Rate of Twist: 1:24"

Depth of Groove: .003"—.004"

Powder: GOI, Pyrodex (P)

Patch: None

Ignition: CCI No. 11

Lube: RIG (over ball)

Powd. Meas.: Uncle Mike 120

Powd. Temp.: 70° F.

LOAD DATA

Projectile/.375" Weight/80-gr. Type/Hornady round ball

Powder Charge (Volume)	Powder Charge (Approx. gr. wt.)	Muzzle Velocity FPS.	Muzzle Energy Ft. Lbs.	Velocity 50 yds.	Energy 50 yds.
10 FFFg	10.5	433	33	355	22
15 FFFg	15.6	730	95	591	62
20 FFFg	20.7	881	138	709	89
23 FFFg	23.5	915	149	737	97
Pyrodex (P)					
10 P	7.7	439	34	360	23
15 P	11.5	701	87	568	57
20 P	15.3	799	113	647	74
24 P*	18.6	954	162	749	100

▶ **23 FFFg or 24 P maximum recommended load**

* Uncle Mike 120 measure set at 24 did work with Pyrodex P in filling the chamber.

COMMENTS

The little Navy Arms 36-caliber Colt replica was enjoyable to fire, and we would place it in the realm of a sidearm used for plinking. It is historical in nature and our copy shot quite well. The accuracy was best in the 15 FFFg load; however, we will call the 23 Pyrodex P load our *optimum load* because of its increased velocity.

See the caution that precedes this section. Note: Maximum load listed in bold should be used with caution.

PENGUIN/HOPPE'S

Ethan Allen M300 Target Pistol (45-cal.)

Caliber: 45

Barrel Length: 7"

Barrel Dim: N.A.

Rate of Twist: 1:25"

Depth of Groove: .010"

Powder: GOI

Patch: .013" pure Irish linen

Ignition: CCI No. 11

Lube: RIG

Powd. Meas.: Uncle Mike 120

Powd. Temp.: 70° F.

LOAD DATA

Projectile/.440" Weight/128-gr. Type/Hornady round ball

Powder Charge (Volume)	Powder Charge (Approx. gr. wt.)	Muzzle Velocity FPS.	Muzzle Energy Ft. Lbs.	Velocity 50 yds.	Energy 50 yds.
25 FFFg	25.8	752	162	647	120

▶ **25 FFFg maximum recommended load**

COMMENTS   The above load is considered an *optimum load* for this target pistol.

See the caution that precedes this section. Note: Maximum load listed in bold should be used with caution.

RICHLAND

Texas New Army Revolver (44-cal.)

Caliber: 44

Barrel Length: 12"

Barrel Dim: Octagonal

Rate of Twist: 1:39"

Depth of Groove: .008"

Powder: GOI, Pyrodex (P)

Patch: None

Ignition: CCI No. 11

Lube: RIG (over ball)

Powd. Meas.: Uncle Mike 120

Powd. Temp.: 72° F.

LOAD DATA—A

Projectile/.454" Weight/141-gr. Type/Speer round ball

Powder Charge (Volume)	Powder Charge (Approx. gr. wt.)	Muzzle Velocity FPS.	Muzzle Energy Ft. Lbs.	Velocity 50 yds.	Energy 50 yds.
20 FFFg	20.7	745	174	647	131
25 FFFg*	25.8	899	253	764	183
30 FFFg	30.9	991	308	823	212
35 FFFg	36.0	1031	333	953	284
Pyrodex (P) 35 P	28.0	967	293	812	308

▶ **35 FFFg or 35 P maximum recommended load**

*Accurate with corn meal filler.

See the caution that precedes this section. Note: Maximum load listed in bold should be used with caution.

▶ All pertinent data for Load Data—B is the same as for Load Data—A except the following:

Projectile: .456, 220-gr. Lee bullet

LOAD DATA—B

Projectile/.456" Weight/220-gr. Type/Lee bullet Mould/456-220-IR

Powder Charge (Volume)	Powder Charge (Approx. gr. wt.)	Muzzle Velocity FPS.	Muzzle Energy Ft. Lbs.	Velocity 50 yds.	Energy 50 yds.
25 FFFg	25.8	845	349	794	308
Pyrodex (P) 25 P	19.7	716	250	675	227

▶ **25 FFFg or 25 P maximum recommended load**

COMMENTS (Loads A&B)

This interesting handgun with the long sight radius was most accurate with 25 FFFg and 141-grain round ball with corn meal filler. It was also accurate with the 25 FFFg charge and the 220 Lee bullet. Either load could be considered an *optimum load*.

See the caution that precedes this section. Note: Maximum load listed in bold should be used with caution.

187

RICHLAND

3rd Hartford Dragoon 1851 Rev. (44 cal.)

Caliber: 44

Barrel Length: 7½"

Barrel Dim: Round

Rate of Twist: 1:39"

Depth of Groove: .008"

Powder: GOI, Pyrodex (P)

Patch: None

Ignition: Navy Arms No. 11

Lube: RIG (over ball)

Powd. Meas.: Uncle Mike 120

Powd. Temp.: 67° F.

LOAD DATA—A

Projectile/.454" Weight/141-gr. Type/Hornady round ball

Powder Charge (Volume)	Powder Charge (Approx. gr. wt.)	Muzzle Velocity FPS.	Muzzle Energy Ft. Lbs.	Velocity 50 yds.	Energy 50 yds.
30 FFFg	30.9	852	227	733	168
40 FFFg	41.2	1025	329	849	226
45 FFFg	46.5	1100	379	891	249
50 FFFg	51.8	1142	408	925	268
Pyrodex (P) 50 P	38.7	908	258	772	187

▶ **50 FFFg or 50 P maximum recommended load**

COMMENTS

While this is not a target model in any sense, the Richland Arms Dragoon is very impressive as a shooter. Our *optimum load* is the 45 FFFg charge.

See the caution that precedes this section. Note: Maximum load listed in bold should be used with caution.

► All pertinent data for Load Data—B is the same as for Load Data—A except the following:

Projectile: Lee .456"
220-gr. bullet

LOAD DATA—B

Projectile/.456" Weight/220-gr. Type/Lee bullet Mould/456-220

Powder Charge (Volume)	Powder Charge (Approx. gr. wt.)	Muzzle Velocity FPS.	Muzzle Energy Ft. Lbs.	Velocity 50 yds.	Energy 50 yds.
40 FFFg	41.2	905	400	846	350

► **40 FFFg maximum recommended load**

See the caution that precedes this section. Note: Maximum load listed in bold should be used with caution.

189

RUGER

Old Army Revolver (44-cal.)

Caliber: 44

Barrel Length: 7½"

Barrel Dim: Round

Rate of Twist: 1:16"

Depth of Groove: .006"

Powder: GOI

Patch: None

Ignition: CCI No. 11

Lube: RIG (over ball)

Powd. Meas.: Uncle Mike 120

Powd. Temp.: 75° F.

LOAD DATA

Projectile/.457" Weight/143-gr. Type/Hornady round ball

Powder Charge (Volume)	Powder Charge (Approx. gr. wt.)	Muzzle Velocity FPS.	Muzzle Energy Ft. Lbs.	Velocity 50 yds.	Energy 50 yds.
20 FFFg	20.7	598	114	520	86
25 FFFg	25.8	701	156	610	118
30 FFFg	30.9	842	225	724	166
40 FFFg	41.2	984	308	827	217
Pyrodex (P)					
20 P	15.3	601	115	523	87
25 P	19.6	763	185	664	140
30 P	24.0	917	267	779	193
40 P	31.0	1047	348	859	234

▶ **40 FFFg or 40 P maximum recommended loads.**

COMMENTS
(Loads A&B)

Our best accuracy was obtained with the .457" Hornady 143-grain round ball and 25 FFFg or 25 Pyrodex P, with a cornmeal filler to take up space in the chamber. Given the superb accuracy of these loads, I would recommend either as the *optimum load*.

See the caution that precedes this section. Note: Maximum load listed in bold should be used with caution.

THOMPSON/CENTER

Patriot (45-cal.)

Caliber: 45

Barrel Length: 9″

Barrel Dim: 13/16″ across flats

Rate of Twist: 1:20″

Depth of Groove: .010″

Powder: GOI, Pyrodex (P)

Patch: .013″ Irish linen/plus cotton over powder patch for 30 grains or more

Ignition: Navy Arms No. 11

Lube: Whale Oil

Powd. Meas.: Uncle Mike 120

Powd. Temp.: 75° F.

LOAD DATA—A

Projectile/.445″ Weight/133-gr. Type/Hornady round ball

Powder Charge (Volume)	Powder Charge (Approx. gr. wt.)	Muzzle Velocity FPS.	Muzzle Energy Ft. Lbs.	Velocity 50 yds.	Energy 50 yds.
20 FFFg	20.7	716	151	623	115
25 FFFg	25.8	821	199	709	148
30 FFFg	30.9	913	246	776	178
35 FFFg	36.0	991	290	823	200
Pyrodex (P) 20 P	15.3	730	157	635	119
25 P	19.6	811	194	702	146
30 P	24.0	931	256	791	185
35 P	27.5	1021	303	838	207

▶ **35 FFFg or 35 P maximum recommended load**

THOMPSON/CENTER

Patriot (45-cal.)

▶ All pertinent data for Load Data—B is the same as for Load Data—A except the following:

Projectile: .440" 129-gr. Hornady round ball

LOAD DATA—B

Projectile/.440" Weight/129-gr. Type/Hornady round ball

Powder Charge (Volume)	Powder Charge (Approx. gr. wt.)	Muzzle Velocity FPS.	Muzzle Energy Ft. Lbs.	Velocity 50 yds.	Energy 50 yds.
20 FFFg	20.7	712	145	619	110
25 FFFg	25.8	802	184	694	138
30 FFFg	30.9	901	233	766	168
35 FFFg	36.0	987	279	844	204
Pyrodex (P) 20 P	15.3	724	150	630	114
25 P	19.6	808	187	699	140
30 P	24.0	922	244	780	174
35 P	27.5	1007	291	836	200

▶ **35 FFFg or 35 P maximum recommended loads**

COMMENTS
(Load Data A&B)

Accuracy was best with 30 FFFg or Pyrodex P (same accuracy with either). Even at 30 FFFg however, there was some patch burnout, and accuracy was improved with a backer patch or a small bit of hornet nest on the powder charge prior to loading the patched round ball. Our tests did not disclose any measurable accuracy differences between the .440" and .445" ball. With the use of a backer patch, the 30 FFFg charge is our *optimum load*. If you don't have and sperm whale oil, J&A Old Slickum will serve well as a substitute.

See the caution that precedes this section. Note: Maximum load listed in bold should be used with caution.

Loading Data

BLACK POWDER METALLICS

> **WARNING:** A recent study has indicated that the use of corn meal, Kapok or any other "filler" can be unsafe in metallic cartridges. While the data may suggest the use of such a filler, we must warn against such practice. Air space in a black powder loaded metallic cartridge may be reduced by going to a coarser granulation of black powder and/or a heavier, safe, black powder charge. Space may also be taken up by deeper bullet seating or the use of a longer/heavier bullet. At least 90 percent of the case space available should be filled with either powder or projectile.

INTRODUCTION

WE HAVE an important and somewhat full chapter on the loading of the black powder metallic cartridges, and the reader is urged to examine this material before loading any rounds of ammo. While the mechanical basics are the same for either smokeless or black powder cartridges, there are some rather important differences as well. That chapter deals with those differences, the aim being to help the reader toward a common goal—safe and accurate black powder metallic ammunition.

But why black powder in the metallics? Won't smokeless do as well or better? Without letting sentiment or romance cloud our vision, there is no doubt that in *some* rifles the use of a recommended smokeless powder in recommended safe amounts is a wise way to go in the old-time black powder metallic.

However, there is a reason for the rather impressive growth of interest in the black powder cartridge. In fact, there are a number of occasions when I much prefer black powder. Mainly, we use black powder in the old-time arms because they were designed for it to begin with. When there is an original and mechanically safe shooting iron around, one can rest assured that the use of black powder will maintain the gun in good repair. Simply, the pressure is lower than it is in most smokeless applications where similar velocities are to be obtained.

Aside from a pressure standpoint, there are many shooters who prefer to use black powder, at least some of the time, in their old-time cartridge guns because it is the traditional and historical fuel. They do not mind the minor cleanup problems, because they prefer the smoke and "thump" that goes with black powder now as it did back in the days when those interesting cartridge guns were invented and used across our land. So, with these two reasons (mildness of pressure and historical purpose), we find a large number of shooters going afield with black powder loaded into the cartridges in their magazines or chambers of their black powder cartridge guns. The bellow from a Sharps firing, for example, 120 grains of Fg or FFg black powder behind a 500- or 550-grain bullet is its own reward for stepping back in time with these old arms. Smokeless powder, while often doing a very fine job in breechloaders designed for that propellant, is not necessarily correct for all situations and purposes.

We urge, once more, that as the reader digests the following black powder loading data, he does not attempt a single load in his own black powder cartridge firearms without first consulting the chapter on this subject. We have included data on proper primers, proper powder amounts and granulations, case cleanup, case length and trimming, information on old cases, bullet diameters for the old guns, and much more in this chapter.

We hope that the person interested in using black powder safely and effectively in his breechloader will enjoy that chapter prepared for his benefit. Meanwhile, here are the loads which we tested and chronographed for a number of black powder cartridge arms.

Single Action Army (45 Colt)

Caliber: 45 Colt

Barrel Length: 7½"

Barrel Dim: Round

Rate of Twist: 1:16"

Depth of Groove: N.A.

Powder: GOI

Patch: None

Ignition: Large pistol primer

Lube: None

Powd. Meas.: Uncle Mike 120

Powd. Temp.: 80° F.

LOAD DATA

Projectile/.451" Weight/255-gr. Type/Lyman bullet Mould/No. 454424

Powder Charge (Volume)	Powder Charge (Approx. gr. wt.)	Muzzle Velocity FPS.	Muzzle Energy Ft. Lbs.	Velocity 50 yds.	Energy 50 yds.
37FFg	38.3	773	338	730	302

▶ **37 FFg maximum recommended load**

COMMENTS

In testing this round with our original Colt Peacemaker, we were not satisfied with the results of our particular load. The rounds had been pre-loaded some time ago with a case full of FFg black powder, duPont brand. However, we felt something was amiss when our velocity averaged at 550 fps at the muzzle. We did, in fact, obtain better ballistics with our fresh loads in this Colt (newly manufactured) 45. The load listed is intended for use in Single Action Army Colt revolvers in good, safe, mechanical condition. If you have any doubts about the SA Colt you intend to fire this load in, have the gun thoroughly checked out by a competent gunsmith. The 37-grain charge of FFg is the *optimum load*.

Case lengths are as follows: *Trim*—1.280"; *Maximum Case*—1.285"; *Maximum Overall*—1.600". **Shell holders** are as follows: *RCBS*—20; *Bonanza*—21; *Lyman*—11; *Pacific*—32.

See the caution that precedes this section. Note: Maximum load listed in bold should be used with caution.

HARRINGTON & RICHARDSON

M171, Trap Door Cav. Carb. (45-70 Gov't.)

Caliber: 45-70 Gov't.

Barrel Length: 22"

Barrel Dim: Round tapered

Rate of Twist: 1:20"

Depth of Groove: .004"

Powder: GOI

Patch: None

Ignition: Large rifle primer

Lube: None

Powd. Meas.: Uncle Mike 120

Powd. Temp.: 64° F.

LOAD DATA

Projectile/.457" Weight/405-gr. Type/Remington JSP

Powder Charge (Volume)	Powder Charge (Approx. gr. wt.)	Muzzle Velocity FPS.	Muzzle Energy Ft. Lbs.	Velocity 100 yds.	Energy 100 yds.
67 FFg	66.7	1202	1300	1058	1007
▶ **67 FFg maximum recommended load**					

COMMENTS

The rifle was a great deal of fun to shoot with black powder cartridges, and we felt that recoil was not a problem. The rifle was very easy to clean, and in 10 minutes the bore was sparkling after a range session of 40 rounds. Standard deviation with our black powder load was lower than was the factory fodder, being 53 fps with the factory ammo and 24 fps with the handloaded black powder ammo. The *optimum load* is 67 FFg.

Case lengths are as follows: *Trim*—2.100"; *Maximum Case*—2.105"; *Maximum Overall*—2.550". **Shell holders** are as follows: *RCBS*—14; *Bonanza*—16; *Lyman*—17; *Pacific*—14.

See the caution that precedes this section. Note: Maximum load listed in bold should be used with caution.

Marlin 1895 S (45-70 Gov't.)

Caliber: 45-70 Gov't.

Barrel Length: 22"

Barrel Dim: Round

Rate of Twist: 1:12"

Depth of Groove: .006"

Powder: GOI

Patch: None

Ignition: Large rifle primer

Lube: None

Powd. Meas.: Uncle Mike 120

Powd. Temp.: 77° F.

LOAD DATA

Projectile/.457" Weight/405-gr. Type/Remington JSP

Powder Charge (Volume)	Powder Charge (Approx. gr. wt.)	Muzzle Velocity FPS.	Muzzle Energy Ft. Lbs.	Velocity 100 yds.	Energy 100 yds.
67 FFg	66.7	1231	1363	1083	1055

▶ **67 FFg maximum recommended load**

COMMENTS

The Marlin 1895S was designed very much in the old-time style, and with the intent of offering a repeater capable of throwing a large caliber bullet. While its black powder load is not as powerful as some of the smokeless loads possible in this rifle, there is no doubt that our black powder load offers sufficient ballistics for close-range hunting. The *optimum load* is 67 grains of FFg.

Case lengths are as follows: *Trim*—2.100"; *Maximum Case*—2.105"; *Maximum Overall*—2.550". **Shell holders** are as follows: *RCBS*—14; *Bonanza*—16; *Lyman*—17; *Pacific*—14.

See the caution that precedes this section. Note: Maximum load listed in bold should be used with caution.

NAVY ARMS

Henry Repeating Rifle/Carbine (44-40 Win.)

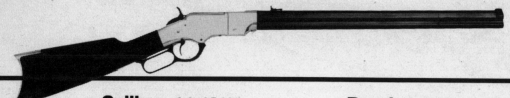

Caliber: 44-40 Win.

Barrel Length: 21"

Barrel Dim: Octagonal

Rate of Twist: 1:36"

Depth of Groove: .003"

Powder: GOI

Patch: None

Ignition: Large rifle primer

Lube: Alox 2138F & bee's wax, 50/50

Powd. Meas.: Uncle Mike 120

Powd. Temp.: 59° F.

LOAD DATA

Projectile/.427" Weight/200-gr. Type/Lyman bullet Mould/No. 42798

Powder Charge (Volume)	Powder Charge (Approx. gr. wt.)	Muzzle Velocity FPS.	Muzzle Energy Ft. Lbs.	Velocity 100 yds.	Energy 100 yds.
35FFg	34.6	1206	646	965	414

▶ **35 FFg maximum recommended load**

COMMENTS

We have gotten up to 1307 fps with the 44-40 and 35 FFg; however, as always, the ballistics vary with the rifle in accord with several factors, including bore dimension, barrel length, powder lots, etc. This particular test arm developed an average velocity of 1206 fps at the muzzle. One can see that the 44-40 is not an extremely powerful cartridge. On the other hand, this round, with black powder loads, has taken and will take deer-sized game at close range. Furthermore, it is a cinch to shoot rapidly, due to low recoil. The *optimum load* is 35 grains of FFg.

Case lengths are as follows: *Trim*—1.582"; *Maximum Case*—1.305"; *Maximum Overall*—1.592". **Shell holders** are as follows: *RCBS*—26 or 28; *Bonanza*—19; *Lyman*—14B; *Pacific*—9.

See the caution that precedes this section. Note: Maximum load listed in bold should be used with caution.

Remington Rolling Block (45-70 Gov't.)

Caliber: 45-70 Gov't.

Barrel Length: 26″

Barrel Dim: 1¹⁄₁₆″ across flats

Rate of Twist: 1:22″

Depth of Groove: .003″

Powder: GOI

Patch: None

Ignition: Large rifle primer

Lube: None

Powd. Meas.: Uncle Mike 120

Powd. Temp.: 67° F.

LOAD DATA

Projectile/.457″ Weight/405-gr. Type/Remington JSP

Powder Charge (Volume)	Powder Charge (Approx. gr. wt.)	Muzzle Velocity FPS.	Muzzle Energy Ft. Lbs.	Velocity 100 yds.	Energy 100 yds.
67 FFg	66.7	1243	1390	1094	1077

▶ **67 FFg maximum recommended load**

COMMENTS

Yet another enjoyable 45-70 with black powder loads was the Navy Arms Remington Rolling Block rifle. Ballistics with the black powder round were totally sufficient for close-range hunting and also for target work. The *optimum* *load* is 67 grains of FFg.

Case lengths are as follows: *Trim*—2.100″; *Maximum Case*—2.105″; *Maximum Overall*—2.550″. **Shell holders** are as follows: *RCBS*—14; *Bonanza*—16; *Lyman*—17; *Pacific*—14.

See the caution that precedes this section. Note: Maximum load listed in bold should be used with caution.

RUGER

No. 3 Single Shot Carbine (45-70 Gov't.)

Caliber: 45-70 Gov't.

Barrel Length: 22"

Barrel Dim: N.A.

Rate of Twist: 1:20"

Depth of Groove: .004" to .0045"

Powder: GOI

Patch: None

Ignition: Large rifle primer

Lube: None

Powd. Meas.: Uncle Mike 120

Powd. Temp.: 62° F.

LOAD DATA

Projectile/.457" Weight/405-gr. Type/Remington JSP

Powder Charge (Volume)	Powder Charge (Approx. gr. wt.)	Muzzle Velocity FPS.	Muzzle Energy Ft. Lbs.	Velocity 100 yds.	Energy 100 yds.
67 FFg	66.7	1213	1324	1067	1024

▶ **67 FFg maximum recommended load**

COMMENTS

The rifle shot well with its 67 FFg black powder charge. The charge was somewhat compressed within the cartridge case. Remember that our modern cases do not hold as much powder as our older cases and 67 grains was capacity with FFg. Standard deviation averaged a very low and very impressive 7 fps in our tests with our black powder loads. Factory loads produced Sds of 50 fps and 51 fps for the tests. The 67 FFg black power load seemed very satisfactory to us, and it produces sufficient ballistics for close-range hunting—it's the *optimum load.*

Case lengths are as follows: *Trim*—2.100"; *Maximum Case*—2.105"; *Maximum Overall*—2.550". **Shell holders** are as follows: *RCBS*—14; *Bonanza*—16; *Lyman*—17; *Pacific*—14.

See the caution that precedes this section. Note: Maximum load listed in bold should be used with caution.

1874 Long Range Express (50x3¼")

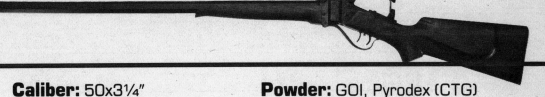

Caliber: 50x3¼"

Barrel Length: 34"

Barrel Dim: Tapered/1.23" to 1.05"

Rate of Twist: 1:36"

Depth of Groove: .005"

Powder: GOI, Pyrodex (CTG)

Patch: None

Ignition: Large rifle primer

Lube: Alox

Powd. Meas.: Tresco 200

Powd. Temp.: 65° F.

LOAD DATA

Powder Charge (Volume)	Powder Charge (Approx. gr. wt.)	Muzzle Velocity FPS.	Muzzle Energy Ft. Lbs.	Velocity 100 yds.	Energy 100 yds.
Projectile/.512" Weight/416-gr. Type/Lyman bullet Mould/No. 512138 (No. 2 alloy*)					
Pyrodex 140 CTG	116.1	1857	3186	1448	1937
Projectile/.512" Weight/462-gr. Type/Hoch bullet (No. 2 alloy*)					
Pyrodex 140 CTG	116.1	1770	3215	1398	2005
Projectile/.512" Weight/540-gr. Type/RCBS 50-515 bullet (wheel wgt. lead)					
Pyrodex 140 CTG	116.1	1688	3164	1384	2127

*See Comments.

See the caution that precedes this section. Note: Maximum load listed in bold should be used with caution.

C. SHARPS

1874 Long Range Express (50x3¼")

Projectile/.510"	Weight/500-gr.	Type/N.E.I. Nesbitt 50-500 (No. 2 alloy*)			
140 Fg	139.5	1489	2462	1251	1738
Pyrodex **140 CTG**	116.1	1696	3450	1390	2317

Projectile/.512"	Weight/638-gr.	Type/N.E.I. Nesbitt 50-625 (pure lead)			
140 Fg	139.5	1396	2762	1173	1950
Pyrodex **140 CTG**	116.1	1413	2829	1187	1997

Projectile/.512"	Weight/462-gr.	Type/Hoch custom 500-462 (No. 2 alloy*)			
140 Fg	139.5	1581	2565	1249	1601

Projectile/.512"	Weight/416-gr.	Type/Lyman bullet Mould/No. 512138 (No. 2 alloy*)			
140 Fg	139.5	1596	2354	1229	1396

Projectile/.512"	Weight/540-gr.	Type/RCBS 50-515 bullet (wheel wgt. lead)			
140 Fg	139.5	1486	2648	1219	1782

*See Comments.

COMMENTS

We took the opportunity of presenting a variety of data for the reader based upon testing with several bullet weights. The use of Fg and Pyrodex CTG was advised by C. Sharps Co. No case space was tolerated. In all loads, a ⅛-inch single card wad *plus* corn meal filler was used when the wad was not sufficient to take up all the extra space inside of the cartridge case. But at no time were loads used in which there was air space. Note: We recommended this procedure in the loading of all black powder cartridges, either filler or wads plus filler. The N.E.I. 638-grain cast bullet and 140 grains of Pyrodex CTG (and one card wad to take up space) proved to be a superb combination. We recommend it as the *optimum load*.

A bullet cast of No. 2 alloy possesses sufficient "give" to upset in the bore of this big rifle. The use of this alloy, in this case, provides the shooter with a bullet that offers better penetration on larger game such as elk or moose.

Case lengths are as follows: *Trim*—3.240"; *Maximum Case*—3.250"; *Maximum Overall*—Variable. **Shell holders** are as follows: *RCBS*—Custom.

See the caution that precedes this section. Note: Maximum load listed in bold should be used with caution.

C. SHARPS

Sporting Rifle No. 3 (45-120-3¼")

Caliber: 45-120-3¼"

Barrel Length: 30"

Barrel Dim: Tapered octagon

Rate of Twist: 1:20"

Depth of Groove: .035"

Powder: GOI

Patch: None

Ignition: Large rifle primer

Lube: 50% Alox 2138F/50% bee's wax

Powd. Meas.: Tresco 200

Powd. Temp.: 71° F.

LOAD DATA

Projectile/.457" Weight/480-gr. Type/Lyman bullet Mould/No. 457121*

Powder Charge (Volume)	Powder Charge (Approx. gr. wt.)	Muzzle Velocity FPS.	Muzzle Energy Ft. Lbs.	Velocity 100 yds.	Energy 100 yds.
110 Fg	109.7	1482	2341	1230	1613

▶ **110 Fg maximum recommended load**

* Our mould threw a bullet that averaged 480 grains in weight.

COMMENTS

Only one load was tested in the 45-120-3¼" Sharps rifle. The bullet was No. 457121, which is listed at 490 grains; however, our mould produced a bullet of 480 grains in weight in Alloy No. 2 lead. Accuracy with this load was good, and in an informal shooting session, we placed 5-shots into a 6-inch bull's-eye with regularity from 200 yards distance on a calm day. The 110 Fg charge is the *optimum load* for this rifle.

Case lengths are as follows: *Trim*—3.240"; *Maximum Case*—3.250"; *Maximum Overall*—Variable. **Shell holders** are as follows: *RCBS*—14; *Bonanza*—16; *Lyman*—17; *Pacific*—14.

See the caution that precedes this section. Note: Maximum load listed in bold should be used with caution.

WINCHESTER (USRACO)

John Wayne Commemorative (32-40 Win.)

Caliber: 32-40 Win.

Barrel Length: 18½"

Barrel Dim: N.A.

Rate of Twist: 1:16"

Depth of Groove: .0025"

Powder: GOI

Patch: None

Ignition: Large rifle primer

Lube: Bee's wax

Powd. Meas.: Uncle Mike 120

Powd. Temp.: 80° F.

LOAD DATA

Projectile/.321" Weight/164-gr. Type/Lyman bullet Mould/No. 32127

Powder Charge (Volume)	Powder Charge (Approx. gr. wt.)	Muzzle Velocity FPS.	Muzzle Energy Ft. Lbs.	Velocity 100 yds.	Energy 100 yds.
35 FFg	34.6	1202	526	986	354

▶ **35 FFg maximum recommended load**

.COMMENTS

This handsome rifle with it s short barrel shot quite well with 35 grains FFg. Thrown with the Uncle Mike measure, that load in volume is also very close to a grains weight charge. The modern case with the cast 155-grain bullet held about 35 FFg without undue air space. The shooter should be careful of air space, filling the case with the proper amount of black powder to avoid large air pockets. The above load is *optimum*.

Some shooters may question our inclusion of this "collectible firearm." Because an original 94 in 32-40 was not available for testing we used this rifle. The data shown is intended for all Winchester Model 94s, in 32-40, in safe shooting condition. **Case lengths** are as follows: *Trim*—2.120"; *Maximum Case*—2.130"; *Maximum Overall*—2.500". **Shell holders** are as follows: *RCBS*—2; *Bonanza*—4; *Lyman*—6; *Pacific*—2.

See the caution that precedes this section. Note: Maximum load listed in bold should be used with caution.

Oliver F. Win. Commem. (38-55 Win.)

Caliber: 38-55 Win.

Barrel Length: 24″

Barrel Dim: N.A.

Rate of Twist: 1:18″

Depth of Groove: .003″

Powder: GOI, Pyrodex (RS)

Patch: None

Ignition: Large rifle primer

Lube: Bee's wax

Powd. Meas.: Uncle Mike 120

Powd. Temp.: 80° F.

LOAD DATA

Projectile/.377″ Weight/250-gr. Type/Lyman bullet Mould/No. 375248*

Powder Charge (Volume)	Powder Charge (Approx. gr. wt.)	Muzzle Velocity FPS.	Muzzle Energy Ft. Lbs.	Velocity 100 yds.	Energy 100 yds.
Pyrodex (RS) 50 RS	36.1	1391	1074	1168	757

▶ **50 RS maximum recommended load**

* Our bullet with this mould averaged at 250 grains.

COMMENTS

The excellent 38-55 bagged many deer prior to the days of high speed ammo, and even into modern times. In the hands of a good shot, the 38-55 is plenty of deer medicine for woods. There are still a great many 38-55 rifles around, not only in the original rifles, but also a modest number of Winchester commemorative rifles. The 50 volume Pyrodex RS load is the *optimum load*.

Testing with this highly collectible rifle was accomplished in an effort to provide our readers with black powder load data for 38-55, Model 94s, in safe shooting condition.

Case lengths are as follows: *Trim—2.118″; Maximum Case—2.1285″; Maximum Overall—2.550″.* **Shell holders** are as follows: RCBS—2; *Bonanza—4; Lyman—6; Pacific—2.*

See the caution that precedes this section. Note: Maximum load listed in bold should be used with caution.

<u>Loading Data</u>

MUZZLE-LOADING SHOTGUNS

INTRODUCTION

THE MUZZLELOADER shotgun loads presented here in our ballistics section were maximized at a volume-for-volume charge, which must be explained. This particular manner of loading the black powder muzzle-loading shotgun has been accepted and proved effective for more years than any of us have walked the planet; however, it is to be considered a maximum load, at least in my opinion. Seldom will a shooter require a volume/volume load, and though we have opted for that here, to give the shotgun a "fair chance" in the performance department, most shooters will find that a little *less* powder with the selected shot charge will offer plenty of punch, with a milder recoil.

The *maximum* black powder shotgun load for the muzzleloader is, remember, a volume-for-volume affair. We never talk weights. Of course the shot charge is considered in ounce measurements, but even here we set a calibrated unit for 1¼ ounces or 1-ounce or whatever is safe or recommended, and we actually toss the shot charge by volume only. It would be a disaster, however, to treat the powder charge in terms of weight.

In the bulk-for-bulk loading practice, which, remember, is our *maximum*, the same volumetric measure which was used to toss the shot charge is used to throw the powder charge. We have given the reader a chart showing how much weight his charge of powder will be at a certain bulk setting. For example, we see that a volumetric shot charge which constituted 1¼ ounces of shot from our Lee measure amounted to about 90 grains of Fg or 92 grains of FFg black powder.

The Lee Shot Measure was used exclusively for our loads. In the field, a hunter who requires maximum power from his black powder muzzleloader would find it easy to use this measure for both volumes of shot and volumes of powder. In my own actual practice, and this is *important*, I usually consider using a somewhat imbalanced shot/powder load in favor of shot. Were I hunting quail with a 12-gauge frontloader shotgun, for example, and if I were measuring my charges in the field, I might drop in 1¼ ounces of 7½ shot by simply setting the measure for 1¼ of course, and then pouring shot from a flask or horn of some sort.

Underneath that shot charge would be a quantity of black powder that would have been tossed with the measure set at the 1-ounce setting for about 70-72 grains of FFg black powder instead of leaving it on the 1¼ setting. Why? I have never needed the velocity for quail shooting, but in a no-choke, straight-tube cylinder bore shotgun, it's nice to have the added shot. I have, in fact, effectively hunted upland game with a shotgun registering only 800 fps over the chronograph screens. For those 20-yard shots, with plenty of shot in the air, a hunter does not need any more velocity for quail and cottontails.

Although authorities have long sanctioned a volume-for-volume method of loading the black powder muzzle-loading shotgun, and while we also subscribe to this practice as an absolute *MAXIMUM* load in new or gunsmith-approved muzzle-loading shotguns, our practice is to call one (1) ounce of shot maximum in the 20-gauge, 1¼ ounces of shot maximum in the 12-gauge and 1½ ounces of shot maximum in the 10-gauge with volume-for-volume charges. In actual field practice, we normally opt for lower powder than shot ratios. As a rule of thumb, we reduce the powder charge by about 20 percent from the bulk for bulk measure. For example, in the 12-gauge we might set the measure on 1-ounce and pour our bulk load of Fg or FFg black powder and then change the measure to the 1¼-ounce setting to throw the shot charge. As field loads, these "less-powder-than-shot" charges not only take game cleanly, they are economical.

In the field, a hunter may also wish to tote his loads premeasured, using small plastic film containers or similar "pop-the-top" holders. And, once again, I'd rarely use a volume-for-volume shotgun loading. However, as we have suggested, the method of volume-for-volume shotgun loads has been with us a long time and in a new, well-made shotgun, it is accepted. It does not render a powder charge which is beyond the recommendations of experts over the years. But I still consider it all the powder I would use, and in 90 percent of the situations where a black powder frontloader is used, it is more powder than I need. Such a volume-for-volume load gives reasonable velocity, and this is its goal. I feel that over the years the shotgun has proved most effective for me when the pattern is *dense*, and hang a few feet per second velocity.

For the shooter interested in the powder charge weight in grains when using the volume-for-volume approach to loading the black powder scattergun, our calibration of the Lee measure is presented in that chapter. The charges are going to be *approximations only*, since the measure is "open top." The charge of powder was leveled off; however, without a funnel to swing into place, I used a sliver of wood to level the charge. I did, however, load the measure to overfull and tap it consistently ten times as I always do with any adjustable black powder measure. This insured a satisfactory level of precision.

Velocity

The highest velocity I have personally obtained with a black powder shotgun is 1400 fps using a 12-gauge with 1¼ ounces of shot and a heavy charge of FFg black powder. Having actual pressure data on hand, and the shotgun being well-constructed, we knew that we had come nowhere close to exceeding the limits of this particular shotgun. While this specific load was over our volume-for-volume maximum, the shooting was conducted under strict test conditions. *Never* exceed our volume-for-volume recommendations.

Energy

There is not much point in trying to list energy ratings for the reader. These are somewhat meaningless. If, for example, we wanted to impress our readers, we could have selected a big 1½-ounce 10-gauge load and shown a muzzle energy of more than 1500 foot-pounds. However, that figure would be based on a shot weight of about 650 grains as one single mass. Our shot does not strike as one single mass, except at ultra-close range. We are dealing instead with individual pellets, all of which are very small in mass, even for the larger No. 2 or 3 shot we might use on geese.

The individual pellet energy is far and away a different matter when compared with the total mass of the shot charge. It's like a march of soldier ants. If only one ant reaches its goal or "target," that's not much "energy," but if many reach the target, then there is much potential for the application of "power." At the muzzle, or nearly so, we could talk energy in terms of mass of the shot charge, since all the pellets might strike that target. Even then, however, the pellets do not act as a single projectile and the figures are not accurate.

Taking a single No. 2 pellet at .15″ diameter, we can compute a weight in pure lead of about 5 grains using our formula for computing the actual weight of a sphere. To be exact, we come up with 5.077 grains per each No. 2 pellet. Now, at 1100 fps at the muzzle, each pellet is worth only 13.4 foot-pounds of energy. However, when a couple of these whack the target, even a big tough bird such as the goose or wild turkey will fall, provided the pellets were in a vital area. At long range, let's say 50 yards, a No. 2 shot beginning its journey at 1100 fps from the muzzle would be down to around 725 fps. At that velocity, each pellet is rated at a KE of about 5.8 foot-pounds.

Powder Granulations

As we have or will discuss over and over, muzzle-loading shotguns seem to fare best with the larger granulations of powder. In my book, Fg and FFg are the better choices, and I do not see a use for FFFg in the shotgun. Naturally, FFg, in keeping with the laws of energy per granulation "cut," delivers more velocity per charge than Fg. In my opinion, the shotgunner should try Fg and FFg for pattern *in his shotgun*, before choosing one over the other.

Sure, velocity is important in shotgunning. It can cut down "lead time," though so slightly per the velocity differences we are dealing with here that it's almost unnoticeable. And we do, again, rely on velocity for energy, mass *in motion*. If it "ain't movin' " there's no energy, except for theoretical potential energy, not kinetic energy. So velocity is important, but in terms of busting a clay pigeon or bagging a mallard, I prefer a dense, well distributed pattern to a few extra feet per second of velocity.

Pressures

Because we are dealing with a large bore (see Chapter 5 on black powder pressures), our shotgun pressures fall into a reasonable realm. This does not mean we should encourage overloading. We are still moving a large mass of shot down that bore, and we must stay within safety limits. And, once again I preach, we do not need to push that shot charge at ultra-high velocities to obtain satisfactory results on target or game within range limitations.

The wad column can have a lot to do with generated pressures in terms of the stress on the walls of the barrel. A wad column, very obviously, has to move out of the way of the expanding gases behind it or something is going to give, such as the breech of the gun. How that wad column moves, and how much it leaks, dictates, in part, what pressures will be generated. Wads for the shotgun are *not the same* in nature as cloth patches for the rifle. When wads blow out, of course, we have leakage and usually a poor pattern. This is why we recommend putting an over-powder nitro card downbore before seating a cushion fiber wad. All too often, the cushion fiber wad alone has a hole blown right through it by the powder charge. When this occurs, it's good bye pattern, since the cushion is now torn, blown through and won't support much of anything.

We used the Ballistic Pattern Driver from Ballistics Products, Inc., for our 10-gauge loads, and we used the BP12 Magnum Shotgun wad coupled with the BPGS gas seal (also from Ballistic Products, Inc.) in the 12-gauge tables. Since we have devoted a chapter to patterns, we will leave the topic of wads for that space. Shooters would find that wads can change velocities appreciably, and I have obtained as much as 200 fps more velocity with one wad column over another wad column.

Shot Sizes

In terms of our velocities, shot size did not matter. The fine Lawrence Brand No. 7½ shot was used for velocity readings. Naturally, any shot size, as long as it amounted to a specific mass somewhat in correspondence with the setting on the measure, would give about the same velocity figures at the muzzle. Of course, when using bulk loadings of shot and powder, there will be some degree of variation in actual weight among shot sizes, as there is less air space around the smaller shot than around the large pellets.

Procedures

The bore was scrubbed with a Hoppe's bristle brush following each and every shot. I especially took care to remove any plastic "wash" that might be in the bore, but did not seem to encounter much of this. I also used a bore light from Sports Specialties to actually look in the bore for any foreign matter that might be present. Also, I tested the nipples by removing them to determine if they were "straight-through" types or if they had the small orifice in the base. In one case, the type of nipple I call "straight-through," which seems to have a hole of about the same diameter from the top of the nipple cone to the base of the nipple, was encountered. I tested with it in place just for my own edification, and here is what occurred: When I switched the nipple to one with a tiny exit hole in the base, the velocity went up by 87 fps on the average with the 1-ounce volume/volume FFg charge, and by an average of 64 fps with the 1¼-ounce volume/volume FFg charge and load.

In Summary

Finally, I would like to sound one small warning—I made it a practice to insure that each charge was down in the breech where it belonged prior to firing the gun. This is best accomplished by maintaining a steady strong pressure upon the loading rod or ramrod while seating the wads. With wads that fit to the bore quite closely, air is trapped between the wad itself and the breech section of the barrel where the powder charge exists. This air, when compressed by the wad, can force the wad(s) back *up* the bore.

By holding the pressure upon the loading rod, the air is forced *through* the powder charge and out the nipple. In fact, the shooter can often hear the air expelling itself through the vent of the nipple. Also, one can feel the ramrod, oftentimes, pushing right back up toward the muzzle. We need to make certain that the *total load*, powder,

wads, shot and overshot card, are all down in the breech until fired.

Approximation of Grains Weight Powder Charge for Lee Shot Measure, with Shotgun Bulk/Bulk Loadings

The shotgun velocities in this book were taken with bulk-/bulk, or volume/volume loads. It has been a black powder practice for many years to use a single *volumetric* (never weight!) measure for *both* shot and powder charge.

In short, if a 1¼-ounce shot measure is used, the same *bulk* volume shot of Fg or FFg black powder is also tossed with that very same shot measure. All the volume-for-volume loads listed should be considered maximum for the guns tested.

The Lee Shot Measure was used for all shotgun loads in this book. Below, we have an approximation of the grains weight for each shot setting on the Lee Measure.

These are approximations only, since the measure does not have a swing-in-line funnel and the powder has to be leveled off by a scrape of a sliver of wood or simply tapped until the topmost portion of the powder charge is removed.

FG GOI black powder

Measure Set on	Approximate Charge Weight in Grains
1 ounce	70 grs.
1⅛ ounces	80 grs.
1¼ ounces	90 grs.
1⅜ ounces	100 grs.
1½ ounces	110 grs.
1⅝ ounces	120 grs.
1¾ ounces	130 grs.
1⅞ ounces	140 grs.

FFG GOI black powder

Measure Set on	Approximate Charge Weight in Grains
1 ounce	72 grs.
1⅛ ounces	82 grs.
1¼ ounces	92 grs.
1⅜ ounces	102 grs.
1½ ounces	112 grs.
1⅝ ounces	122 grs.
1¾ ounces	132 grs.
1⅞ ounces	142 grs.

ARMSPORT

Double Barrel No. 5125 (10-gauge)

Caliber: 10-gauge

Barrel Length: 29″

Rate of Twist: Smoothbore

Powder: GOI

Patch: None

Ignition: Navy Arms No. 11

Lube: None

Powd. Meas.: Lee Shot Measure

Powd. Temp.: 70° F.

LOAD DATA

Projectile/Lawrence Brand No. 7½ chilled shot

Powder/Shot Charge	Lee Shot Measure Setting	Muzzle Velocity FPS.
90 FFg/1¼ oz. shot	1¼	969
▶ **90 FFg with 1¼ oz. shot maximum recommended load**		

COMMENTS

The *optimum load* is 90 FFg with 1¼ oz. shot.
Wad: The wad used in this load was a Ballistic Products, Inc. Pattern Driver with 10-gauge black powder over shot wad.

See the caution that precedes this section. Note: Maximum load listed in bold should be used with caution.

Western M1212 Hammer (12-gauge)

Caliber: 12-gauge

Barrel Length: 20"

Rate of Twist: Smoothbore

Powder: GOI

Case: Instant Muzzleloader

Patch: .015" Ox-Yoke Precision Blue-Striped

Ignition: CCI No. 11

Lube: RIG

Powd. Meas.: Tresco 200

Powd. Temp.: 75° F.

LOAD DATA

Projectile/.690"* Weight/502-gr. Type/Denver Bullet Co. round ball

Powder Charge (Volume)	Powder Charge (Approx. gr. wt.)	Muzzle Velocity FPS.	Muzzle Energy Ft. Lbs.	Velocity 100 yds.	Energy 100 yds.
110 FFg	109.7	1115	1386	881	865
110 Fg	109.7	900	903	743	502
120 Fg	119.8	992	1097	794	703
130 Fg	129.7	1107	1366	875	854

▶ **130 Fg maximum recommended load**

* The .690" round ball actually miked out at .695"

COMMENTS

While a modern version of an old-time hammer gun, this "stage coach style" double barrel, I felt, was well suited to black powder shooting and the hammer gun was included in our test runs. The aim was to produce a powerful load with a .690"-.695" round ball. An interesting unit was used as a shotgun shell, this being the "Instant Muzzle Loader" shotgun "case," a fully metallic unit from Sports Specialities which uses standard No. 11 percussion caps fitted to a "nipple" at the base of the unit. The "Instant Muzzle Loader" unit was loaded with black powder and the ball was inserted tightly patched. A CCI No. 11 cap was then seated and the round fired. The *optimum load* is 130 grains of Fg.

Note: The use of the Instant Muzzleloader device may not be legal in your area for Primitive black powder hunts. Check your state's Primitive-hunt regulations before using this device.

See the caution that precedes this section. Note: Maximum load listed in bold should be used with caution.

EUROARMS

Magnum Cape Gun (12-gauge)

Caliber: 12-gauge

Barrel Length: 32"

Rate of Twist: Smoothbore

Powder: GOI

Patch: None

Ignition: CCI No. 11

Lube: None

Powd. Meas.: Lee Shot Measure

Powd. Temp.: 67° F.

LOAD DATA—A

Projectile/Lawrence Brand No. 7½ chilled shot

Powder/Shot Charge	Lee Shot Measure Setting	Muzzle Velocity FPS.
70 FFg/1 oz. shot	1	966
80 FFg/1⅛ oz. shot	1⅛	1010
90 FFg/1¼ oz. shot	1¼	1021

▶ **90 FFg/1¼ oz. shot maximum recommended load**

COMMENTS

We viewed the Magnum Cape Gun as an upland shotgun, as well as a fowler, as well as an all-around single-shot capable of old-time smoothbore function, where a gun might be used for deer as well as birds. From the "shotgun" side of the picture, we found the 90 FFg/1¼-ounce shot charge to be our *optimum load* for upland game.
Wads: 1 Ballistic Products BPGS wad with Magnum Shot Cup and black powder 12-ga. over-shot wad.

See the caution that precedes this section. Note: Maximum load listed in bold should be used with caution.

EUROARMS

▶ All pertinent data for Load Data—B is the same as for Load Data—A except the following:

Patch: .015″ Ox-Yoke Precision Blue-Striped
Lube: RIG
Powd. Meas. Tresco 200
Powd. Temp.: 69° F.

LOAD DATA—B

Projectile/.690″ Weight/494-gr. Type/Denver Bullet Co.

Powder Charge (Volume)	Powder Charge (Approx. gr. wt.)	Muzzle Velocity FPS.	Muzzle Energy Ft. Lbs.	Velocity 100 yds.	Energy 100 yds.
80 Fg	79.9	1006	1110	805	711
80 FFg	80.1	1042	1191	823	743

▶ **80 FFg maximum recommended load**

COMMENTS

There was little gain in going from Fg to FFg black powder in this particular shotgun in this particular test. We recommend the 80 Fg charge as *optimum* for close-range deer hunting in the Magnum Cape Gun. Because of the heavy breech section, with its built-up style, the shooter might wish to investigate the use of a rear sight, *provided* that the breech area is *not weakened* by screw holes and/or slots. A gunsmith should be consulted. The addition of a rear aiming point might be of value for the deer hunter using the single round patched ball in this smoothbore.

See the caution that precedes this section. Note: Maximum load listed in bold should be used with caution.

BERETTA

Tricentennial Model 100 (12-gauge)

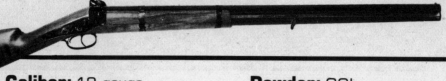

Caliber: 12-gauge

Barrel Length: 29"

Rate of Twist: Smoothbore

Powder: GOI

Patch: None

Ignition: CCI No. 11

Lube: None

Powd. Meas.: Lee Shot Measure

Powd. Temp.: 64° F.

LOAD DATA—A

Projectile/Lawrence Brand No. 7½ chilled shot

Powder/Shot Charge	Lee Shot Measure Setting	Muzzle Velocity FPS.
70 FFg/1 oz. shot	1	971
80 FFg/1⅛ oz. shot	1⅛	1016
90 FFg/1¼ oz. shot	1¼	1127

▶ **90 FFg/1¼ oz. shot maximum recommended load**

COMMENTS

We wanted to check this over/under shotgun with a load of 1¼ ounces of shot. If anything, we view this shotgun as an uplander, and 1¼ ounces of shot will handle any of the upland game birds. The light gun is a backaction, that is, the lock is the backaction variety, once somewhat popular, still a very good lock design. As a result of testing, we found that for general all around use the 1-ounce FFg load was ideal, it is our *optimum load*.

Wads: 1 Ballistic Products BPGS wad with Magnum Shot Cup and black powder 12-ga. over-shot wad.

See the caution that precedes this section. Note: Maximum load listed in bold should be used with caution.

BERETTA

Tricentennial Model 100 (12-gauge)

▶ All pertinent data for Load Data—B is the same as for Load Data—A except the following:

Patch: .015" Ox-Yoke Precision Blue-Striped
Lube: RIG
Powd. Meas.: Uncle Mike 120

LOAD DATA—B

Projectile/.690" Weight/494-gr. Type/Denver Bullet Co. round ball

Powder Charge (Volume)	Powder Charge (Approx. gr. wt.)	Muzzle Velocity FPS.	Muzzle Energy Ft. Lbs.	Velocity 100 yds.	Energy 100 yds.
80 Fg	81.2	809	718	680	507
80 FFg	81.0	851	795	704	544

▶ **80 FFg maximum recommended load**

COMMENTS

As we have stated throughout the book, firearms will vary because they are truly individual in nature. In the rifles we find depth-of-groove differences and twist variations, not to mention the particular configuration of the rifling, hence drag differences in the bore. However, we also found shotguns somewhat individual in ballistic nature. But no firearm in any caliber was sub-par due to a problem in the bore. We would choose the 80 Fg charge here with the big round ball for deer hunting at close range. In effect, one could have two fast shots at a deer in the woods, with two .690" spheres of lead each weighing 494 grains. Because of the somewhat lower pressure. I would recommend the 80 Fg load as an *optimum load*.

See the caution that precedes this section. Note: Maximum load listed in bold should be used with caution.

GREEN RIVER

Northwest Trade Gun (20-gauge)

Caliber: 20-gauge

Barrel Length: 30"

Barrel Dim: Tapered

Rate of Twist: Smoothbore

Powder: GOI

Patch: .024" sailcloth

Ignition: FFFFg pan powder

Lube: RIG

Powd. Meas.: Tresco 200

Powd. Temp.: 66° F.

LOAD DATA

Projectile/.570" Weight/280-gr. Type/Denver Bullet Co. round ball

Powder Charge (Volume)	Powder Charge (Approx. gr. wt.)	Muzzle Velocity FPS.	Muzzle Energy Ft. Lbs.	Velocity 100 yds.	Energy 100 yds.
70 FFg	70.1	1215	918	840	439
80 FFg	80.1	1296	1045	876	477
90 FFg	90.0	1369	1166	904	508
70 FFg *	70.1	1015			

▶ **90 FFg maximum recommended load**

* This load was with 1 oz. No. 7½ shot, and a Remington one-piece plastic wad

COMMENTS

Many shooters still prefer a smoothbore for reasons of versatility and ease of cleaning, and Green River Forge has answered their requests with this historical piece. It is a 20-gauge, and it did shoot standard, open bore, 20-gauge patterns. However, the smoothbore will also handle a patched round ball. The .595" to .600" cast ball is preferred. We were unable to obtain this size ball; therefore, we used a heavy .024" patching with a standard .570" round ball. The results were quite reasonable. Our recommended *optimum load* is 90 FFg. We also fired an ounce of 7½ Lawrence brand shot with 70 FFg and a Remington Power Piston No. W29944 with a Circle Fly black powder 20-gauge over-shot wad and achieved over 1000 fps average muzzle velocity. That is our *optimum load* with shot. If a shooter wanted the all-around smoothbore advantage, he would have both shotgun and round-ball gun in the Northwest model.

See the caution that precedes this section. Note: Maximum load listed in bold should be used with caution.

Ethan Allen(12-gauge)

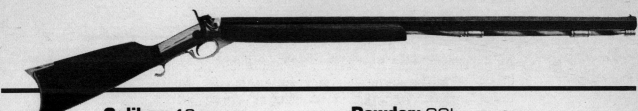

Caliber: 12-gauge

Barrel Length: 32"

Barrel Dim: 1" across flats

Rate of Twist: Smoothbore

Powder: GOI

Patch: None

Ignition: Navy Arms No. 11

Lube: None

Powd. Meas.: Lee Shot Measure

Powd. Temp.: 70° F.

LOAD DATA—A

Projectile/Lawrence Brand No. 7½ chilled shot

Powder/Shot Charge	Lee Shot Measure Setting	Muzzle Velocity FPS.
70 FFg/1 oz. shot	1	991
90 FFg/1¼ oz. shot	1¼	1051

▶ **90 FFg/1¼ oz. shot maximum recommended load**

COMMENTS

This interesting single shot 12-gauge develops good strong ballistics and used within reasonable ranges would suffice for any game normally hunted with a 12-gauge shotgun. For general, all around use, the 1¼-oz. shot, 90-grain (3⅓ Dram Equiv.) FFg load is *optimum*.

Wads: BP 12-gauge Magnum shot cup with BPGS 12-gauge gas seal from Ballistic Products, Inc. with 12-gauge black powder over-shot wad.

See the caution that precedes this section. Note: Maximum load listed in bold should be used with caution.

MOWREY

Ethan Allen(12-gauge)

▶ All pertinent data for Load Data—B is the same as for Load Data—A except the following:

Patch: (See Comments)
Ignition: CCI No. 11
Lube: Whale oil
Powd. Meas.: Tresco
Powd. Temp.: 75° F.

LOAD DATA—B

Projectile/.690" Weight/494-gr. Type/Denver Bullet Co. round ball

Powder Charge (Volume)	Powder Charge (Approx. gr. wt.)	Muzzle Velocity FPS.	Muzzle Energy Ft. Lbs.	Velocity 100 yds.	Energy 100 yds.
80 Fg	79.9	1001	1099	801	704

▶ **80 Fg maximum recommended load**

COMMENTS

I felt that a maximum charge of 80 Fg would be best—it proved to be our *optimum load*. Above 80 Fg, patches, even with the elaborate setup described here, were failing. With the 80-gr. charge of Fg, this shotgun would serve as a musket of sufficient power for big game at close range.

Patching: A Ballistics Products, Inc., nitro card wad was placed directly upon the powder charge, followed by a cushion wad lubed with sperm whale oil. The ball was patched with a single .017" Ox-Yoke Precision Blue-Striped patch lubed with whale oil. If you are unable to locate any sperm whale oil, J&A Old Slickum may be used as a substitute.

See the caution that precedes this section. Note: Maximum load listed in bold should be used with caution.

218

Classic Side-by-Side (12-gauge)

Caliber: 12-gauge

Barrel Length: 28″

Rate of Twist: Smoothbore

Powder: GOI

Patch: None

Ignition: Navy Arms No. 11

Lube: None

Powd. Meas.: Lee Shot Measure

Powd. Temp.: 70°F.

LOAD DATA

Projectile/Lawrence Brand No. 7½ chilled shot

Powder/Shot Charge	Lee Shot Measure Setting	Muzzle Velocity FPS.
70 FFg/1 oz. shot	1	966
90 FFg/1¼ oz. shot	1¼	1021

▶ **90 FFg/1¼ oz. shot maximum recommended load**

COMMENTS

The Navy Arms Classic shotgun produced black powder ballistics which make it suitable for any game normally hunted with a 12-gauge shotgun, kept of course, within its patterning ability. The 1¼-ounce load tested against a modern shotshell with 1¼-ounce loads proved to be very similar in velocity. For general, all around shotgunning the 90-grain (3⅓ Dram Equiv.), 1¼-ounce load would be about *optimum*.

Wad: BP 12-gauge Magnum shot cup with the BPGS 12-gauge gas-seal and 12-gauge black powder over-shot wad from Ballistic Products, Inc.

See the caution that precedes this section. Note: Maximum load listed in bold should be used with caution.

Terry Texas Ranger (12-gauge)

Caliber: 12-gauge

Barrel Length: 14″

Rate of Twist: Smoothbore

Powder: GOI

Patch: None

Ignition: Navy Arms No. 11

Lube: None

Powd. Meas.: Lee Shot Measure

Powd. Temp.: 64°F.

LOAD DATA

Projectile/Lawrence Brand No. 7½ chilled shot

Powder/Shot Charge	Lee Shot Measure Setting	Muzzle Velocity FPS.
70 FFg/1 oz. shot	1	902
90 FFg/1¼ oz. shot	1¼	868
▶ **90 FFg/1¼ oz. shot maximum recommended load**		

COMMENTS

This little shotgun is on par with the Sile Cavalry, but is not the same in overall exterior dimensions. It proved to be a very useful scattergun for short-range work, and the ballistics were certainly sufficient for all such shotgunning. Backpackers interested in a short, powerful gun would be interested in this class of muzzle-loading shotgun. The loads shown were tested several times with the same results. Inasmuch as the velocities are quite close, you may select your *optimum load* based upon your shot-charge requirement.

Wad: BP 12-gauge Magnum shot cup with the BPGS 12-gauge gas seal and 12-gauge over-shot wad from Ballistic Products, Inc.

See the caution that precedes this section. Note: Maximum load listed in bold should be used with caution.

Confederate Cavalry (12-gauge)

Caliber: 12-gauge

Barrel Length: 14"

Rate of Twist: Smoothbore

Powder: GOI

Patch: None

Ignition: Navy Arms No. 11

Lube: None

Powd. Meas.: Lee Shot Measure

Powd. Temp.: 64°F.

LOAD DATA

Projectile/Lawrence Brand No. 7½ chilled shot

Powder/Shot Charge	Lee Shot Measure Setting	Muzzle Velocity FPS.
70 FFg/1 oz. shot	1	887
90 FFg/1¼ oz. shot	1¼	845

▶ **90 FFg/1¼ oz. shot maximum recommended load**

COMMENTS

In spite of the short barrel, the little Cavalry shotgun has plenty of ballistics for close-range quail shooting, and would suffice for any other game normally hunted with a shotgun. (See chapter on patterns for mention of Cavalry patterning.) The two loads shown were tested several times with the same results. Inasmuch as the velocities are quite close, you may select your *optimum load* based on your shot-charge requirements.

Wad: BP 12-gauge Magnum shot cup with BPGS 12-gauge gas seal and 12-gauge black powder over-shot wad.

See the caution that precedes this section. Note: Maximum load listed in bold should be used with caution.

Loading Data

INTRODUCTION TO THE BLACK POWDER SHOTSHELL

UNFORTUNATELY, we could not gain the blessings of the powder manufacturers in terms of loading for and shooting the old-time Damascus or "twist" shotgun barrels. The reader must understand that these companies are forced to observe "safety-first" attitudes at all times, and certainly they cannot, nor can we, sit back here and put the OK on a firearm we have not even seen, that may not have been properly checked out by a black powder gunsmith, and which could, possibly, hold a flaw in the steel that would cause a burst gun and perhaps an injury to the shooter.

Why bother then? What uses would one have for a black powder shotgun shell? As a matter of fact, there are many thousands upon thousands of non-Damascus shotguns out there from the "olden days," and while these shotguns are well-constructed and while they are indeed made of the best steels known at the time, there may be question as to firing them with a modern smokeless powder shotgun shell. These thousands of sound, gunsmith-checked shotguns, however, are deemed all right to fire with black powder shotgun shells and this is why we have presented a short section here on such loads.

Also, and this is important, we have offered the black powder shotgun shooter who is interested in using the shell an entire chapter devoted to tips and tricks designed to help the shooter maintain his firearm in safety as well as reasonable performance. *The shooter must read this chapter before he begins loading his black powder shotgun shells.* That chapter explains wad columns in the black powder shotshell, as well as points concerning the function of such shotshells and the care required to clean the shotguns following black powder shotshell use.

BLACK POWDER SHOTGUN SHELL DATA
Shotgun: Remington 870 Remington pump, 30-inch barrel
Hull: Winchester Mark V 12-Ga. Standard Winchester Primer
LOADS*

1. 90 GOI FFg black powder
   two (2) .135" Nitro Card Wads
   1¼ ounces, No. 4 shot

   Velocity: 1,224 fps

2. 90 GOI FFg black powder
   two (2) .135" Nitro Card Wads
   1½ ounces, No. 4 shot

   Velocity: 1,213 fps

3. 90 GOI FFg black powder
   one (1) .135" Nitro Card Wad
   one (1) Ballistics Products, Inc., felt wad
   1⅛ ounces, No. 4 shot

   Velocity: 1,255 fps

4. 90 GOI FFg black powder
   one (1) .135" Nitro Card Wad
   one (1) Ballistics Products, Inc., felt wad
   1⅜ ounces, No. 4 shot

   Velocity: 1,146 fps

---

*The loads listed here are *not* intended for use in Damascus (twist-steel) barreled shotguns. These loads are for use in modern shotguns, designed for use with smokeless powder loads.

Math and Formulas for the Black Powder Shooter

EVERY SHOOTER enjoys looking at a few "paper theories and laws" now and then, and this brief glance delves into a few such rules. Hopefully, the reader will find these useful, as well as interesting.

Energy

Every ammunition company in the world that I know of uses the standard kinetic energy formula by Newton. Energy, whether kinetic or latent, is the *potential* to do *work*, and the Newtonian law supplies its figures in terms of foot-pounds of energy. Working the formula is easier than talking about it. It goes like this:

Step One: Square the velocity in feet per second.
Step Two: Divide the result by 7000 to reduce from grains to pounds.
Step Three: Divide by 64.32 (a constant equal to 2g, the acceleration of gravity).
Step Four: Multiply the last figure obtained by the weight of the projectile in grains weights.

Let's do an example, and at the same time compare two loads, a modern and an old-time black powder recipe. First, we'll take the modern. Let's make it the snappy 25-06, using a 100-grain bullet at 3300 fps at the muzzle. Now, by the numbers, we will come up with the KE at the muzzle:

1. We square 3300 and get: 10890000.
2. We divide that number by 7000 to reduce from grains to pounds, and we have: 1555.7143
3. Now we divide by twice the acceleration of gravity, a constant in the formula and we arrive at: 24.1871
4. But 24.1871 is the energy in only one grain, so we must multiply this figure times the total weight of the bullet in grains. Our 25-06 bullet, in this case, weighs 100 grains, and 24.1871 times 100 equals: 2,418.71, or to round it off, 2,419. What is that? It is 2,419 foot-pounds of muzzle energy.

Now we will look at our second firearm, the smokepole. I am going to choose a 54-caliber shooting a round ball because I have cleanly bagged elk, deer, bison and other big game with one shot each from this caliber using the round ball. We can get just about 2000 fps from the 54 with stout, but safe loads, in *some* rifles, depending upon rifling, twist and so forth. My own 54 earns about 1,975 fps with a 225-grain round ball. So, let's figure the KE on it: it comes to 1,949 foot-pounds of muzzle energy. But nothing is shot at the muzzle. So, let's take the energies of the 25-06 and the 54 at 50 yards. I can stalk to within 50 yards if I'm willing to hunt hard and work for my shot.

At 50 yards, the 25-06 is still smoking along at about 3150 fps (estimated). This is a KE of 2,204 foot-pounds. But the 54 ball is down to a velocity of only 1,475 fps. And that is worth a KE of 1,087 foot-pounds. Having hunted with both the 25-06 and the 54, I do not see that much difference in "real life performance" at 50 yards. But at the same time, there is no doubt that the high energy smack of a 25-06 is impressive, nor does the KE formula show the 54 as worthless, so let's use the KE theory, but let no one suggest that it is the only criterion in the world for expressing "power."

Precision vs Accuracy

As my friend Admiral Schneider says, "Precision and accuracy are *not* the same. When we refer to our data, we are hoping for accuracy! Remember this: with precision, when referring to data, we may get the same results every time, and yet those results could be *wrong*. Sure, they are consistent. But if we got 1500 fps time after time, it would show precision, but maybe not accuracy. With accuracy, the data are correct.

I have a good example on the tip of my memory. A fellow called me and said that his 50-caliber Ithaca was getting more velocity than my printed data in an article, and he chronographed over and over again and by the beard of General Jackson, he got the same figures over and over, so my data must be wrong. Well, I've been wrong before and will be again, so I went out and tested my rifle. Of course, no two rifles will yield the same velocity exactly, but we were 200 fps apart.

Finally, we compared load chains. Heck, he was using the one I recommended. So we had the same patch arrangement, the same powder brand and granulation and the same lube with the same percussion cap, yet he was getting 200 fps more than I was getting. This time, for a change, I decided my data were correct. And here is why: He was shooting 10-shot strings and then cleaning up *after* the 10 shots were fired. Well, as the fouling built up, so did the pressure, so by the time he averaged those 10 shots for his score, he had some real wild velocities in there. This time, he was precise but I was accurate.

Powder and Ball Size

In an earlier chapter, we spoke of kinetic energy of rotation between the 60-caliber ball and the 50-caliber round ball. We used true 60s and 50s for our argument, that is, the balls were .60" and .50" in size, not .595" and .495". Recall that we said the following:

$$\frac{.6^3}{.5^3} \times \frac{.6}{.5} = 2.07$$

The 2.07 was the figure saying that the .60" ball had 2.07 times more energy of rotation than the .50" ball, but not 2.07 times more translational KE. Now let's look at it another way, since this is our "play games with numbers" chapter. Let's do the following:

$$\frac{.6^3}{.5^3} = 1.73$$

This time, we will find that the .60" does have *about* (it won't come out on the money) 1.73 times more KE than the .50" ball. Let's see if this is true in "real life." Let's keep the velocity of both balls the same. We will say they both leave the muzzle at 1800 fps. Now, a .50" ball will weigh 188 grains and a .60" ball will weigh 325 grains. So, working the KE, as we did above, we get 1,353 foot-pounds of energy KE for the .50" at 1800 fps, and we get 2,339 foot-pounds of energy for the .60" ball. Is that a real difference of 1.73 times? Well, we said the .60" was 1.73 times more "powerful" in terms of KE than the .50". So if the .50" got an energy rating of 1,353 foot-pounds, we should be able to take 1.73 times that and end up with the energy of the .60". If we do take 1.73 times 1,353 we end up with 2,340.69, which is mighty close to 2,339, right?

Not totally convinced? Let's do one more real fast. Let's take a .50" against a true .70" ball. The .50" weighs 188 grains. We already established that. The .70" ball goes 516 grains. Here we go:

$$\frac{.7^3}{.5^3} = \frac{.343}{.125} = 2.74$$

If we take 2.74 times the energy of the .50" ball at 1800 fps (remember, the velocity is the same with both .70" and .50" here) we get 2.74 times 1353 or 3,707.22. Now the true KE of the .70" ball at 1800 fps is actually 3,713 KE. That's pretty close again. All we care about here is showing that ball size, with velocity remaining the same, means an awful lot to "power."

Figuring Round Ball Mass

This is easy, fun and useful. It serves two purposes. First, our gauging the mass of round balls will show the reader how fast that mass rises with increase in ball size or diameter. Second, we can find out if our lead spherical projectiles are truly pure of lead or mixed with tin, antimony and other "impurities." The formula goes like this:

1. We want to figure the VOLUME of a sphere (ball) first. This is the old grammar school formula that goes: D^3 times .5236. (Remember figuring the volume of a sphere?) The resulting number is multiplied times 2,873.5, which is the weight of a cubic inch of pure lead in *grains* weight (437.5 grains in an ounce). Let's do one: we mike a ball to .310" size. So, .310" times .310" times .310" is .029791", times .5236, or .01559857, and this times 2,873.5, or 44.822482, or rounded off to 44.8. Now we know that a ball of .310" size for the .32 squirrel rifle is supposed to weigh out at 44.8 grains *in pure lead*.

So, if we mike our own cast round balls at .310" caliber, they should weigh pretty darn close to 44.8 grains if they are accurately composed of pure lead and not agents which will lighten them up, such as tin and antimony. Just for fun, here is a Hornady .310" swaged ball from the factory. I grabbed 10 out of the box at total random, and the 10 averaged out at 44.7 grains. I really do not think a shooter can ask for much more in terms of pure lead and the spread was minimal from the weight of one ball to the next as well.

Therefore, with this little formula we can find out if our own lead pills are pure of lead by miking the ball for true diameter, and then using the formula. Then we merely weigh our products on the powder/bullet scale to see if they actually match up with the "theoretical perfect" weight of a pure lead round ball of that size. Also, this formula shows us swiftly how fast a ball rises in mass as the diameter increases.

For example, a .350" ball for the 36-caliber rifle weighs 65 grains. If we double the size of the ball to 70-caliber, that ball, in pure lead will go 516 grains. Obviously, doubling the diameter did far more than doubling the mass of the projectile. The 70 is almost 8 times heavier than the .350" ball.

We'll leave this one, but first I want to say once more that I am aware of the fine field work accomplished by expert shots with the smaller black powder rifles. The average round ball of our own early America was something like 38-caliber in size. Yet, the leatherstocking men of the eastern seaboard won a war and fed their families with their fine rifles. I think it is worth a brief glance at one historical battle in which our American riflemen's love of accuracy saved the day. This was the Battle of New Orleans, January 8, 1815. And it is told in the *Dictionary of American History*, by Drs. Jameson and Buel. The history goes like this:

> As they [the British] advanced to the charge they were killed by the hundreds, yet did not falter. When within 200 yards of the American line, the Kentucky and Tennessee riflemen, deadly shots, four ranks deep, fired line by line. The slaughter was terrible, but the British, now reinforced by General Keane's troops, pressed on up to the very parapets. But Generals Pakenham and Gibbs were both mortally wounded. General Keane and Major Wilkinson, the next in command, were so severely wounded that they were carried from the field and the British fell back in disorder. Colonel Thornton's division had meantime captured General Morgan's position on the right bank of the river, but was recalled in view of the defeat on the other side. The British lost in this battle 700 killed, 1,400 wounded, and 500 prisoners. The American loss was eight killed and thirteen wounded. (p. 33-34)